GREAT ENGLISH

AND AMERICAN ESSAYS

GREAT ENGLISH AND AMERICAN ESSAYS

EDITED BY DOUGLASS S. MEAD

REVISED AND ENLARGED

Holt, Rinehart and Winston

NEW YORK · CHICAGO · SAN FRANCISCO

TORONTO

FOREWORD

The essays in this volume have been chosen with several considerations in view. I have attempted, in the first place, to select pieces which are representative of successive periods in the literary history of England and America, and thus to provide some sense of the development of the essay form in our literature. I have selected only pieces which seemed to me to have some permanent literary value; the collection therefore illustrates a high standard of writing in a variety of essay forms. The essays all seem to me provocative in one way or another, and they represent an intentionally wide variety of themes and points of view. If the collection achieves its purpose, it should be well adapted for class discussion of both content and form. I have attempted to achieve a fruitful balance between the familiar and the new, between classic essayists and less well-known writers. If the reader looks in vain for certain of his favorite essays, it must be confessed that some of the editor's too are missing. I hope that the fresh material I have been able to include will more than compensate for any specific omissions. For the essays of the earlier periods I have provided explanatory footnotes, since many of the references in such pieces are unfamiliar to the contemporary student, especially to the freshman or sophomore. For modern essays, however, since these represent a level of good reading the student can reasonably be expected to carry out on his own, I have provided few footnotes or none at all.

It is manifestly impossible to cite individually all those who, in one way or another, have helped me in the preparation of this volume. Many persons have been kind. To all of them I offer my grateful thanks.

DOUGLASS S. MEAD

State College, Pennsylvania
January, 1950

A WORD ABOUT THE REVISION

The change in contents of this revised edition comes as a result of experience. Some of the essays which seemed less attractive than others have been replaced and a somewhat larger representation of the modern era has been included. The book still demonstrates the extensive variety of essay styles and themes and is adaptable to many uses. Although the publisher has eliminated some of the "white space" in the first edition in order to hold down the length and price of the volume, the number of essays has been increased from thirty to thirty-five.

Thanks are due to all those who over a broad area have been generous in constructive criticism, including Professors Richard S. Beal, D. R. Cherry, R. F. Grady, S.J., John C. Sherwood, and William W. Watt. Most especially do I thank my friends and colleagues, Brice Harris, Pauline Locklin, Arthur Lewis, Ralph Condee, Bernard Jerman, Chadwick Hansen, and Stanley Weintraub. These people have used the book and have happily been most helpful with suggestions.

D. S. M.

University Park, Pa.
February, 1957

CONTENTS

vii

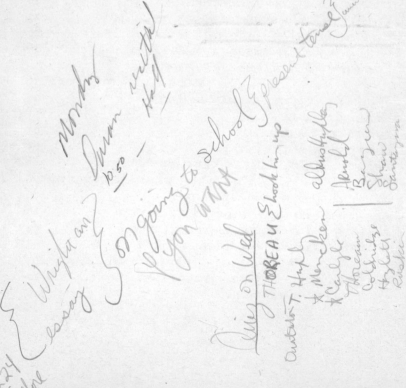

GREAT ENGLISH
AND AMERICAN ESSAYS

THE MISERY OF BEING OLD
AND IGNORANT

OWEN FELLTHAM (1602?-1668)

From *Resolves*, 1620. Felltham is known for his penetrating analyses of
human conduct, to which he added a personal "resolve." In the present
essay he wants to make sure that when he talks to himself as an old man
he will have an intelligent listener.

'Tis a capital misery for a man to be at once both old and
ignorant. If he were only old, and had some knowledge, he
might abate the tediousness of decrepit age by the divine rap-
tures of contemplation. If he were young, though he knew
nothing, yet his years would serve him to labor and learn;
whereby in the winter of his time he might beguile the weariness of his pillow and chair. But now his body being withered
by the stealing length of his days, and his limbs wholly disabled
for either motion or exercise, these, together with a mind un-
furnished of those contenting speculations of admired science,
cannot but delineate the portraiture of a man wretched. A
gray head with a wise mind is a treasury of grave precepts,
experience, and judgment. But foolish old age is a barren vine
in autumn, or an university to study folly in: every action is a
pattern of infirmity: while his body sits still he knows not how
to find his mind action: and tell me if there be any life more irksome than idleness. I have numbered yet but a few days,[1] and
those, I know, I have neglected; I am not sure they shall be
more, nor can I promise my head it shall have a snowy hair.

[1] Written before he was twenty.

What then? Knowledge is not hurtful, but helps a good mind; anything that is laudable I desire to learn. If I die to-morrow, my life to-day shall be somewhat the sweeter for knowledge: and if my day prove a summer one, it shall not be amiss to have provided something that in the evening of my age may make my mind my companion. Notable was the answer that Antisthenes[2] gave when he was asked what fruit he had reaped of all his studies. "By them," saith he, "I have learned both to live and to talk with myself."

OF MARRIAGE AND SINGLE LIFE

FRANCIS BACON (1561-1626)

From *Essays and Counsels, Civil and Moral,* 1625. Bacon thought of the essay as a series of random thoughts expressed in terse statements called aphorisms. "Of Marriage and Single Life" combines this aphoristic style with the practical analysis of a problem which young people perennially face. The reader might not always agree.

———

He that hath wife and children hath given hostages to fortune; for they are impediments to great enterprises, either of virtue or mischief. Certainly the best works, and of greatest merit for the public, have proceeded from the unmarried or childless men, which, both in affection and means, have married and endowed the public. Yet it were great reason that those that have children should have greatest care of future times, unto which they know they must transmit their dearest pledges. Some there are, who, though they lead a single life, yet their thoughts do end with themselves, and account future times impertinences;[1] nay, there are some other that account wife and children but as bills of charges; nay, more, there are

---

[2] Athenian philosopher, *ca.* 444-365 B.C.
[1] Matters of no importance.

some foolish rich covetous men that take pride in having no children, because they may be thought so much the richer; for, perhaps, they have heard some talk, "Such a one is a great rich man," and another except to it, "Yea, but he hath a great charge of children," as if it were an abatement to-his riches. But the most ordinary cause of a single life is liberty, especially in certain self-pleasing and humorous[2] minds, which are so sensible of every restraint, as they will go near to think their girdles and garters to be bonds and shackles. Unmarried men are best friends, best masters, best servants, but not always best subjects; for they are light to run away, and almost all fugitives are of that condition. A single life doth well with churchmen, for charity will hardly water the ground where it must first fill a pool. It is indifferent for judges and magistrates, for if they be facile and corrupt you shall have a servant five times worse than a wife. For soldiers, I find the generals commonly, in their hortatives, put men in mind of their wives and children. And I think the despising of marriage amongst the Turks maketh the vulgar soldier more base. Certainly, wife and children are a kind of discipline of humanity; and single men, though they be many times more charitable, because their means are less exhaust, yet, on the other side, they are more cruel and hard-hearted, good to make severe inquisitors, because their tenderness is not so oft called upon. Grave natures, led by custom, and therefore constant, are commonly loving husbands; as was said of Ulysses, "*Vetulam suam praetulit immortalitati.*" [3] Chaste women are often proud and froward, as presuming upon the merit of their chastity. It is one of the best bonds, both of chastity and obedience, in the wife if she think her husband wise, which she will never do if she find him jealous. Wives are young men's mistresses, companions for middle age, and old men's nurses; so as a man may have a quarrel [4] to marry when he will. But yet he was reputed one of the wise men[5] that made

---

[2] Eccentric.
[3] He preferred his old wife to immortality.
[4] Pretext.
[5] Thales, an ancient Greek philosopher.

answer to the question when a man should marry, "A young man not yet, an elder man not at all." It is often seen that bad husbands have very good wives; whether it be that it raiseth the price of their husband's kindness when it comes, or that the wives take a pride in their patience; but this never fails, if the bad husbands were of their own choosing, against their friends' consent; for then they will be sure to make good their own folly.

A DOWNRIGHT SCHOLAR

JOHN EARLE (1600?-1665)

From *Microcosmography*, 1628. Earle is famous for his "Characters," a variety of essay which displays familiar types of humanity by a sequence of actions. Readers have always been able to fit the descriptions to "people I know," and "the downright scholar" is no exception.

Is one that has much learning in the ore, unwrought and un-tried, which time and experience fashions and refines. He is good metal in the inside, though rough and unscoured with-out, and therefore hated of the courtier, that is quite contrary. The time has got a vein of making him ridiculous, and men laugh at him by tradition, and no unlucky absurdity but is put upon his profession, and done like a scholar. But his fault is only this, that his mind is somewhat too much taken up with his mind, and his thoughts not loaden with any carriage besides. He has not put on the quaint garb of the age, which is now a man's *imprimis* and all the *item*.[1] He has not humbled his meditations to the industry of compliment, nor afflicted his brain in an elaborate leg. His body is not set upon nice pins, to be turning and flexible for every motion, but his scrape[2] is homely and his nod worse. He cannot kiss his hand and cry,

---

[1] All in all.
[2] Bow.

"Madam," nor talk idly enough to bear her company. His smacking of a gentlewoman is somewhat too savory, and he mistakes her nose for her lip. A very woodcock would puzzle him in carving, and he wants the logic of a capon. He has not the glib faculty of sliding over a tale, but his words come squeamishly out of his mouth, and the laughter commonly before the jest. He names this word college too often, and his discourse bears too much on the university. The perplexity of mannerliness will not let him feed, and he is sharp set at an argument when he should cut his meat. He is discarded for a gamester at all games but one and thirty,[3] and at tables he reaches not beyond doublets.[4] His fingers are not long and drawn out to handle a fiddle, but his fist is clunched with the habit of disputing. He ascends a horse somewhat sinisterly, though not on the left side, and they both go jogging in grief together. He is exceedingly censured by the Inns of Court men for that heinous vice, being out of fashion. He cannot speak to a dog in his own dialect, and understands Greek better than the language of a falconer. He has been used to a dark room, and dark clothes, and his eyes dazzle at a satin doublet. The hermitage of his study has made him somewhat uncouth in the world, and men make him worse by staring on him. Thus is he silly and ridiculous, and it continues with him for some quarter of a year out of the university. But practise him a little in men, and brush him o'er with good company, and he shall outbalance those glisterers as far as a solid substance does a feather, or gold, gold-lace.

THE GOOD SCHOOLMASTER

THOMAS FULLER (1608-1661)

From *Holy and Profane States*, 1642. Fuller put life into the character essay by adding illustrations and examples, with the result that the "good

---

[3] Similar to modern blackjack.
[4] Backgammon

schoolmaster" takes on the stature of a lovable human being. The reader will also be surprised to learn how much of the pedagogy of the seventeenth century is still valid.

There is scarce any profession in the commonwealth more necessary which is so slightly performed. The reasons whereof I conceive to be these: first, young scholars make this calling their refuge, yea, perchance, before they have taken any degree in the university, commence schoolmasters in the country, as if nothing else were required to set up this profession but only a rod and a ferula. Secondly, others who are able use it only as a passage to better preferment, to patch the rents in their present fortune till they can provide a new one, and betake themselves to some more gainful calling. Thirdly, they are disheartened from doing their best with the miserable reward which in some places they receive, being masters to the children and slaves to their parents. Fourthly, being grown rich, they grow negligent, and scorn to touch the school but by the proxy of an usher. But see how well our schoolmaster behaves himself.

His genius inclines him with delight to his profession. Some men had as lief be schoolboys as schoolmasters, to be tied to the school, as Cooper's "Dictionary" and Scapula's "Lexicon" are chained to the desks therein; and though great scholars, and skilful in other arts, are bunglers in this: but God of His goodness hath fitted several men for several callings, that the necessity of Church and State in all conditions may be provided for. So that he who beholds the fabric thereof may say, "God hewed out this stone, and appointed it to lie in this very place, for it would fit none other so well, and here it doth most excellent." And thus God mouldeth some for a schoolmaster's life, undertaking it with desire and delight, and discharging it with dexterity and happy success.

He studieth his scholars' natures as carefully as they their books, and ranks their dispositions into several forms. And though it may seem difficult for him in a great school to descend to all particulars, yet experienced schoolmasters may quickly make a grammar of boy's natures, and reduce them all, saving some few exceptions, to these general rules:

1. Those that are ingenious and industrious. The conjunction of two such planets in a youth presages much good unto him. To such a lad a frown may be a whipping, and a whipping a death; yea, where their master whips them once, shame whips them all the week after. Such natures he useth with all gentleness.

2. Those that are ingenious and idle. These think, with the hare in the fable, that running with snails (so they count the rest of their schoolfellows) they shall come soon enough to the post, though sleeping a good while before their starting. Oh, a good rod would finely take them napping.

3. Those that are dull and diligent. Wines, the stronger they be, the more lees they have when they are new. Many boys are muddy-headed till they be clarified with age, and such afterwards prove the best. Bristol diamonds[1] are both bright and squared and pointed by nature, and yet are soft and worthless; whereas orient ones in India are rough and rugged naturally. Hard, rugged, and dull natures of youth acquit themselves afterwards the jewels of the country, and therefore their dullness at first is to borne with, if they be diligent. That schoolmaster deserves to be beaten himself who beats nature in a boy for a fault. And I question whether all the whipping in the world can make their parts, which are naturally sluggish, rise one minute before the hour nature hath appointed.

4. Those that are invincibly dull and negligent also. Correction may reform the latter, not amend the former. All the whetting in the world can never set a razor's edge on that which hath no steel in it. Such boys he consigneth over to other professions. Shipwrights and boatmakers will choose those crooked pieces of timber which other carpenters refuse. Those may make excellent merchants and mechanics who will not serve for scholars.

---

[1] Rock crystals.

He is able, diligent, and methodical in his teaching; not leading them rather in a circle than forwards. He minces his precepts for children to swallow, hanging clogs on the nimbleness of his own soul, that his scholars may go along with him.

He is and will be known to be an absolute monarch in his school. If cockering mothers proffer him money to purchase their sons an exemption from his rod (to live as it were in a peculiar, out of their master's jurisdiction), with disdain he refuseth it, and scorns the late custom, in some places, of commuting whipping into money, and ransoming boys from the rod at a set price. If he hath a stubborn youth, correction-proof, he debaseth not his authority by contesting with him, but fairly, if he can, puts him away before his obstinacy hath affected others.

He is moderate in inflicting deserved correction. Many a schoolmaster better answereth the name παιδοτρίβης than παιδαγωγός, rather tearing his scholars' flesh with whipping than giving them good education. No wonder if his scholars hate the muses, being presented unto them in the shapes of fiends and furies. Junius complains *de insolenti carnificina*[2] of his schoolmaster, by whom *conscindebatur flagris septies aut octies in dies singulos*.[3] Yea, hear the lamentable verses of poor Tusser in his own life:

> "*From Paul's I went, to Eton sent,*
> *To learn straightways the Latin phrase,*
> *Where fifty-three stripes, given to me*
> > *At once I had.*
>
> "*For fault but small, or none at all,*
> *It came to pass thus beat I was;*
> *See Udall, see, the mercy of thee,*
> > *To me, poor lad.*"

Such an Orbilius[4] mars more scholars than he makes: their

[2] Of harsh brutality.
[3] He was torn with whips seven or eight times a day.
[4] Teacher of the poet Horace and notorious for his flogging.

tyranny hath caused many tongues to stammer, which spake plain by nature, and whose stuttering at first was nothing else but fears quavering on their speech at their master's presence; and whose mauling them about their heads hath dulled those who, in quickness, exceeded their master.

He makes his school free to him who sues to him *in forma pauperis.*[5] And surely learning is the greatest alms that can be given. But he is a beast who, because the poor scholar cannot pay him his wages, pays the scholar in his whipping. Rather are diligent lads to be encouraged with all excitements to learning. This minds me of what I have heard concerning Mr. Bust, that worthy late schoolmaster of Eton, who would never suffer any wandering begging scholar (such as justly the statute hath ranked in the forefront of rogues) to come into his school, but would thrust him out with earnestness (however privately charitable unto him), lest his schoolboys should be disheartened from their books by seeing some scholars, after their studying in the university, preferred to beggary.

He spoils not a good school to make thereof a bad college, therein to teach his scholars logic. For, besides that logic may have an action of trespass against grammar for encroaching on her liberties, syllogisms are solecisms taught in the school, and oftentimes they are forced afterwards in the university to unlearn the fumbling skill they had before.

Out of his school he is no whit pedantical in carriage or discourse; contenting himself to be rich in Latin, though he doth not jingle with it in every company wherein he comes.

To conclude, let this amongst other motives make schoolmasters careful in their place, that the eminencies of their scholars have commended the memories of their schoolmasters to posterity, who otherwise in obscurity had altogether been forgotten. Who had ever heard of R. Bond, in Lancashire, but for the breeding of learned Ascham, his scholar? or of Hartgrave, in Brundly school, in the same county, but because he was the first did teach worthy Dr. Whitaker? Nor do I honour the memory of Mulcaster for anything so much as for his

---

[5] As a pauper.

scholar, that gulf of learning, Bishop Andrews. This made the
Athenians, the day before the great feast of Theseus, their
founder, to sacrifice a ram to the memory of Conidas, his
schoolmaster that first instructed him.

A SUPERSTITIOUS HOUSEHOLD

JOSEPH ADDISON (1672-1719)

The Spectator for March 8, 1711. Joseph Addison and his equally famous
collaborator Richard Steele perfected the periodical essay. Day after day
The Spectator offered its readers serious discourse, wholesome entertainment, or a pleasant corrective for social foibles. This gentle satire on be-
setting superstitions is apt to nudge those people who are forever
knocking on wood.

Somnia, terrores magicos, miracula, sagas,
Nocturnos lemures, portentaque Thessala rides? [1]

Horace

Going yesterday to dine with an old acquaintance, I had the
misfortune to find his whole family very much dejected.
Upon asking him the occasion of it, he told me that his wife
had dreamt a very strange dream the night before, which
they were afraid portended some misfortune to themselves
or to their children. At her coming into the room, I observed a
settled melancholy in her countenance, which I should have
been troubled for, had I not heard from whence it proceeded.
We were no sooner sat down, but, after having looked upon
me a little while, "My dear," says she, turning to her husband,
"you may now see the stranger that was in the candle last
night." Soon after this, as they began to talk of family affairs,

---

[1] "Can you make sport of portents, gipsy crones,
Hobgoblins, dreams, raw head and bloody bones?"
—John Conington

a little boy at the lower end of the table told her that he was to go into join-hand [2] on Thursday. "Thursday?" says she, "no, child, if it please God, you shall not begin upon Childermas Day;[3] tell your writing master that Friday will be soon enough." I was reflecting with myself on the oddness of her fancy, and wondering that anybody would establish it as a rule to lose a day in every week. In the midst of these my musings, she desired me to reach her a little salt upon the point of my knife, which I did in such a trepidation and hurry of obedience, that I let it drop by the way; at which she immediately startled, and said it fell towards her. Upon this I looked very blank; and, observing the concern of the whole table, began to consider myself, with some confusion, as a person that had brought a disaster upon the family. The lady however recovering herself, after a little space, said to her husband with a sigh, "My dear, misfortunes never come single." My friend, I found, acted but an under part at his table, and being a man of more good nature than understanding, thinks himself obliged to fall in with all the passions and humors of his yoke-fellow. "Do not you remember, child," says she, "that the pigeon-house fell the very afternoon that our careless wench spilt the salt upon the table?" "Yes," says he, "my dear, and the next post brought us an account of the battle of Almanza." The reader may guess at the figure I made, after having done all this mischief. I despatched my dinner as soon as I could, with my usual taciturnity; when, to my utter confusion, the lady seeing me cleaning my knife and fork, and laying them across one another upon my plate, desired me that I would humor her so far as to take them out of that figure, and place them side by side. What the absurdity was which I had committed I did not know, but I suppose there was some traditionary superstition in it; and therefore, in obedience to the lady of the house, I disposed of my knife and fork in two parallel lines, which is the figure I shall always lay them in for the future, though I do not know any reason for it.

[2] A flowing style of hand-writing.
[3] December 28, supposedly a day of bad fortune.

It is not difficult for a man to see that a person has conceived an aversion to him. For my own part, I quickly found,
by the lady's looks, that she regarded me as a very odd kind of
fellow, with an unfortunate aspect: for which reason I took my
leave immediately after dinner, and withdrew to my own
lodgings. Upon my return home, I fell into a profound contemplation on the evils that attend these superstitious follies of
mankind; how they subject us to imaginary afflictions, and
additional sorrows, that do not properly come within our lot.
As if the natural calamities of life were not sufficient for it, we
turn the most indifferent circumstances into misfortunes, and
suffer as much from trifling accidents as from real evils. I have
known the shooting of a star spoil a night's rest; and have seen
a man in love grow pale and lose his appetite upon the plucking
of a merry-thought.[4] A screech owl at midnight has alarmed a
family more than a band of robbers; nay, the voice of a cricket
hath struck more terror than the roaring of a lion. There is
nothing so inconsiderable, which may not appear dreadful to
an imagination that is filled with omens and prognostics. A
rusty nail, or a crooked pin, shoot up into prodigies.

I remember I was once in a mixed assembly, that was full
of noise and mirth, when on a sudden an old woman unluckily
observed there were thirteen of us in company. This remark
struck a panic terror into several who were present, insomuch
that one or two of the ladies were going to leave the room; but
a friend of mine taking notice that one of our female companions was big with child, affirmed there were fourteen in
the room, and that, instead of portending one of the company
should die, it plainly foretold one of them should be born. Had
not my friend found this expedient to break the omen, I question not but half the women in the company would have fallen
sick that very night.

An old maid, that is troubled with the vapors, produces
infinite disturbances of this kind among her friends and
neighbors. I know a maiden aunt of a great family, who is

---

[4] A wishbone.

one of these antiquated Sibyls, that forebodes and prophesies from one end of the year to the other. She is always seeing apparitions, and hearing death-watches,[5] and was the other day almost frighted out of her wits by the great house-dog, that howled in the stable at a time when she lay ill of the tooth-ache. Such an extravagant cast of mind engages multitudes of people not only in impertinent terrors, but in supernumerary duties of life; and arises from that fear and ignorance which are natural to the soul of man. The horror with which we entertain the thoughts of death (or indeed of any future evil) and the uncertainty of its approach, fill a melancholy mind with innumerable apprehensions and suspicions, and consequently dispose it to the observation of such groundless prodigies and predictions. For as it is the chief concern of wise men to retrench the evils of life by the reasonings of philosophy; it is the employment of fools to multiply them by the sentiments of superstition.

For my own part, I should be very much troubled were I endowed with this divining quality, though it should inform me truly of every thing that can befall me. I would not anticipate the relish of any happiness, nor feel the weight of any misery, before it actually arrives.

I know but one way of fortifying my soul against these gloomy presages and terrors of mind, and that is, by securing to myself the friendship and protection of that Being who disposes of events, and governs futurity. He sees, at one view, the whole thread of my existence, not only that part of it which I have already passed through, but that which runs forward into all the depths of eternity. When I lay me down to sleep, I recommend myself to his care; when I awake, I give myself up to his direction. Amidst all the evils that threaten me, I will look up to him for help, and question not but he will either avert them, or turn them to my advantage. Though I know neither the time nor the manner of the death I am to die, I am not at all solicitous about it; because I am sure that he knows

[5] Ticking beetles.

them both, and that he will not fail to comfort and support me under them.

GULLIVER EXPLAINS WARFARE

JONATHAN SWIFT (1667-1745)

From *Gulliver's Travels*, Part IV, Ch. 5, 1726. Swift made use of bitter irony to expose the disgusting and sordid side of human nature. Gulliver finds himself in a land governed by the Houyhnhnms, a race of benevolent horses, whereas the counterpart of man is the dirty, filthy beast called the Yahoo. In great humiliation Gulliver discovers that he is a Yahoo. In an effort to explain the exalted position of Yahoos in other lands he expostulates zealously upon the wonders of European culture, but unwittingly he makes a mockery of his world. The exultant account of European warfare contains a powerful undercurrent of ridicule.

The reader may please to observe that the following extract of many conversations I had with my master, contains a summary of the most material points which were discoursed at several times, for above two years, his Honor often desiring fuller satisfaction, as I farther improved in the Houyhnhnm tongue. I laid before him, as well as I could, the whole state of Europe; I discoursed of trade and manufactures, of arts and sciences; and the answers I gave to all the questions he made, as they arose upon several subjects, were a fund of conversation not to be exhausted. But I shall here only set down the substance of what passed between us concerning my own country, reducing it into order as well as I can, without any regard to time, or other circumstances, while I strictly adhere to truth. My only concern is, that I shall hardly be able to do justice to my master's arguments and expressions, which must needs suffer by my want of capacity, as well as by a translation into our barbarous English.

In obedience, therefore, to his Honor's commands, I related to him the revolution under the Prince of Orange; the long war with France entered into by the said Prince, and renewed by his successor the present Queen, wherein the greatest powers of Christendom were engaged, and which still continued; I computed, at his request, that about a million of Yahoos might have been killed in the whole progress of it, and perhaps a hundred or more cities taken, and five times as many ships burnt or sunk.

He asked me what were the usual causes or motives that made one country go to war with another. I answered they were innumerable; but I should only mention a few of the chief. Sometimes the ambition of princes, who never think they have land or people enough to govern; sometimes the corruption of ministers, who engage their master in a war in order to stifle or divert the clamor of the subjects against their evil administration. Difference in opinion hath cost many millions of lives: for instance, whether flesh be bread, or bread be flesh; whether the juice of a certain berry be blood or wine; whether whistling be a vice or virtue; whether it be better to kiss a post, or throw it into the fire; what is the best color for a coat,—whether black, white, red, or gray; and whether it should be long or short, narrow or wide, dirty or clean; with many more. Neither are any wars so furious and bloody, or of so long continuance, as those occasioned by difference in opinion, especially if it be in things indifferent.

Sometimes the quarrel between two princes is to decide which of them shall dispossess a third of his dominions, where neither of them pretend to any right. Sometimes one prince quarreleth with another, for fear the other should quarrel with him. Sometimes a war is entered upon, because the enemy is too strong; and sometimes because he is too weak. Sometimes our neighbors want the things which we have, or have the things which we want; and we both fight, till they take ours, or give us theirs. It is a very justifiable cause of a war, to invade a country, after the people have been wasted by famine, destroyed by pestilence, or embroiled by factions among themselves. It is justifiable to enter into war against our nearest ally, when one of his towns lies convenient for us, or a territory of land, that would render our dominions round and complete. If a prince sends forces into a nation where the people are poor and ignorant, he may lawfully put half of them to death, and make slaves of the rest, in order to civilize and reduce them from their barbarous way of living. It is a very kingly, honorable, and frequent practice, when one prince desires the assistance of another to secure him against an invasion, that the assistant, when he hath driven out the invader, should seize on the dominions himself, and kill, imprison, or banish the prince he came to relieve. Alliance by blood or marriage is a frequent cause of war between princes; and the nearer the kindred is, the greater is their disposition to quarrel. Poor nations are hungry, and rich nations are proud; and pride and hunger will ever be at variance. For these reasons, the trade of a soldier is held the most honorable of all others; because a soldier is a Yahoo hired to kill in cold blood as many of his own species, who had never offended him, as possibly he can.

There is likewise a kind of beggarly princes in Europe, not able to make war by themselves, who hire out their troops to richer nations, for so much a day to each man; of which they keep three fourths to themselves, and it is the best part of their maintenance; such are those in many northern parts of Europe.

What you have told me, (said my master) upon the subject of war, does indeed discover most admirably the effects of that reason you pretend to: however, it is happy that the shame is greater than the danger; and that nature hath left you utterly uncapable of doing much mischief.

For your mouths lying flat with your faces, you can hardly bite each other to any purpose, unless by consent. Then as to the claws upon your feet before and behind, they are so short and tender, that one of our *Yahoos* would drive a dozen of yours before him. And therefore in recounting the numbers of those who have been killed in battle, I cannot but think that you have *said the thing which is not.*

I could not forbear shaking my head, and smiling a little at his ignorance. And being no stranger to the art of war, I gave him a description of cannons, culverins, muskets, carabines, pistols, bullets, powder, swords, bayonets, battles, sieges, retreats, attacks, undermines, countermines, bombardments, sea fights; ships sunk with a thousand men, twenty thousand killed on each side; dying groans, limbs flying in the air, smoke, noise, confusion, trampling to death under horses' feet; flight, pursuit, victory; fields strewed with carcases left for food to dogs, and wolves, and birds of prey; plundering, stripping, ravishing, burning and destroying. And to set forth the valour of my own dear countrymen, I assured him, that I had seen them blow up a hundred enemies at once in a siege, and as many in a ship, and beheld the dead bodies drop down in pieces from the clouds, to the great diversion of the spectators.

I was going on to more particulars, when my master commanded me silence. He said, whoever understood the nature of *Yahoos* might easily believe it possible for so vile an animal, to be capable of every action I had named, if their strength and cunning equalled their malice. But as my discourse had increased his abhorrence of the whole species, so he found it gave him a disturbance in his mind, to which he was wholly a stranger before. He thought his ears being used to such abominable words, might by degrees admit them with less detestation. That although he hated the *Yahoos* of this country, yet he no more blamed them for their odious qualities, than he did a *gnnayh* (a bird of prey) for its cruelty, or a sharp stone for cutting his hoof. But when a creature pretending to reason, could be capable of such enormities, he dreaded lest the corruption of that faculty might be worse than brutality itself. He seemed therefore confident, that instead of reason, we were only possessed of some quality fitted to increase our natural vices; as the reflection from a troubled stream returns the image of an ill shapen body, not only larger, but more distorted.

HOW TO PLEASE

LORD CHESTERFIELD (1694-1773)

From *Letters to His Son*. Chesterfield wanted his son to be a scholar, a gentleman, and a career diplomat. The letters are a correspondence course adapted to the peculiar needs of his son. Lest the boy should falter in the competitive social whirl, his father emphasizes suave deportment and astute tact as requisites for success. Perhaps he overdoes it.

LONDON, OCTOBER 16, O.S. 1747.

DEAR BOY:

The art of pleasing is a very necessary one to possess, but a very difficult one to acquire. It can hardly be reduced to rules; and your own good sense and observation will teach you more of it than I can. "Do as you would be done by," is the surest method that I know of pleasing. Observe carefully what pleases you in others, and probably the same things in you will please others. If you are pleased with the complaisance and attention of others to your humours, your tastes, or your weaknesses, depend upon it, the same complaisance and attention on your part to theirs will equally please them. Take the tone of the company that you are in, and do not pretend to give it; be serious, gay, or even trifling, as you find the present humour of the company; this is an attention due from every individual to the majority. Do not tell stories in company; there is nothing more tedious and disagreeable; if by chance you know a very short story, and exceedingly applicable to the present subject of conversation, tell it in as few words as possible; and even then, throw out that you do not love to tell stories, but that the shortness of it tempted you.

Of all things, banish the egotism out of your conversation,

and never think of entertaining people with your own personal concerns or private affairs; though they are interesting to you, they are tedious and impertinent to everybody else; besides that, one cannot keep one's own private affairs too secret. Whatever you think your own excellencies may be, do not affectedly display them in company; nor labour, as many people do, to give that turn to the conversation, which may supply you with an opportunity of exhibiting them. If they are real, they will infallibly be discovered, without your pointing them out yourself, and with much more advantage. Never maintain an argument with heat and clamour, though you think or know yourself to be in the right; but give your opinion modestly and coolly, which is the only way to convince; and, if that does not do, try to change the conversation, by saying, with good-humour, "We shall hardly convince one another; nor is it necessary that we should, so let us talk of something else."

Remember that there is a local propriety to be observed in all companies; and that what is extremely proper in one company may be, and often is, highly improper in another.

The jokes, the *bon-mots*, the little adventures, which may do very well in one company, will seem flat and tedious, when related in another. The particular characters, the habits, the cant of one company may give merit to a word, or a gesture, which would have none at all if divested of those accidental circumstances. Here people very commonly err; and fond of something that has entertained them in one company, and in certain circumstances, repeat it with emphasis in another, where it is either insipid, or, it may be, offensive, by being ill-timed or misplaced. Nay, they often do it with this silly preamble: "I will tell you an excellent thing," or, "I will tell you the best thing in the world." This raises expectations, which, when absolutely disappointed, make the relator of this excellent thing look, very deservedly, like a fool.

If you would particularly gain the affection and friendship of particular people, whether men or women, endeavour to find out their predominant excellency, if they have one, and their prevailing weakness, which everybody has; and do justice to the one, and something more than justice to the other. Men have various objects in which they may excel, or at least would be thought to excel; and, though they love to hear justice done to them, where they know that they excel, yet they are most and best flattered upon those points where they wish to excel, and yet are doubtful whether they do or not. As for example: Cardinal Richelieu, who was undoubtedly the ablest statesman of his time, or perhaps of any other, had the idle vanity of being thought the best poet too; he envied the great Corneille his reputation, and ordered a criticism to be written upon the *Cid*. Those, therefore, who flattered skilfully, said little to him of his abilities in state affairs, or at least but *en passant*, and as it might naturally occur. But the incense which they gave him, the smoke of which they knew would turn his head in their favour, was as a *bel esprit* and a poet. Why? Because he was sure of one excellency, and distrustful as to the other.

You will easily discover every man's prevailing vanity by observing his favourite topic of conversation; for every man talks most of what he has most a mind to be thought to excel in. Touch him but there, and you touch him to the quick. The late Sir Robert Walpole (who was certainly an able man) was little open to flattery upon that head, for he was in no doubt himself about it; but his prevailing weakness was, to be thought to have a polite and happy turn to gallantry —of which he had undoubtedly less than any man living. It was his favourite and frequent subject of conversation, which proved to those who had any penetration that it was his prevailing weakness, and they applied to it with success.

Women have, in general, but one object, which is their beauty; upon which scarce any flattery is too gross for them to follow. Nature has hardly formed a woman ugly enough to be insensible to flattery upon her person; if her face is so shocking that she must, in some degree, be conscious of it, her figure and air, she trusts, make ample amends for it. If her figure is deformed, her face, she thinks, counterbalances it. If they are both bad, she comforts herself that she has graces, a certain manner, a *je ne sçais quoi* still more engaging than beauty. This truth is evident from the studied and elaborate dress of the ugliest woman in the world. An undoubted, uncontested, conscious beauty is, of all women, the least sensible of flattery upon that head; she knows it is her due, and is therefore obliged to nobody for giving it her. She must be flattered upon her understanding; which, though she may possibly not doubt of herself, yet she suspects that men may distrust.

Do not mistake me, and think that I mean to recommend to you abject and criminal flattery: no; flatter nobody's vices or crimes: on the contrary, abhor and discourage them. But there is no living in the world without a complaisant indulgence for people's weaknesses, and innocent, though ridiculous vanities. If a man has a mind to be thought wiser, and a woman handsomer, than they really are, their error is a comfortable one to themselves, and an innocent one with regard to other people; and I would rather make them my friends by indulging them in it, than my enemies by endeavouring (and that to no purpose) to undeceive them.

There are little attentions, likewise, which are infinitely engaging, and which sensibly affect that degree of pride and self-love, which is inseparable from human nature, as they are unquestionable proofs of the regard and consideration which we have for the persons to whom we pay them. As, for example, to observe the little habits, the likings, the antipathies, and the tastes of those whom we would gain; and then take care to provide them with the one, and to secure them from the other; giving them, genteelly, to understand, that you had observed they liked such a dish, or such a room, for which reason you had prepared it: or, on the contrary, that having observed they had an aversion to such a dish, a dislike to such a person, etc., you had taken care to avoid presenting them. Such attention to such trifles flatters self-love much more than greater things, as it makes people think themselves almost the only objects of your thoughts and care.

These are some of the arcana necessary for your initiation

in the great society of the world. I wish I had known them
better at your age; I have paid the price of three and fifty years
for them, and shall not grudge it if you reap the advantage.
Adieu.

THE STAGE-COACH

SAMUEL JOHNSON (1709-1784)

The Adventurer for August 25, 1753. Johnson, learned and sometimes
ponderous, could temper his philosophy to the interests of his fellow
commoners. Time has qualified a few points in this essay but not many.
"Reaching to glory" is a trait of the human species ever old and ever
new. Years after Johnson, O. Henry made use of a similar episode in
Transients in Arcadia.

———

> ———*Tolle periclum,*
> *Jam vaga prosiliet frænis natura remotis.*
>   Horace

> But take the danger and the shame away,
> And vagrant nature bounds upon her prey.
>   Francis

To the *Adventurer*

SIR,
It has been observed, I think, by Sir WILLIAM TEMPLE, and
after him by almost every other writer, that England affords a
greater variety of characters, than the rest of the world. This
is ascribed to the liberty prevailing amongst us, which gives
every man the privilege of being wise or foolish his own way,
and preserves him from the necessity of hypocrisy, or the
servility of imitation.

That the position itself is true, I am not completely satisfied.

To be nearly acquainted with the people of different countries can happen to very few; and in life, as in every thing else beheld at a distance, there appears an even uniformity; the petty discriminations which diversify the natural character, are not discoverable but by a close inspection; we therefore find them most at home, because there we have most opportunities of remarking them. Much less am I convinced, that this peculiar diversification, if it be real, is the consequence of peculiar liberty: for where is the government to be found, that superintends individuals with so much vigilance, as not to leave their private conduct without restraint? Can it enter into a reasonable mind to imagine, that men of every other nation are not equally masters of their own time or houses with ourselves, and equally at liberty to be parsimonious or profuse, frolic or sullen, abstinent or luxurious? Liberty is certainly necessary to the full play of predominant humours; but such liberty is to be found alike under the government of the many or the few; in monarchies or in commonwealths.

How readily the predominant passion snatches an interval of liberty, and how fast it expands itself when the weight of restraint is taken away, I had lately an opportunity to discover, as I took a short journey into the country in a stage coach; which, as every journey is a kind of adventure, may be very properly related to you, though I can display no such extraordinary assembly as CERVANTES has collected at DON QUIXOTE's inn.

In a stage coach the passengers are for the most part wholly unknown to one another, and without expectation of ever meeting again when their journey is at an end; one should therefore imagine, that it was of little importance to any of them, what conjectures the rest should form concerning him. Yet so it is, that as all think themselves secure from detection, all assume that character of which they are most desirous, and on no occasion is the general ambition of superiority more apparently indulged.

On the day of our departure, in the twilight of the morning, I ascended the vehicle with three men and two women, my fellow-travelers. It was easy to observe the affected elevation of mien with which everyone entered, and the supercilious civility with which they paid their compliments to each other. When the first ceremony was dispatched, we sat silent for a long time, all employed in collecting importance into our faces, and endeavouring to strike reverence and submission into our companions.

It is always observable that silence propagates itself, and that the longer talk has been suspended the more difficult it is to find anything to say. We began now to wish for conversation; but no one seemed inclined to descend from his dignity, or first propose a topic of discourse. At last a corpulent gentleman, who had equipped himself for this expedition with a scarlet surtout and a large hat with a broad lace, drew out his watch, looked on it in silence, and then held it dangling at his finger. This was, I suppose, understood by all the company as an invitation to ask the time of the day, but nobody appeared to heed his overture; and his desire to be talking so far overcame his resentment that he let us know of his own accord that it was past five, and that in two hours we should be at breakfast.

His condescension was thrown away; we continued all obdurate; the ladies held up their heads; I amused myself with watching their behaviour; and of the other two, one seemed to employ himself in counting the trees as we drove by them, the other drew his hat over his eyes and counterfeited a slumber. The man of benevolence, to show that he was not depressed by our neglect, hummed a tune and beat time upon his snuff-box.

Thus universally displeased with one another, and not much delighted with ourselves, we came at last to the little inn appointed for our repast; and all began at once to recompense themselves for the constraint of silence by innumerable questions and orders to the people that attended us. At last, what everyone had called for was got, or declared impossible to be got at that time, and we were persuaded to sit round the same table; when the gentleman in the red surtout looked again upon his watch, told us that we had half an hour to spare, but he was sorry to see so little merriment among us; that all fellow-travellers were for the time upon the level, and that it was always his way to make himself one of the company. "I remember," says he, "it was on just such a morning as this that I and my Lord Mumble and the Duke of Tenterden were out upon a ramble: we called at a little house as it might be this; and my landlady, I warrant you, not suspecting to whom she was talking, was so jocular and facetious, and made so many merry answers to our questions, that we were all ready to burst with laughter. At last the good woman happening to overhear me whisper the Duke and call him by his title, was so surprised and confounded that we could scarcely get a word from her; and the Duke never met me from that day to this but he talks of the little house, and quarrels with me for terrifying the landlady."

He had scarcely time to congratulate himself on the veneration which this narrative must have procured him from the company, when one of the ladies, having reached out for a plate on a distant part of the table, began to remark the inconveniences of travelling and the difficulty which they who never sat at home without a great number of attendants found in performing for themselves such offices as the road required; but that people of quality often travelled in disguise, and might be generally known from the vulgar by their condescension to poor innkeepers and the allowance which they made for any defect in their entertainment; that for her part, while people were civil and meant well, it was never her custom to find fault, for one was not to expect upon a journey all that one enjoyed at one's own house.

A general emulation seemed now to be excited. One of the men, who had hitherto said nothing, called for the last newspaper; and having perused it a while with deep pensiveness, "It is impossible," says he, "for any man to guess how to act with regard to the stocks; last week it was the general opinion that they would fall; and I sold out twenty thousand pounds in order to a purchase: they have now risen unexpectedly, and I make no doubt but at my return to London I shall risk thirty thousand pounds among them again."

A young man, who had hitherto distinguished himself only by the vivacity of his look and a frequent diversion of his eyes from one object to another, upon this closed his snuff-box and told us that he had a hundred times talked with the chancellor and the judges on the subject of the stocks; that for his part he did not pretend to be well acquainted with the principles on which they were established, but had always heard them reckoned pernicious to trade, uncertain in their produce, and unsolid in their foundation; and that he had been advised by three judges, his most intimate friends, never to venture his money in the funds, but to put it out upon land security, till he could light upon an estate in his own country.

It might be expected that, upon these glimpses of latent dignity, we should all have begun to look round us with veneration, and have behaved like the princes of romance when the enchantment that disguises them is dissolved and they discover the dignity of each other: yet it happened that none of these hints made much impression on the company; everyone was apparently suspected of endeavouring to impose false appearances upon the rest; all continued their haughtiness, in hopes to enforce their claims; and all grew every hour more sullen, because they found their representations of themselves without effect.

Thus we travelled on four days with malevolence perpetually increasing, and without any endeavour but to outvie each other in superciliousness and neglect; and when any two of us could separate ourselves for a moment, we vented our indignation at the sauciness of the rest.

At length the journey was at an end, and time and chance, that strip off all disguises, have discovered that the intimate of lords and dukes is a nobleman's butler, who has furnished a shop with the money he has saved; the man who deals so largely in the funds, is a clerk of a broker in Change-alley; the lady who so carefully concealed her quality, keeps a cook-shop behind the Exchange; and the young man, who is so happy in the friendship of the judges, engrosses and transcribes for bread in a garret of the Temple. Of one of the women only I could make no disadvantageous detection, because she had assumed no character, but accommodated herself to the scene before her, without any struggle for distinction or superiority.

I could not forbear to reflect on the folly of practising a fraud, which as the event shewed, had been already practised too often to succeed, and by the success of which no advantage could have been obtained; of assuming a character, which was to end with the day; and of claiming upon false pretences honours which must perish with the breath that paid them.

But Mr. ADVENTURER, let not those who laugh at me and my companions, think this folly confined to a stage coach. Every man in the journey of life takes the same advantage of the ignorance of his fellow travellers, disguises himself in counterfeited merit, and hears those praises with complacency which his conscience reproaches him for accepting. Every man deceives himself while he thinks he is deceiving others; and forgets that the time is at hand when every illusion shall cease; when fictitious excellence shall be torn away; and ALL must be shown to ALL in their real state.

I am, SIR,

Your humble Servant,

VIATOR.

AN ELECTION

OLIVER GOLDSMITH (1728-1774)

From *The Citizen of the World*, Letter CXII, 1762. Goldsmith posed as a visiting Chinese who was writing his impressions of England to a friend back home. The device permitted him a playful exaggeraton in his satire on contemporary conventions. Could it be that he somehow foresaw the twentieth-century "kick-off" dinner and the recurrent electioneering fanfare?

FROM LIEN CHI ALTANGI TO FUM HOAM, FIRST PRESIDENT OF THE CEREMONIAL ACADEMY AT PEKIN, IN CHINA.

The English are at present employed in celebrating a feast which becomes general every seventh year; the parliament of the nation being then dissolved, and another appointed to be chosen. This solemnity falls infinitely short of our Feast of the Lanterns in magnificence and splendour; it is also surpassed by others of the East in unanimity and pure devotion; but no festival in the world can compare with it for eating. Their eating, indeed, amazes me; had I five hundred heads, and were each head furnished with brains, yet would they all be insufficient to compute the number of cows, pigs, geese, and turkeys which upon this occasion die for the good of their country.

To say the truth, eating seems to make a grand ingredient in all English parties of zeal, business, or amusement. When a church is to be built or an hospital endowed, the directors assemble and, instead of consulting upon it, they eat upon it, by which means the business goes forward with success. When the poor are to be relieved, the officers appointed to dole out public charity assemble and eat upon it. Nor has it ever been known that they filled the bellies of the poor till they had previously satisfied their own. But in the election of magistrates the people seem to exceed all bounds; the merits of a candidate are often measured by the number of his treats; his constituents assemble, eat upon him, and lend their applause, not to his integrity or sense, but to the quantities of his beef and brandy.

And yet I could forgive this people their plentiful meals on this occasion, as it is extremely natural for every man to eat a great deal when he gets it for nothing; but what amazes me is that all this good living no way contributes to improve their good-humour. On the contrary, they seem to lose their temper as they lose their appetites; every morsel they swallow, and every glass they pour down, serves to increase their animosity. Many an honest man, before as harmless as a tame rabbit, when loaded with a single election dinner has become more dangerous than a charged culverin. Upon one of these occasions I have actually seen a bloody-minded man-milliner sally forth at the head of a mob, determined to face a desperate pastry-cook who was general of the opposite party.

But you must not suppose they are without a pretext for thus beating each other. On the contrary, no man here is so un-

civilized as to beat his neighbour without producing very
sufficient reasons. One candidate, for instance, treats with gin,
a spirit of their own manufacture; another always drinks
brandy, imported from abroad. Brandy is a wholesome liquor;
gin, a liquor wholly their own. This, then, furnishes an obvious
cause of quarrel—whether it be most reasonable to get drunk
with gin or get drunk with brandy? The mob meet upon the
debate, fight themselves sober, and then draw off to get drunk
again, and charge for another encounter. So that the English
may now properly be said to be engaged in war; since, while
they are subduing their enemies abroad, they are breaking each
other's heads at home.

I lately made an excursion to a neighbouring village, in order
to be a spectator of the ceremonies practised upon this occasion.
I left town in company with three fiddlers, nine dozen of hams,
and a corporation poet, which were designed as reinforcements
to the gin-drinking party. We entered the town with a very
good face; the fiddlers, no way intimidated by the enemy, kept
handling their arms up the principal street. By this prudent
manœuvre, they took peaceable possession of their head-
quarters, amidst the shouts of multitudes, who seemed perfectly
rejoiced at hearing their music, but above all at seeing their
bacon.

I must own, I could not avoid being pleased to see all ranks of
people, on this occasion, levelled into an equality, and the poor,
in some measure, enjoying the primitive privileges of nature. If
there was any distinction shown, the lowest of the people
seemed to receive it from the rich. I could perceive a cobbler
with a levee at his door, and a haberdasher giving audience
from behind his counter.

But my reflections were soon interrupted by a mob, who
demanded whether I was for the distillery or the brewery? As
these were terms with which I was totally unacquainted, I
chose at first to be silent; however, I know not what might
have been the consequence of my reserve, had not the attention
of the mob been called off to a skirmish between a brandy-
drinker's cow and a gin-drinker's mastiff, which turned out,

greatly to the satisfaction of the mob, in favour of the mastiff.

This spectacle, which afforded high entertainment, was at last ended by the appearance of one of the candidates, who came to harangue the mob: he made a very pathetic speech upon the late excessive importation of foreign drams, and the downfall of the distillery; I could see some of the audience shed tears. He was accompanied in his procession by Mrs. Deputy and Mrs. Mayoress. Mrs. Deputy was not in the least in liquor; and as for Mrs. Mayoress, one of the spectators assured me in my ear, that—she was a very fine woman before she had the small-pox.

Mixing with the crowd, I was now conducted to the hall where the magistrates are chosen: but what tongue can describe this scene of confusion! the whole crowd seemed equally inspired with anger, jealousy, politics, patriotism, and punch. I remarked one figure that was carried up by two men upon this occasion. I at first began to pity his infirmities as natural, but soon found the fellow so drunk that he could not stand; another made his appearance to give his vote, but though he could stand, he actually lost the use of his tongue, and remained silent; a third, who, though excessively drunk, could both stand and speak, being asked the candidate's name for whom he voted, could be prevailed upon to make no other answer but "Tobacco and brandy." In short, an election hall seems to be a theatre, where every passion is seen without disguise; a school where fools may readily become worse, and where philosophers may gather wisdom.—Adieu.

OF SOCIETY AND CIVILIZATION

THOMAS PAINE (1738-1809)

From *The Rights of Man*, Part Second, Ch. 1, 1791. Out of the milieu that produced the doctrine that all men are created equal came Tom Paine. In his opinion all governments were oppressive, whereas mankind, untrammeled and uncoerced, would display his innate nobility and live amicably with his neighbor. It can be seen that Paine was neither wholly right nor wholly wrong.

Great part of that order which reigns among mankind is not the effect of government. It has its origin in the principles of society and the natural constitution of man. It existed prior to government, and would exist if the formality of government was abolished. The mutual dependence and reciprocal interest which man has upon man, and all the parts of a civilised community upon each other, create that great chain of connection which holds it together. The landholder, the farmer, the manufacturer, the merchant, the tradesman, and every occupation, prospers by the aid which each receives from the other, and from the whole. Common interest regulates their concerns, and forms their law; and the laws which common usage ordains, have a greater influence than the laws of government. In fine, society performs for itself almost everything which is ascribed to government.

To understand the nature and quantity of government proper for man, it is necessary to attend to his character. As nature created him for social life, she fitted him for the station she intended. In all cases she made his natural wants greater than his individual powers. No one man is capable, without the aid of society, of supplying his own wants; and those wants, acting upon every individual, impel the whole of them into society, as naturally as gravitation acts to a centre.

But she has gone further. She has not only forced man into society by a diversity of wants which the reciprocal aid of each other can supply, but she has implanted in him a system of social affections, which, though not necessary to his existence, are essential to his happiness. There is no period in life when this love for society ceases to act. It begins and ends with our being.

If we examine with attention the composition and constitution of man, the diversity of his wants and talents in different men for reciprocally accommodating the wants of each other, his propensity to society, and consequently to preserve the advantages resulting from it, we shall easily discover that a great part of what is called government is mere imposition.

Government is no farther necessary than to supply the few cases to which society and civilisation are not conveniently competent; and instances are not wanting to show, that everything which government can usefully add thereto, has been performed by the common consent of society, without government.

For upwards of two years from the commencement of the American War, and to a longer period in several of the American States, there were no established forms of government. The old governments had been abolished, and the country was too much occupied in defence to employ its attention in establishing new governments; yet during this interval order and harmony were preserved as inviolate as in any country in Europe. There is a natural aptness in man, and more so in society, because it embraces a greater variety of abilities and resources, to accommodate itself to whatever situation it is in. The instant formal government is abolished, society begins to act: a general association takes place, and common interest produces common security.

So far is it from being true, as has been pretended, that the abolition of any formal government is the dissolution of society, that it acts by a contrary impulse, and brings the latter the closer together. All that part of its organization which it had committed to its government, devolves again upon itself, and acts through its medium. When men, as well from natural instinct as from reciprocal benefits, have habituated themselves to social and civilised life, there is always enough of its principles in practice to carry them through any changes they may find necessary or convenient to make in their government. In short, man is so naturally a creature of society that it is almost impossible to put him out of it.

Formal government makes but a small part of civilised life; and when even the best that human wisdom can devise is established, it is a thing more in name and idea than in fact. It is to the great and fundamental principles of society and civilisation—to the common usage universally consented to, and mutually and reciprocally maintained—to the unceasing circulation of interest, which, passing through its million channels, invigorates the whole mass of civilised man—it is to these things, infinitely more than to anything which even the best instituted government can perform, that the safety and prosperity of the individual and of the whole depends.

The more perfect civilisation is, the less occasion has it for government, because the more it does regulate its own affairs, and govern itself; but so contrary is the practice of old governments to the reason of the case, that the expenses of them increase in the proportion they ought to diminish. It is but few general laws that civilised life requires, and those of such common usefulness, that whether they are enforced by the forms of government or not, the effect will be nearly the same. If we consider what the principles are that first condense men into society, and what the motives that regulate their mutual intercourse afterwards, we shall find, by the time we arrive at what is called government, that nearly the whole of the business is performed by the natural operation of the parts upon each other.

Man, with respect to all those matters, is more a creature of consistency than he is aware, or than governments would wish him to believe. All the great laws of society are laws of nature. Those of trade and commerce, whether with respect to the intercourse of individuals or of nations, are laws of mutual and reciprocal interests. They are followed and obeyed, because it is the interest of the parties so to do, and not on account of any formal laws their governments may impose or interpose.

But how often is the natural propensity to society disturbed or destroyed by the operations of government! When the latter, instead of being ingrafted on the principles of the former, assumes to exist for itself, and acts by partialities of favour and oppression, it becomes the cause of the mischiefs it ought to prevent.

If we look back to the riots and tumults which at various times have happened in England, we shall find that they did not proceed from the want of a government, but that government was itself the generating cause: instead of consolidating society it divided it; it deprived it of its natural cohesion, and engendered discontents and disorders which otherwise would not have existed. In those associations, which men promiscuously form for the purpose of trade, or of any concern in which government is totally out of the question, and in which they act merely on the principles of society, we see how naturally the various parties unite; and this shows, by comparison, that governments, so far from being always the cause or means of order, are often the destruction of it. The riots of 1780[1] had no other source than the remains of those prejudices which the Government of itself had encouraged. But with respect to England there are also other causes.

Excess and inequality of taxation, however disguised in the means, never fail to appear in their effects. As a great mass of the community are thrown thereby into poverty and discontent, they are constantly on the brink of commotion; and deprived, as they unfortunately are, of the means of information, are easily heated to outrage. Whatever the apparent cause of any riots may be, the real one is always want of happiness. It shows that something is wrong in the system of government that injures the felicity by which society is to be preserved.

But as fact is superior to reasoning, the instance of America presents itself to confirm these observations. If there is a country in the world where concord, according to common calculation, would be least expected, it is America. Made up

---

[1] The George Gordon riots.

as it is of people from different nations, accustomed to different forms and habits of government, speaking different languages, and more different in their modes of worship, it would appear that the union of such a people was impracticable; but by the simple operation of constructing government on the principles of society and the rights of man, every difficulty retires, and all the parts are brought into cordial unison. There the poor are not oppressed, the rich are not privileged. Industry is not mortified by the splendid extravagance of a Court rioting at its expense. Their taxes are few, because their government is just: and as there is nothing to render them wretched, there is nothing to engender riots and tumults.

A metaphysical man, like Mr. Burke,[2] would have tortured his invention to discover how such a people could be governed. He would have supposed that some must be managed by fraud, others by force, and all by some contrivance; that genius must be hired to impose upon ignorance, and show and parade to fascinate the vulgar. Lost in the abundance of his researches, he would have resolved and re-resolved, and finally overlooked the plain and easy road that lay directly before him.

One of the great advantages of the American Revolution has been, that it led to a discovery of the principles, and laid open the imposition of governments. All the Revolutions till then had been worked within the small sphere of a Court, and never on the great floor of a Nation. The parties were always of the class of courtiers; and whatever was their rage for reformation, they carefully preserved the fraud of the profession.

In all cases they took care to represent government as a thing made up of mysteries, which only themselves understood; and they hid from the understanding of the Nation the only thing that was beneficial to know, namely, *that government is nothing more than a national association acting on the principles of society.*

---

[2] Edmund Burke, author of *Reflections on the French Revolution,* to which Paine's book is a reply.

CHARACTERISTICS OF SHAKESPEARE'S DRAMAS

SAMUEL TAYLOR COLERIDGE (1772-1834)

From *Lectures on Shakespeare*, 1818. Full of the then new romantic fervor, Coleridge sought to present Shakespeare to the world in a new light. The lecture which follows is therefore aimed to strike the key note of Shakespeare's genius. Modern scholarship has seen fit to alter very little of Coleridge's masterful evaluation.

In lectures of which amusement forms a large part of the object, there are some peculiar difficulties. The architect places his foundation out of sight, and the musician tunes his instrument before he makes his appearance; but the lecturer has to try his chords in the presence of the assembly, an operation not likely, indeed, to produce much pleasure, but yet indispensably necessary to a right understanding of the subject to be developed.

Poetry in essence is as familiar to barbarous as to civilized nations. The Laplander and the savage Indian are cheered by it as well as the inhabitants of London and Paris; its spirit takes up and incorporates surrounding materials, as a plant clothes itself with soil and climate, whilst it exhibits the working of a vital principle within, independent of all accidental circumstances. And to judge with fairness of an author's works, we ought to distinguish what is inward and essential from what is outward and circumstantial. It is essential to poetry that it be simple, and appeal to the elements and primary laws of our nature; that it be sensuous, and by its imagery elicit truth at a flash; that it be impassioned, and be able to move our feelings and awaken our affections. In comparing different poets with each other, we should inquire which have brought into the fullest play our imagination and our reason, or have created the greatest excitement and produced the completest harmony. If we consider great exquisiteness of language and sweetness of meter alone, it is impossible to deny to Pope the character of a delightful writer; but whether he be a poet must depend upon our definition of the word; and doubtless, if everything that pleases be poetry, Pope's satires and epistles must be poetry. This I must say, that poetry, as distinguished from other modes of composition, does not rest in meter, and that it is not poetry if it make no appeal to our passions or our imagination. One character belongs to all true poets, that they write from a principle within, not originating in anything without; and that the true poet's work in its form, its shapings, and its modifications, is distinguished from all other works that assume to belong to the class of poetry, as a natural from an artificial flower, or as the mimic garden of a child from an enameled meadow. In the former the flowers are broken from their stems and stuck into the ground; they are beautiful to the eye and fragrant to the sense, but their colors soon fade, and their odor is transient as the smile of the planter; while the meadow may be visited again and again with renewed delight; its beauty is innate in the soil, and its bloom is of the freshness of nature.

The next ground of critical judgment, and point of comparison, will be as to how far a given poet has been influenced by accidental circumstances. As a living poet must surely write, not for the ages past, but for that in which he lives, and those which are to follow, it is, on the one hand, natural that he should not violate, and on the other, necessary that he should not depend on, the mere manners and modes of his day. See how little does Shakespeare leave us to regret that he was born in his particular age!

I have said, and I say it again, that great as was the genius of Shakespeare, his judgment was at least equal to it. Of this any one will be convinced, who attentively considers those points in which the dramas of Greece and England differ, from the dissimilitude of circumstances by which each was modified and influenced. The Greek stage had its origin in the ceremonies of a sacrifice, such as of the goat to Bacchus, whom we most erroneously regard as merely the jolly god of wine;— for among the ancients he was venerable, as the symbol of that power which acts without our consciousness in the vital energies of nature,—the *vinum mundi*,[1]—as Apollo was that of the conscious agency of our intellectual being. The heroes of old under the influences of this Bacchic enthusiasm performed more than human actions;—hence tales of the favorite champions soon passed into dialogue. On the Greek stage the chorus was always before the audience; the curtain was never dropped, as we should say; and change of place being therefore, in general, impossible, the absurd notion of condemning it merely as improbable in itself was never entertained by any one. If we can believe ourselves at Thebes in one act, we may believe ourselves at Athens in the next. If a story lasts twenty-four hours or twenty-four years, it is equally improbable. There seems to be no just boundary but what the feelings prescribe. But on the Greek stage where the same persons were perpetually before the audience, great judgment was necessary in venturing on any such change. The poets never, therefore, attempted to impose on the senses by bringing places to men, but they did bring men to places, as in the well known instance in the *Eumenides*,[2] where, during an evident retirement of the chorus from the orchestra, the scene is changed to Athens, and Orestes[3] is first introduced in the temple of Minerva, and the chorus of Furies come in afterwards in pursuit of him.

In the Greek drama there were no formal divisions into scenes and acts; there were no means, therefore, of allowing for the necessary lapse of time between one part of the dialogue and another, and unity of time in a strict sense was, of course, impossible. To overcome that difficulty of accounting for time, which is effected on the modern stage by dropping a curtain, the judgment and great genius of the ancients supplied music and measured motion, and with the lyric ode filled up the

---

[1] Wine of the world.
[2] By Aeschylus.
[3] Son of Agamemnon, he slew his mother and Aegisthus, her lover, for their murder of his father.

vacuity. In the story of the *Agamemnon* of Aeschylus, the capture of Troy is supposed to be announced by a fire lighted on the Asiatic shore and the transmission of the signal by successive beacons to Mycenae. The signal is first seen at the 21st line, and the herald from Troy itself enters at 486th, and Agamemnon himself at the 783rd line. But the practical absurdity of this was not felt by the audience, who, in imagination stretched the minutes into hours, while they listened to the lofty narrative odes of the chorus which almost entirely filled up the interspace. Another fact deserves attention here, namely, that regularly on the Greek stage a drama, or acted story, consisted in reality of three dramas, called together a trilogy, and performed consecutively in the course of one day. Now you may conceive a tragedy of Shakespeare's as a trilogy connected in one single representation. Divide *Lear* into three parts, and each would be a play with the ancients; or take the three Aeschylean dramas of *Agamemnon*,[4] and divide them into, or call them, as many acts, and they together would be one play. The first act would comprise the usurpation of Aegisthus and the murder of Agamemnon; the second, the revenge of Orestes and the murder of his mother; and the third, the penance and absolution of Orestes;—occupying a period of twenty-two years.

The stage in Shakespeare's time was a naked room with a blanket for a curtain; but he made it a field for monarchs. That law of unity, which has its foundations, not in the factitious necessity of custom, but in nature itself, the unity of feeling, is everywhere and at all times observed by Shakespeare in his plays. Read *Romeo and Juliet:* all is youth and spring; youth with its follies, its virtues, its precipitancies; spring with its odors, its flowers, and its transciency. It is one and the same feeling that commences, goes through, and ends the play. The old men, the Capulets and the Montagues, are not common old men; they have an eagerness, a heartiness, a vehemence, the effect of spring; with Romeo, his change of passion, his sudden marriage, and his rash death, are all the

---

[4] *Agamemnon, Choephoroi,* and *Eumenides.*

effects of youth; whilst in Juliet, love has all that is tender and melancholy in the nightingale, all that is voluptuous in the rose, with whatever is sweet in the freshness of spring; but it ends with a long deep sigh like the last breeze of the Italian evening. This unity of feeling and character pervades every drama of Shakespeare.

It seems to me that his plays are distinguished from those of all other dramatic poets by the following characteristics:

1. Expectation in preference to surprise. It is like the true reading of the passage: "God said, Let there be light, and there was *light*"; not there *was* light. As the feeling with which we startle at a shooting star compared with that of watching the sunrise at the pre-established moment, such and so low is surprise compared with expectation.

2. Signal adherence to the great law of nature, that all opposites tend to attract and temper each other. Passion in Shakespeare generally displays libertinism, but involves morality; and if there are exceptions to this, they are—independently of their intrinsic value—all of them indicative of individual character, and, like the farewell admonitions of a parent, have an end beyond the parental relation. Thus the Countess's beautiful precepts to Bertram,[5] by elevating her character, raise that of Helena her favourite, and soften down the point in her which Shakespeare does not mean us not to see, but to see and to forgive, and at length to justify. And so it is in Polonius, who is the personified memory of wisdom no longer actually possessed. This admirable character is always misrepresented on the stage. Shakespeare never intended to exhibit him as a buffoon; for although it was natural that Hamlet—a young man of fire and genius, detesting formality, and disliking Polonius on political grounds, as imagining that he had assisted his uncle in his usurpation—should express himself satirically, yet this must not be taken as exactly the poet's conception of him. In Polonius a certain induration of character had arisen from long habits of business; but take his advice to Laertes, and Ophelia's reverence for his memory, and we shall see that

[5] *All's Well*, Act I, Sc. i.

he was meant to be represented as a statesman somewhat past his faculties,—his recollections of life all full of wisdom, and showing a knowledge of human nature, whilst what immediately takes place before him, and escapes from him, is indicative of weakness. But as in Homer all the deities are in armour, even Venus, so in Shakespeare all the characters are strong. Hence real folly and dulness are made by him the vehicles of wisdom. There is no difficulty for one being a fool to imitate a fool; but to be, remain, and speak like a wise man and a great wit, and yet so as to give a vivid representation of a veritable fool, *hic labor, hoc opus est.*[6] A drunken constable is not uncommon, nor hard to draw; but see and examine what goes to make up a Dogberry.[7]

3. Keeping at all times in the high road of life. Shakespeare has no innocent adulteries, no interesting incests, no virtuous vice; he never renders that amiable which religion and reason alike teach us to detest, or clothes impurity in the garb of virtue, like Beaumont and Fletcher, the Kotzebues[8] of the day. Shakespeare's fathers are roused by ingratitude, his husbands stung by unfaithfulness; in him, in short, the affections are wounded in those points in which all may—nay, must—feel. Let the morality of Shakespeare be contrasted with that of the writers of his own or the succeeding age, or of those of the present day, who boast their superiority in this respect. No one can dispute that the result of such a comparison is altogether in favour of Shakespeare; even the letters of women of high rank in his age were often coarser than his writings. If he occasionally disgusts a keen sense of delicacy, he never injures the mind; he neither excites nor flatters passion, in order to degrade the subject of it; he does not use the faulty thing for a faulty purpose, nor carries on warfare against virtue by causing wickedness to appear as no wickedness, through the medium of a morbid sympathy with the unfortunate. In Shakespeare vice never walks as in twilight; nothing is purposely out of place; he inverts not the order of nature and propriety,—

---

[6] This is the labor, this is the work.
[7] In *Much Ado.*
[8] Kotzebue was a popular German dramatist.

does not make every magistrate a drunkard or glutton, nor every poor man meek, humane, and temperate; he has no benevolent butchers, or sentimental rat-catchers.

4. Independence of the dramatic interest on the plot. The interest in the plot is always in fact on account of the characters, not *vice versa*, as in almost all other writers; the plot is a mere canvas and no more. Hence arises the true justification of the same stratagem being used in regard to Benedick and Beatrice,—the vanity in each being alike. Take away from the *Much Ado about Nothing* all that which is not indispensable to the plot, either as having little to do with it, or, at best, like Dogberry and his comrades, forced into the service when any other less ingeniously absurd watchmen and night-constables would have answered the mere necessities of the action; take away Benedick, Beatrice, Dogberry, and the reaction of the former on the character of Hero, and what will remain? In other writers the main agent of the plot is always the prominent character; in Shakespeare it is so, or is not so, as the character is in itself calculated, or not calculated, to form the plot. Don John is the main-spring of the plot of this play; but he is merely shown and then withdrawn.

5. Independence of the interest on the story as the groundwork of the plot. Hence Shakespeare never took the trouble of inventing stories. It was enough for him to select from those that had been already invented or recorded such as had one or other, or both, of two recommendations, namely, suitableness to his particular purpose, and their being parts of popular tradition—names of which we had often heard, and of their fortunes, and as to which all we wanted was, to see the man himself. So it is just the man himself, the Lear, the Shylock, the Richard, that Shakespeare makes us for the first time acquainted with. Omit the first scene in *Lear*, and yet everything will remain; so the first and second scenes in *The Merchant of Venice*. Indeed it is universally true.

6. Interfusion of the lyrical (that which in its very essence is poetical) not only with the dramatic, as in the plays of Metastasio,[9] where at the end of the scenes comes the *aria*

---

[9] An eighteenth-century Italian.

as the *exit* speech of the character, but also in and through the dramatic. Songs in Shakespeare are introduced as songs only, just as songs are in real life, beautifully as some of them are characteristic of the person who has sung or called for them, as Desdemona's "Willow," [10] and Ophelia's wild snatches, and the sweet carollings in *As You Like It*. But the whole of the *Midsummer-Night's Dream* is one continued specimen of the dramatized lyrical. And observe how exquisitely the dramatic of Hotspur:

> *Marry and I'm glad on't with all my heart;*
> *I'd rather be a kitten and cry mew, &c.*

melts away into the lyric of Mortimer:

> *I understand thy looks: that pretty Welsh*
> *Which thou pour'st down from these swelling heavens*
> *I am too perfect in, &c.*
>
> *1 Henry IV*, III, i

7. The characters of the *dramatis personae*, like those in real life, are to be inferred by the reader; they are not told to him. And it is well worth remarking that Shakespeare's characters, like those in real life, are very commonly misunderstood, and almost always understood by different persons in different ways. The causes are the same in either case. If you take only what the friends of the character say, you may be deceived, and still more so, if that which his enemies say; nay, even the character himself sees through the medium of his character, and not exactly as he is. Take all together, not omitting a shrewd hint from the clown, or the fool, and perhaps your impression will be right; and you may know whether you have in fact discovered the poet's own idea, by all the speeches receiving light from it, and attesting its reality by reflecting it.

Lastly, in Shakespeare the heterogeneous is united, as it is in nature. You must not suppose a pressure or passion always acting on or in the character. Passion in Shakespeare is that by

---

[10] Song in *Othello*, Act IV, Sc. iii.

which the individual is distinguished from others, not that which makes a different kind of him. Shakespeare followed the main march of the human affections. He entered into no analysis of the passions or faiths of men, but assured himself that such and such passions and faiths were grounded in our common nature, and not in the mere accidents of ignorance or disease. This is an important consideration and constitutes our Shakespeare the morning star, the guide and the pioneer, of true philosophy.

THE INDIAN JUGGLERS

WILLIAM HAZLITT (1778-1830)

From *Table Talk*, 1822. In Hazlitt there is a blend of the critic, the artist, and the philosopher. Here he is led to consider the differences between awesome dexterity and inspired fumbling, egocentric vision and dynamic comprehension, talent and genius.

Coming forward and seating himself on the ground in his white dress and tightened turban, the chief of the Indian Jugglers begins with tossing up two brass balls, which is what any of us could do, and concludes with keeping up four at the same time, which is what none of us could do to save our lives, nor if we were to take our whole lives to do it in. Is it then a trifling power we see at work, or is it not something next to miraculous? It is the utmost stretch of human ingenuity, which nothing but the bending the faculties of body and mind to it from the tenderest infancy with incessant, ever-anxious application up to manhood, can accomplish or make even a slight approach to. Man, thou art a wonderful animal, and thy ways past finding out! Thou canst do strange things, but thou turnest them to little account!—To conceive of this effort of extraordinary dexterity distracts the imagination and makes admiration breathless. Yet it costs nothing to the performer, any more than if it were a mere mechanical deception with which he had nothing to do but to watch and laugh at the astonishment of the spectators. A single error of a hair's-breadth, of the smallest conceivable portion of time, would be fatal: the precision of the movements must be like a mathematical truth, their rapidity is like lightning. To catch four balls in succession in less than a second of time, and deliver them back so as to return with seeming consciousness to the hand again, to make them revolve round him at certain intervals, like the planets in their spheres, to make them chase one another like sparkles of fire, or shoot up like flowers or meteors, to throw them behind his back and twine them round his neck like ribbons or like serpents, to do what appears an impossibility, and to do it with all the ease, the grace, the carelessness imaginable, to laugh at, to play with the glittering mockeries, to follow them with his eye as if he could fascinate them with its lambent fire, or if he had only to see that they kept time with the music on the stage —there is something in all this which he who does not admire may be quite sure he never really admired any thing in the whole course of his life. It is skill surmounting difficulty, and beauty triumphing over skill. It seems as if the difficulty once mastered naturally resolved itself into ease and grace, and as if to be overcome at all, it must be overcome without an effort. The smallest awkwardness or want of pliancy or self-possession would stop the whole process. It is the work of witchcraft, and yet sport for children. Some of the other feats are quite as curious and wonderful, such as the balancing the artificial tree and shooting a bird from each branch through a quill; though none of them have the elegance or facility of the keeping up of the brass balls. You are in pain for the result, and glad when the experiment is over; they are not accompanied with the same unmixed, unchecked delight as the former; and I would not give much to be merely astonished without being pleased at the same time. As to the swallowing of the sword, the police ought to interfere to prevent it. When I saw the Indian Juggler do the same things before, his feet were bare, and he had large rings on the toes, which kept turning round all the time of the performance, as if they moved of themselves.—The hearing a speech in Parliament, drawled or stammered out by the Honourable Member or the Noble Lord, the ringing the changes on their common-places, which any one could repeat after them as well as they, stirs me not a jot, shakes not my good opinion of myself: but the seeing the Indian Jugglers does. It makes me ashamed of myself. I ask what there is that I can do as well as this? Nothing. What have I been doing all my life? Have I been idle, or have I nothing to shew for all my labour and pains? Or have I passed my time in pouring words like water into empty sieves, rolling a stone up a hill and then down again, trying to prove an argument in the teeth of facts, and looking for causes in the dark, and not finding them? Is there no one thing in which I can challenge competition, that I can bring as an instance of exact perfection, in which others cannot find a flaw? The utmost I can pretend to is to write a description of what this fellow can do. I can write a book: so can many others who have not even learned to spell. What abortions are these Essays! What errors, what ill-pieced transitions, what crooked reasons, what lame conclusions! How little is made out, and that little how ill! Yet they are the best I can do. I endeavour to recollect all I have ever observed or thought upon a subject, and to express it as nearly as I can. Instead of writing on four subjects at a time, it is as much as I can manage to keep the thread of one discourse clear and unentangled. I have also time on my hands to correct my opinions, and polish my periods: but the one I cannot, and the other I will not do. I am fond of arguing: yet with a good deal of pains and practice it is often as much as I can do to beat my man; though he may be a very indifferent hand. A common fencer would disarm his adversary in the twinkling of an eye, unless he were a professor like himself. A stroke of wit will sometimes produce this effect, but there is no such power or superiority in sense or reasoning. There is no complete mastery of execution to be shewn there: and you hardly know the professor from the impudent pretender or the mere clown.[1]

I have always had this feeling of the inefficacy and slow progress of intellectual compared to mechanical excellence, and it has always made me somewhat dissatisfied. It is a great many years since I saw Richer, the famous rope-dancer, perform at Sadler's Wells. He was matchless in his art, and added to his extraordinary skill exquisite ease, and unaffected natural grace. I was at that time employed in copying a half-length picture of Sir Joshua Reynolds's; and it put me out of conceit with it. How ill this part was made out in the drawing! How heavy, how slovenly this other was painted! I could not help saying to myself, "If the rope-dancer had performed his task in this manner, leaving so many gaps and botches in his work, he would have broke his neck long ago; I should never have seen that vigorous elasticity of nerve and precision of movement!" —Is it then so easy an undertaking (comparatively) to dance on a tight-rope? Let any one, who thinks so, get up and try. There is the thing. It is that which at first we cannot do at all, which in the end is done to such perfection. To account for this in some degree, I might observe that mechanical dexterity is confined to doing some one particular thing, which you can repeat as often as you please, in which you know whether you succeed or fail, and where the point of perfection consists in succeeding in a given undertaking.—In mechanical efforts, you improve by perpetual practice, and you do so infallibly, because

---

[1] The celebrated Peter Pindar (Dr Wolcot) first discovered and brought out the talents of the late Mr Opie, the painter. He was a poor Cornish boy, and was out at work in the fields, when the poet went in search of him. 'Well, my lad, can you go and bring me your very best picture?' The other flew like lightning, and soon came back with what he considered as his master-piece. The stranger looked at it, and the young artist, after waiting for some time without his giving any opinion, at length exclaimed eagerly, 'Well, what do you think of it?'—'Think of it?' said Wolcot, 'why I think you ought to be ashamed of it—that you who might do so well, do no better!' The same answer would have applied to this artist's latest performances, that had been suggested by one of his earliest efforts. [Hazlitt's note.]

the object to be attained is not a matter of taste or fancy or opinion, but of actual experiment, in which you must either do the thing or not do it. If a man is put to aim at a mark with a bow and arrow, he must hit it or miss it, that's certain. He cannot deceive himself, and go on shooting wide or falling short, and still fancy he is making progress. The distinction between right and wrong, between true and false, is here palpable; and he must either correct his aim or persevere in his error with his eyes open, for which there is neither excuse nor temptation. If a man is learning to dance on a rope, if he does not mind what he is about, he will break his neck. After that, it will be in vain for him to argue that he did not make a false step. His situation is not like that of Goldsmith's pedagogue.—

> *In argument they own'd his wondrous skill,*
> *And e'en though vanquish'd, he could argue still.*[2]

Danger is a good teacher, and makes apt scholars. So are disgrace, defeat, exposure to immediate scorn and laughter. There is no opportunity in such cases for self-delusion, no idling time away, no being off your guard (or you must take the consequences)—neither is there any room for humour or caprice or prejudice. If the Indian Jugglers were to play tricks in throwing up the three case-knives, which keep their positions like the leaves of a crocus in the air, he would cut his fingers. I can make a very bad antithesis without cutting my fingers. The tact of style is more ambiguous than that of double-edged instruments. If the Juggler were told that by flinging himself under the wheels of the Jaggernaut,[3] when the idol issues forth on a gaudy day, he would immediately be transported into Paradise, he might believe it, and nobody could disprove it. So the Brahmins may say what they please on that subject, may build up dogmas and mysteries without end, and not be detected: but their ingenious countryman cannot persuade

---

[2] From *The Deserted Village.*

[3] A Hindu god whose car on a certain day made a triumphal procession. Devotees threw themselves beneath the wheels in the hope of gaining entrance to Paradise.

the frequenters of the Olympic Theatre that he performs a number of astonishing feats without actually giving proofs of what he says.—There is then in this sort of manual dexterity, first a gradual aptitude acquired to a given exertion of muscular power, from constant repetition, and in the next place, an exact knowledge how much is still wanting and necessary to be supplied. The obvious test is to increase the effort or nicety of the operation, and still to find it come true. The muscles ply instinctively to the dictates of habit. Certain movements and impressions of the hand and eye, having been repeated together an infinite number of times, are unconsciously but unavoidably cemented into closer and closer union; the limbs require little more than to be put in motion for them to follow a regular track with ease and certainty; so that the mere intention of the will acts mathematically, like touching the spring of a machine,* and you come with Locksley in Ivanhoe, in shooting at a mark, "to allow for the wind."

Farther, what is meant by perfection in mechanical exercises is the performing certain feats to a uniform nicety, that is, in fact, undertaking no more than you can perform. You task yourself, the limit you fix is optional, and no more than human industry and skill can attain to: but you have no abstract, independent standard of difficulty or excellence (other than the extent of your own powers). Thus he who can keep up four brass balls does this *to perfection;* but he cannot keep up five at the same instant, and would fail every time he attempted it. That is, the mechanical performer undertakes to emulate himself, not to equal another.[4] But the artist undertakes to imitate another, or to do what nature has done, and this it appears is more difficult, *viz.* to copy what she has set before us in the face of nature or "human face divine," entire and without a blemish, than to keep up four brass balls at the same instant; for the one is done by the power of human skill and industry, and the other never was nor will be. Upon the whole, therefore, I have more respect for Reynolds, than I have for

* If two persons play each other at any game, one of them necessarily fails. [Hazlitt's note.]

Richer; for, happen how it will, there have been more people
in the world who could dance on a rope like the one than who
could paint like Sir Joshua. The latter was but a bungler in his
profession to the other, it is true; but then he had a harder task-
master to obey, whose will was more wayward and obscure,
and whose instructions it was more difficult to practise. You
can put a child apprentice to a tumbler or rope-dancer with a
comfortable prospect of success, if they are but sound of wind
and limb: but you cannot do the same thing in painting. The
odds are a million to one. You may make indeed as many
H——s and H——s,[5] as you put into that sort of machine, but
not one Reynolds amongst them all, with his grace, his grandeur, his blandness of *gusto*, "in tones and gestures hit," unless
you could make the man over again. To snatch this grace
beyond the reach of art is then the height of art—where fine
art begins, and where mechanical skill ends. The soft suffusion
of the soul, the speechless breathing eloquence, the looks
"commercing with the skies," the ever-shifting forms of an
eternal principle, that which is seen but for a moment, but
dwells in the heart always, and is only seized as it passes by
strong and secret sympathy, must be taught by nature and
genius, not by rules or study. It is suggested by feeling, not by
laborious microscopic inspection: in seeking for it without, we
lose the harmonious clue to it within: and in aiming to grasp
the substance, we let the very spirit of art evaporate. In a word,
the objects of fine art are not the objects of sight but as these
last are the objects of taste and imagination, that is, as they
appeal to the sense of beauty, of pleasure, and of power in
the human breast, and are explained by that finer sense, and
revealed in their innner structure to the eye in return. Nature
is also a language. Objects, like words, have a meaning; and
the true artist is the interpreter of this language, which he can
only do by knowing its application to a thousand other objects
in a thousand other situations. Thus the eye is too blind a guide
of itself to distinguish between the warm or cold tone of a

---

[5] Probably Benjamin Haydon and John Hoppner, two painters whom
Hazlitt esteemed little.

deep blue sky, but another sense acts as a monitor to it, and does not err. The colour of the leaves in autumn would be nothing without the feeling that accompanies it; but it is that feeling that stamps them on the canvas, faded, seared, blighted, shrinking from the winter's flaw, and makes the sight as true as touch—

> And visions, as poetic eyes avow,
> Cling to each leaf and hang on every bough.[6]

The more ethereal, evanescent, more refined and sublime part of art is the seeing nature through the medium of sentiment and passion, as each object is a symbol of the affections and a link in the chain of our endless being. But the unravelling this mysterious web of thought and feeling is alone in the Muse's gift, namely, in the power of that trembling sensibility which is awake to every change and every modification of its ever-varying impressions, that

> Thrills in each nerve, and lives along the line.[7]

This power is indifferently called genius, imagination, feeling, taste; but the manner in which it acts upon the mind can neither be defined by abstract rules, as is the case in science, nor verified by continual unvarying experiments, as is the case in mechanical performances. The mechanical excellence of the Dutch painters in colouring and handling is that which comes the nearest in fine art to the perfection of certain manual exhibitions of skill. The truth of the effect and the facility with which it is produced are equally admirable. Up to a certain point, every thing is faultless. The hand and eye have done their part. There is only a want of taste and genius. It is after we enter upon that enchanted ground that the human mind begins to droop and flag as in a strange road, or in a thick mist, benighted and making little way with many

---

[6] From a letter of Thomas Gray to Horace Walpole.

[7] Probably an inaccurate quotation from a poem of Joseph Addison dealing with the Polyphemus story in Virgil's *Aeneid*.

attempts and many failures, and that the best of us only escape with half a triumph. The undefined and the imaginary are the regions that we must pass like Satan, difficult and doubtful, "half flying, half on foot." The object in sense is a positive thing, and execution comes with practice.

Cleverness is a certain *knack* or aptitude at doing certain things, which depend more on a particular adroitness and off-hand readiness than on force or perseverance, such as making puns, making epigrams, making extempore verses, mimicking the company, mimicking a style, &c. Cleverness is either liveliness and smartness, or something answering to *sleight of hand,* like letting a glass fall sideways off a table, or else a trick, like knowing the secret spring of a watch. Accomplishments are certain external graces, which are to be learnt from others, and which are easily displayed to the admiration of the beholder, *viz.* dancing, riding, fencing, music, and so on. These ornamental acquirements are only proper to those who are at ease in mind and fortune. . . . Talent is the capacity of doing anything that depends on application and industry, such as writing a criticism, making a speech, studying the law. Talent differs from genius, as voluntary differs from involuntary power. Ingenuity is genius in trifles, greatness is genius in undertakings of much pith and moment. A clever or ingenious man is one who can do any thing well, whether it is worth doing or not: a great man is one who can do that which when done is of the highest importance. Themistocles[8] said he could not play on the flute, but that he could make of a small city a great one. This gives one a pretty good idea of the distinction in question.

Greatness is great power, producing great effects. It is not enough that a man has great power in himself, he must shew it to all the world, in a way that cannot be hid or gainsaid. He must fill up a certain idea in the public mind. I have no other notion of greatness than this two-fold definition, great results springing from great inherent energy. The great in visible objects has relation to that which extends over space: the great in mental ones has to do with space and time. No

---

[8] The famous Greek statesman and soldier (525-459 B.C.).

man is truly great, who is great only in his life-time. The test of greatness is the page of history. Nothing can be said to be great that has a distinct limit, or that borders on something evidently greater than itself. Besides, what is short-lived and pampered into mere notoriety, is of a gross and vulgar quality in itself. A Lord Mayor is hardly a great man. A city orator or patriot of the day only shew, by reaching the height of their wishes, the distance they are at from any true ambition. Popularity is neither fame nor greatness. A king (as such) is not a great man. He has great power, but it is not his own. He merely wields the lever of the state, which a child, an idiot, or a madman can do. It is the office, not the man we gaze at. Any one else in the same situation would be just as much an object of abject curiosity. We laugh at the country girl who having seen a king expressed her disappointment by saying, "Why, he is only a man!" Yet, knowing this, we run to see a king as if he was something more than a man.— To display the greatest powers, unless they are applied to great purposes, makes nothing for the character of greatness. To throw a barley-corn through the eye of a needle, to multiply nine figures by nine in the memory, argues infinite dexterity of body and capacity of mind, but nothing comes of either. There is a surprising power at work, but the effects are not proportionate, or such as take hold of the imagination. To impress the idea of power on others, they must be made in some way to feel it. It must be communicated to their understandings in the shape of an increase of knowledge, or it must subdue and overawe them by subjecting their wills. Admiration, to be solid and lasting, must be founded on proofs from which we have no means of escaping; it is neither a slight nor a voluntary gift. A mathematician who solves a profound problem, a poet who creates an image of beauty in the mind that was not there before, imparts knowledge and power to others, in which his greatness and his fame consists, and on which it reposes. Jedediah Buxton[9] will be forgotten; but Napier's bones[10] will live. Lawgivers, philosophers, founders of

---

[9] A wizard at mental calculation but otherwise illiterate.
[10] John Napier (1550-1617) invented logarithms. The "bones" was a calculating device something like the modern slide rule.

religion, conquerors and heroes, inventors and great geniuses in arts and sciences, are great men; for they are great public benefactors, or formidable scourges to mankind. Among ourselves, Shakespear, Newton, Bacon, Milton, Cromwell, were great men; for they shewed great power by acts and thoughts, which have not yet been consigned to oblivion. They must needs be men of lofty stature, whose shadows lengthen out to remote posterity. A great farce-writer may be a great man; for Moliere was but a great farce-writer. In my mind, the author of Don Quixote was a great man. So have there been many others. A great chess-player is not a great man, for he leaves the world as he found it. No act terminating in itself constitutes greatness. This will apply to all displays of power or trials of skill, which are confined to the momentary, individual effort, and construct no permanent image or trophy of themselves without them. . . . A man at the top of his profession is not therefore a great man. He is great in his way, but that is all, unless he shews the marks of a great moving intellect, so that we trace the master-mind, and can sympathise with the springs that urge him on. The rest is but a craft or *mystery*.[11]

OLD CHINA

CHARLES LAMB (1775-1834)

From *The London Magazine*, March, 1823. Into his informal essays Lamb poured the riches of his personality. He loved people, he loved books, he loved living; and over the years he acquired a discriminating sense of values. In "Old China" he chats of some of the things that have made life worth while.

———

I have an almost feminine partiality for old china. When I go to see any great house, I inquire for the china-closet,

---

[11] A knowledge or proficiency peculiar to one's own self.

and next for the picture-gallery. I cannot defend the order of preference, but by saying that we have all some taste or other, of too ancient a date to admit of our remembering distinctly that it was an acquired one. I can call to mind the first play, and the first exhibition, that I was taken to; but I am not conscious of a time when china jars and saucers were introduced into my imagination.

I had no repugnance then—why should I now have?—to those little, lawless, azure-tinctured grotesques, that under the notion of men and women, float about, uncircumscribed by any element, in that world before perspective—a china tea-cup.

I like to see my old friends—whom distance cannot diminish—figuring up in the air (so they appear to our optics), yet on *terra firma* still—for so we must in courtesy interpret that speck of deeper blue, which the decorous artist, to prevent absurdity, had made to spring up beneath their sandals.

I love the men with women's faces, and the women, if possible, with still more womanish expressions.

Here is a young and courtly Mandarin, handing tea to a lady from a salver—two miles off. See how distance seems to set off respect! And here the same lady, or another—for likeness is identity on tea-cups—is stepping into a little fairy boat, moored on the hither side of this calm garden river, with a dainty mincing foot, which in a right angle of incidence (as angles go in our world) must infallibly land her in the midst of a flowery mead—a furlong off on the other side of the same strange stream!

Farther on—if far or near can be predicted of their world—see horses, trees, pagodas, dancing the hays.

Here—a cow and rabbit couchant, and co-extensive—so objects show, seen through the lucid atmosphere of fine Cathay.

I was pointing out to my cousin last evening, over our Hyson (which we are old fashioned enough to drink unmixed still of an afternoon) some of these *speciosa miracula*[1] upon a set of extraordinary old blue china (a recent purchase) which we

---

[1] Brilliant wonders.

were now for the first time using; and could not help remarking how favourable circumstances had been to us of late years,
that we could afford to please the eye sometimes with trifles of
this sort—when a passing sentiment seemed to overshade the
brows of my companion. I am quick at detecting these summer
clouds in Bridget.[2]

"I wish the good old times would come again," she said,
"when we were not quite so rich. I do not mean that I want
to be poor; but there was a middle state"—so she was pleased
to ramble on,—"in which I am sure we were a great deal
happier. A purchase is but a purchase, now that you have
money enough and to spare. Formerly it used to be a triumph.
When we coveted a cheap luxury (and, O! how much ado
I had to get you to consent in those times!)—we were used
to have a debate two or three days before, and to weigh the
for and *against*, and think what we might spare it out of, and
what saving we could hit upon, that should be an equivalent.
A thing was worth buying then, when we felt the money that
we paid for it.

"Do you remember the brown suit, which you made to
hang upon you, till all your friends cried shame upon you, it
grew so thread-bare—and all because of that folio Beaumont
and Fletcher, which you dragged home late at night from
Barker's in Covent-garden? Do you remember how we eyed
it for weeks before we could make up our minds to the
purchase, and had not come to a determination till it was near
ten o'clock of the Saturday night, when you set off from
Islington, fearing you should be too late—and when the old
bookseller with some grumbling opened his shop, and by the
twinkling taper (for he was setting bedwards) lighted out the
relic from his dusty treasures—and when you lugged it home,
wishing it were twice as cumbersome—and when you presented it to me—and when we were exploring the perfectness
of it (*collating*, you called it)—and while I was repairing some
of the loose leaves with paste, which your impatience would
not suffer to be left till day-break—was there no pleasure in

---

[2] Lamb's sister Mary.

being a poor man? or can those neat black clothes which you wear now, and are so careful to keep brushed, since we have become rich and finical—give you half the honest vanity with which you flaunted it about in that over-worn suit—your old corbeau—for four or five weeks longer than you should have done, to pacify your conscience for the mighty sum of fifteen —or sixteen shillings was it?—a great affair we thought it then—which you had lavished on the old folio. Now you can afford to buy any book that pleases you, but I do not see that you ever bring me home any nice old purchases now.

"When you came home with twenty apologies for laying out a less number of shillings upon that print after Lionardo, which we christened the 'Lady Blanch';[3] when you looked at the purchase, and thought of the money—and thought of the money, and looked again at the picture—was there no pleasure in being a poor man? Now, you have nothing to do but to walk into Colnaghi's, and buy a wilderness of Lionardos. Yet do you?

"Then, do you remember our pleasant walks to Enfield, and Potter's Bar, and Waltham, when we had a holyday— holydays, and all other fun, are gone, now we are rich—and the little handbasket in which I used to deposit our day's fare of savoury cold lamb and salad—and how you would pry about at noon-tide for some decent house, where we might go in, and produce our store—only paying for the ale that you must call for—and speculate upon the looks of the land-lady, and whether she was likely to allow us a table-cloth— and wish for such another honest hostess as Isaak Walton has described many a one on the pleasant banks of the Lea, when he went a-fishing—and sometimes they would prove obliging enough, and sometimes they would look grudgingly upon us— but we had cheerful looks still for one another, and would eat our plain food savourily, scarcely grudging Piscator[4] his Trout Hall? Now—when we go out a day's pleasuring, which is seldom moreover, we *ride* part of the way, and go into a fine

---

[3] The picture was "Modesty and Vanity." The Lambs renamed it in fun because Mary had written a poem about it.

[4] The fisherman in Walton's *Compleat Angler.*

inn, and order the best dinners, never debating the expense—which, after all, never has half the relish of those chance country snaps, when we were at the mercy of uncertain usage, and a precarious welcome.

"You are too proud to see a play anywhere now but in the pit. Do you remember where it was we used to sit, when we saw the Battle of Hexham, and the Surrender of Calais,[5] and Bannister and Mrs. Bland in the Children in the Wood [6] —when we squeezed out our shillings a-piece to sit three or four times in a season in the one-shilling gallery—where you felt all the time that you ought not to have brought me—and more strongly I felt obligation to you for having brought me—and the pleasure was the better for a little shame—and when the curtain drew up, what cared we for our place in the house, or what mattered it where we were sitting, when our thoughts were with Rosalind in Arden, or with Viola at the Court of Illyria? You used to say, that the gallery was the best place of all for enjoying a play socially—that the relish of such exhibitions must be in proportion to the infrequency of going—that the company we met there, not being in general readers of plays, were obliged to attend the more, and did attend, to what was going on, on the stage—because a word lost would have been a chasm, which it was impossible for them to fill up. With such reflections we consoled our pride then—and I appeal to you, whether, as a woman, I met generally with less attention and accommodation than I have done since in more expensive situations in the house? The getting in, indeed, and the crowding up those inconvenient staircases was bad enough,—but there was still a law of civility to women recognized to quite as great an extent as we ever found in the other passages—and how a little difficulty overcome heightened the snug seat, and the play, afterwards! Now we can only pay our money and walk in. You cannot see, you say, in the galleries now. I am sure we saw, and heard too, well enough then—but sight, and all, I think, is gone with our poverty.

[5] Plays by George Colman.
[6] By Thomas Morton.

"There was pleasure in eating strawberries, before they became quite common—in the first dish of peas, while they were yet dear—to have them for a nice supper, a treat. What treat can we have now? If we were to treat ourselves now—that is, to have dainties a little above our means, it would be selfish and wicked. It is the very little more that we allow ourselves beyond what the actual poor can get at, that makes what I call a treat—when two people living together, as we have done, now and then indulge themselves in a cheap luxury, which both like; while each apologises, and is willing to take both halves of the blame to his single share. I see no harm in people making much of themselves in that sense of the word. It may give them a hint how to make much of others. But now—what I mean by the word—we never do make much of ourselves. None but the poor can do it. I do not mean the veriest poor of all, but persons as we were, just above poverty.

"I know what you were going to say, that it is mighty pleasant at the end of the year to make all meet,—and much ado we used to have every Thirty-first Night of December to account for our exceedings—many a long face did you make over your puzzled accounts, and in contriving to make it out how we had spent so much—or that we had not spent so much —or that it was impossible we should spend so much next year—and still we found our slender capital decreasing—but then, betwixt ways, and projects, and compromises of one sort or another, and talk of curtailing this charge, and doing without that for the future—and the hope that youth brings, and laughing spirits (in which you were never poor till now) we pocketed up our loss, and in conclusion, with 'lusty brimmers' (as you used to quote it out of *hearty cheerful Mr. Cotton,*[7] as you called him), we used to welcome in the 'coming guest.' Now we have no reckoning at all at the end of the old year— no flattering promises about the new year doing better for us."

Bridget is so sparing of her speech on most occasions that when she gets into a rhetorical vein, I am careful how I interrupt it. I could not help, however, smiling at the phantom

---

[7] Charles Cotton, a seventeenth-century poet.

of wealth which her dear imagination had conjured up out of
a clear income of poor —— hundred pounds a year. "It is true
we were happier when we were poorer, but we were also
younger, my cousin. I am afraid we must put up with the
excess, for if we were to shake the superflux into the sea, we
should not much mend ourselves. That we had much to
struggle with, as we grew up together, we have reason to be
most thankful. It strengthened, and knit our compact closer.
We could never have been what we have been to each other,
if we had always had the sufficiency which you now complain of. The resisting power—those natural dilations of the
youthful spirit, which circumstances cannot straiten—with us
are long since passed away. Competence to age is supplemen-
tary youth; a sorry supplement indeed, but I fear the best that
is to be had. We must ride, where we formerly walked: live
better, and lie softer—and shall be wise to do so—than we had
means to do in those good old days you speak of. Yet could
those days return—could you and I once more walk our thirty
miles a day—could Bannister and Mrs. Bland again be young,
and you and I be young to see them—could the good old one-
shilling gallery days return—they are dreams, my cousin, now
—but could you and I at this moment, instead of this quiet
argument, by our well-carpeted fire-side, sitting on this luxurious sofa—be once more struggling up those inconvenient
stair-cases, pushed about, and squeezed, and elbowed by the
poorest rabble of poor gallery scramblers—could I once more
hear those anxious shrieks of yours—and the delicious *Thank
God, we are safe*, which always followed when the topmost
stair, conquered, let in the first light of the whole cheerful
theatre down beneath us—I know not the fathom line that ever
touched a descent so deep as I would be willing to bury more
wealth in than Croesus had, or the great Jew R——[8] is supposed
to have, to purchase it. And now do just look at that merry
little Chinese waiter holding an umbrella, big enough for a
bed-tester, over the head of that pretty insipid half Madonna-ish
chit of a lady in that very blue summer-house."

[8] Nathan Rothschild.

LABOR

THOMAS CARLYLE (1795-1881)

From *Past and Present*, Book III, Ch. XI, 1843. Carlyle's corrective for the confusion, suffering, and despair of his age was work. With his peculiar vigorous style he challenges heroic man to burst through the obstacles and win a new world.

———

For there is a perennial nobleness, and even sacredness, in Work. Were he never so benighted, forgetful of his high calling, there is always hope in a man that actually and earnestly works: in Idleness alone is there perpetual despair. Work, never so Mammonish, mean, *is* in communication with Nature; the real desire to get Work done will itself lead one more and more to truth, to Nature's appointments and regulations, which are truth.

The latest Gospel in this world is, Know thy work and do it. "Know thyself": long enough has that poor "self" of thine tormented thee; thou wilt never get to "know" it, I believe! Think it not thy business, this of knowing thyself; thou art an unknowable individual: know what thou canst work at; and work at it, like a Hercules! That will be thy better plan.

It has been written, "an endless significance lies in Work"; a man perfects himself by working. Foul jungles are cleared away; fair seedfields rise instead, and stately cities; and withal the man himself first ceases to be a jungle and foul unwholesome desert thereby. Consider how, even in the meanest sorts of Labor, the whole soul of a man is composed into a kind of real harmony, the instant he sets himself to work! Doubt, Desire, Sorrow, Remorse, Indignation, Despair itself, all these like helldogs lie beleaguering the soul of the poor dayworker, as of every man: but he bends himself with free valor against his task, and all these are stilled, all these shrink murmuring far off into their caves. The man is now a man. The blessed glow of Labor in him, is it not as purifying fire, wherein all poison is burnt up, and of sour smoke itself there is made bright blessed flame!

Destiny, on the whole, has no other way of cultivating us. A formless Chaos, once set it *revolving*, grows round and ever rounder; ranges itself, by mere force of gravity, into strata, spherical courses; is no longer a Chaos, but a round compacted World. What would become of the Earth, did she cease to revolve? In the poor old Earth, so long as she revolves, all inequalities, irregularities disperse themselves; all irregularities are incessantly becoming regular. Hast thou looked on the Potter's wheel,—one of the venerablest objects; old as the Prophet Ezechiel [1] and far older? Rude lumps of clay, how they spin themselves up, by mere quick whirling, into beautiful circular dishes. And fancy the most assiduous Potter, but without his wheel; reduced to make dishes or rather amorphous botches, by mere kneading and baking! Even such a Potter were Destiny, with a human soul that would rest and lie at ease, that would not work and spin! Of an idle unrevolving man the kindest Destiny, like the most assiduous Potter without wheel, can bake and knead nothing other than a botch; let her spend on him what expensive coloring, what gilding and enameling she will, he is but a botch. Not a dish; no, a bulging, kneaded, crooked, shambling, squint-cornered, amorphous botch,—a mere enameled vessel of dishonor! Let the idle think of this.

Blessed is he who has found his work; let him ask no other blessedness. He has a work, a life-purpose; he has found it, and will follow it! How, as a free-flowing channel, dug and torn by noble force through the sour mud-swamp of one's existence, like an ever-deepening river there, it runs and flows; —draining-off the sour festering water, gradually from the root of the remotest grass-blade; making, instead of pestilential

---

[1] Not in Ezekiel, but Jeremiah, 18: 1-6.

swamp, a green fruitful meadow with its clear-flowing stream. How blessed for the meadow itself, let the stream and *its* value be great or small! Labor is Life: from the inmost heart of the Worker rises his god-given Force, the sacred celestial Life-essence breathed into him by Almighty God; from his inmost heart awakens him to all nobleness,—to all knowledge, "self-knowledge" and much else, so soon as Work fitly begins. Knowledge? The knowledge that will hold good in working, cleave thou to that; for Nature herself accredits that, says Yea to that. Properly thou hast no other knowledge but what thou hast got by working: the rest is yet all a hypothesis of knowledge; a thing to be argued of in schools, a thing floating in the clouds, in endless logic-vortices, till we try it and fix it. "Doubt, of whatever kind, can be ended by Action alone."

And again, hast thou valued Patience, Courage, Perseverance, Openness to light; readiness to own thyself mistaken, to do better next time? All these, all virtues, in wrestling with the dim brute Powers of Fact, in ordering of thy fellows in such wrestle, there and elsewhere not at all, thou wilt continually learn. Set down a brave Sir Christopher[2] in the middle of black ruined Stone-heaps, of foolish unarchitectural Bishops, red-tape Officials, idle Nell-Gwyn Defenders of the Faith;[3] and see whether he will ever raise a Paul's Cathedral out of all that, yea or no! Rough, rude, contradictory are all things and persons, from the mutinous masons and Irish hodmen, up to the idle Nell-Gwyn Defenders, to blustering redtape Officials, foolish unarchitectural Bishops. All these things and persons are there not for Christopher's sake and his Cathedral's; they are there for their own sake mainly! Christopher will have to conquer and constrain all these,—if he be able. All these are against him. Equitable Nature herself, who carries her mathematics and architectonics not on the face of her, but deep in the hidden heart of her,—Nature herself is but partially for him; will be wholly against him, if he constrain her not! His very money, where is it to come from? The pious munificence of England

[2] Sir Christopher Wren, architect.
[3] A satirical allusion to immoral kings who held the title. Nell Gwyn was the mistress of Charles II.

lies far-scattered, distant, unable to speak, and say, "I am here";
—must be spoken to before it can speak. Pious munificence,
and all help, is so silent, invisible like the gods; impediment,
contradictions manifold are so loud and near! O brave Sir
Christopher, trust thou in those notwithstanding, and front all
these; understand all these; by valiant patience, noble effort,
insight, by man's-strength, vanquish and compel all these,—and,
on the whole, strike down victoriously the last topstone of that
Paul's Edifice; thy monument for certain centuries, the stamp
"Great Man" impressed very legibly on Portland-stone there!

Yes, all manner of help, and pious response from Men or
Nature, is always what we call silent; cannot speak or come to
light, till it be seen, till it be spoken to. Every noble work is at
first "impossible." In very truth, for every noble work the
possibilities will lie diffused through Immensity; inarticulate,
undiscoverable except to faith. Like Gideon thou shalt spread
out thy fleece at the door of thy tent;[4] see whether under the
wide arch of Heaven there be any bounteous moisture, or none.
Thy heart and life-purpose shall be as a miraculous Gideon's
fleece, spread out in silent appeal to Heaven: and from the kind
Immensities, what from the poor unkind Localities and town
and country Parishes there never could, blessed dew-moisture
to suffice thee shall have fallen!

Work is of a religious nature:—work is of a *brave* nature;
which it is the aim of all religion to be. All work of man is as
the swimmer's: a waste ocean threatens to devour him; if he
front it not bravely, it will keep its word. By incessant wise
defiance of it, lusty rebuke and buffet of it, behold how it
loyally supports him, bears him as its conqueror along. "It is
so," says Goethe, "with all things that man undertakes in this
world."

Brave Sea-captain, Norse Sea-king,—Columbus, my hero,
royalest Sea-king of all! it is no friendly environment this of
thine, in the waste deep waters; around thee mutinous discouraged souls, behind thee disgrace and ruin, before thee

---

[4] If the fleece gathered dew and the ground was dry, or vice versa,
Gideon knew that God would help him. Judges 6: 36-38.

the unpenetrated veil of Night. Brother, these wild water-mountains, bounding from their deep bases (ten miles deep, I am told) are not entirely there on thy behalf! Meseems *they* have other work than floating thee forward:—and the huge Winds, that sweep from Ursa Major to the Tropics and Equators, dancing their giant-waltz through the kingdoms of Chaos and Immensity, they care little about filling rightly or filling wrongly the small shoulder-of-mutton sails in this cockle-skiff of thine! Thou art not among articulate-speaking friends, my brother; thou art among immeasurable dumb monsters, tumbling, howling wide as the world here. Secret, far off, invisible to all hearts but thine, there lies a help in them: see how thou wilt get at that. Patiently thou wilt wait till the mad Southwester spend itself, saving thyself by dextrous science of defence, the while: valiantly, with swift decision, wilt thou strike in, when the favouring East, the Possible, springs up. Mutiny of men thou wilt sternly repress; weakness, despondency, thou wilt cheerily encourage: thou wilt swallow down complaint, unreason, weariness, weakness of others and thyself; —how much wilt thou swallow down! There shall be a depth of Silence in thee, deeper than this Sea, which is but ten miles deep: a Silence unsoundable; known to God only. Thou shalt be a Great Man. Yes, my World-Soldier, thou of the World Marine-service,—thou wilt have to be *greater* than this tumultuous unmeasured World here round thee is; thou, in thy strong soul, as with wrestler's arms, shalt embrace it, harness it down; and make it bear thee on,—to new Americas, or whither God wills!

GIFTS [1]

RALPH WALDO EMERSON (1803-1862)

From *Essays*, 2nd Series, 1844. The essays of Emerson contain the substance of his transcendental philosophy. "Gifts," although short, yet is

[1] Used with the courtesy of Houghton Mifflin Co., the authorized publishers.

typical in that it elevates a material formality to a spiritual plane. It causes one to reconsider the motives which actuate and perpetuate the custom of giving and receiving.

> *Gifts of one who loved me,—*
> *'Twas high time they came;*
> *When he ceased to love me,*
> *Time they stopped for shame.*

It is said that the world is in a state of bankruptcy, that the world owes the world more than the world can pay, and ought to go into chancery, and be sold. I do not think this general insolvency, which involves in some sort all the population, to be the reason of the difficulty experienced at Christmas and New Year, and other times, in bestowing gifts; since it is always so pleasant to be generous, though very vexatious to pay debts. But the impediment lies in the choosing. If, at any time, it comes into my head that a present is due from me to somebody, I am puzzled what to give until the opportunity is gone. Flowers and fruits are always fit presents; flowers, because they are a proud assertion that a ray of beauty outvalues all the utilities of the world. These gay natures contrast with the somewhat stern countenance of ordinary nature; they are like music heard out of a workhouse. Nature does not cocker us: we are children, not pets: she is not fond: everything is dealt to us without fear or favor, after severe universal laws. Yet these delicate flowers look like the frolic and interference of love and beauty. Men used to tell us that we love flattery, even though we are not deceived by it, because it shows that we are of importance enough to be courted. Something like that pleasure, the flowers give us: what am I to whom these sweet hints are addressed? Fruits are acceptable gifts, because they are the flower of commodities, and admit of fantastic values being attached to them. If a man should send to me to come a hundred miles to visit him, and should set before me a basket of fine summer-fruit, I should think there was some proportion between the labour and the reward.

For common gifts, necessity makes pertinences[2] and beauty every day, and one is glad when an imperative leaves him no option, since if the man at the door has no shoes you have not to consider whether you could procure him a paint-box. And as it is always pleasing to see a man eat bread, or drink water, in the house or out of doors, so it is always a great satisfaction to supply these first wants. Necessity does everything well. In our condition of universal dependence, it seems heroic to let the petitioner be the judge of his necessity, and to give all that is asked, though at great inconvenience. If it be a fantastic desire, it is better to leave to others the office of punishing him. I can think of many parts I should prefer playing to that of the Furies. Next to things of necessity, the rule for a gift, which one of my friends prescribed, is, that we might convey to some person that which properly belonged to his character, and was easily associated with him in thought. But our tokens of compliment and love are for the most part barbarous. Rings and other jewels are not gifts, but apologies for gifts. The only gift is a portion of thyself. Thou must bleed for me. Therefore the poet brings his poem; the shepherd, his lamb; the farmer, corn; the miner, a gem; the sailor, coral and shells; the painter, his picture; the girl, a handkerchief of her own sewing. This is right and pleasing, for it restores society in so far to its primary basis, when a man's biography is conveyed in his gift, and every mans' wealth is an index of his merit. But it is a cold, lifeless business when you go to the shops to buy me something, which does not represent your life and talent, but a goldsmith's. This is fit for kings, and rich men who represent kings, and a false state of property, to make presents of gold and silver stuffs, as a kind of symbolical sin-offering, or payment of black-mail.

The law of benefits is a difficult channel, which requires careful sailing, or rude boats. It is not the office of a man to receive gifts. How dare you give them? We wish to be self-

[2] Appropriate occasions.

sustained. We do not quite forgive a giver. The hand that feeds us is in some danger of being bitten. We can receive anything from love, for that is a way of receiving it from ourselves; but not from anyone who assumes to bestow. We sometimes hate the meat which we eat, because there seems something of degrading dependence in living by it.

> "*Brother, if Jove to thee a present make,*
> *Take heed that from his hands thou nothing take.*" [3]

We ask the whole. Nothing less will content us. We arraign society if it do not give us besides earth, and fire, and water, opportunity, love, reverence, and objects of veneration.

He is a good man who can receive a gift well. We are either glad or sorry at a gift, and both emotions are unbecoming. Some violence, I think, is done, some degradation borne, when I rejoice or grieve at a gift. I am sorry when my independence is invaded, or when a gift comes from such as do not know my spirit, and so the act is not supported; and if the gift pleases me overmuch, then I should be ashamed that the donor should read my heart, and see that I love his commodity, and not him. The gift, to be true, must be the flowing of the giver unto me, correspondent to my flowing unto him. When the waters are at a level, then my goods pass to him, and his to me. All his are mine, all mine his. I say to him, "How can you give me this pot of oil, or this flagon of wine, when all your oil and wine is mine?" which belief of mine this gift seems to deny. Hence the fitness of beautiful, not useful things for gifts. This giving is flat usurpation, and therefore when the beneficiary is ungrateful, as all beneficiaries hate all Timons, not at all considering the value of the gift, but looking back to the greater store it was taken from, I rather sympathize with the beneficiary than with the anger of my lord Timon.[4] For, the expectation of gratitude is mean, and is continually punished by the total insensibility of the obliged person. It is a great happiness to get off without

[3] From Hesiod.

[4] Timon of Athens became a misanthrope when, after he had lavished his wealth upon them, his friends deserted him.

injury and heart-burning from one who has had the ill luck to
be served by you. It is a very onerous business, this of being
served, and the debtor naturally wishes to give you a slap. A
golden text for these gentlemen is that which I so admire in the
Buddhist, who never thanks, and who says, "Do not flatter your
benefactors."

The reason of these discords I conceive to be, that there is
no commensurability between a man and any gift. You cannot
give anything to a magnanimous person. After you have served
him, he at once puts you in debt by his magnanimity. The
service a man renders his friend is trivial and selfish, compared
with the service he knows his friend stood in readiness to yield
him, alike before he had begun to serve his friend, and now
also. Compared with that goodwill I bear my friend, the benefit
it is in my power to render him seems small. Besides, our action
on each other, good as well as evil, is so incidental and at random, that we can seldom hear the acknowledgements of any
person who would thank us for a benefit without some shame
and humiliation. We can rarely strike a direct stroke, but must
be content with an oblique one; we seldom have the satisfaction
of yielding a direct benefit which is directly received. But
rectitude scatters favors on every side without knowing it, and
receives with wonder the thanks of all people.

I fear to breathe any treason against the majesty of love,
which is the genius and god of gifts and to whom we must not
affect to prescribe. Let him give kingdoms or flower leaves
indifferently. There are persons from whom we always expect
fairy tokens; let us not cease to expect them. This is prerogative,
and not to be limited by our municipal rules. For the rest, I
like to see that we cannot be bought and sold. The best of hos-
pitality and of generosity is also not in the will, but in fate. I
find that I am not much to you; you do not need me; you do
not feel me; then am I thrust out of doors, though you proffer
me house and lands. No services are of any value, but only likeness.[5] When I have attempted to join myself to others by
services, it proved an intellectual trick—no more. They eat

_____

[5] Affinity of taste and emotion.

your service like apples, and leave you out. But love them, and
they feel you and delight in you all the time.

LITERATURE OF KNOWLEDGE
AND LITERATURE OF POWER

THOMAS DE QUINCEY (1785-1859)

From "Alexander Pope," in *The North British Review*, 1848. The term
"literature" is used so loosely that it is apt to apply to everything in print.
De Quincey makes a nice distinction between the literature of utility and
the *belles lettres*, but it is of course obvious that border line cases might
pose difficulties.

What is it that we mean by *literature?* Popularly, and amongst
the thoughtless, it is held to include everything that is printed
in a book. Little logic is required to disturb *that* definition. The
most thoughtless person is easily made aware that in the idea
of *literature* one essential element is some relation to a general
and common interest of man,—so that what applies only to a
local, or professional, or merely personal interest, even though
presenting itself in the shape of a book, will not belong to
Literature. So far the definition is easily narrowed; and it is
as easily expanded. For not only is much that takes a station in
books not literature, but inversely, much that really *is* literature
never reaches a station in books. The weekly sermons of Christendom, that vast pulpit literature which acts so extensively
upon the popular mind—to warn, to uphold, to renew, to comfort, to alarm—does not attain the sanctuary of libraries in the
ten-thousandth part of its extent. The drama again,—as, for
instance, the finest part of Shakespeare's plays in England, and
all leading Athenian plays in the noontide of the Attic stage,—
operated as a literature on the public mind, and were (according to the strictest letter of that term) *published* through the

audiences that witnessed their representation some time before they were published as things to be read; and they were published in this scenical mode of publication with much more effect than they could have had as books during ages of costly copying or of costly printing.

Books, therefore, do not suggest an idea coextensixe and interchangeable with the idea of literature; since much literature, scenic, forensic, or didactic (as from lecturers and public orators), may never come into books, and much that does come into books may connect itself with no literary interest. But a far more important correction, applicable to the common vague idea of literature, is to be sought not so much in a better definition of literature as in a sharper distinction of the two functions which it fulfils. In that great social organ which, collectively, we call literature, there may be distinguished two separate offices, that may blend and often do so, but capable, severally, of a severe insulation, and naturally fitted for reciprocal repulsion. There is, first, the literature of *knowledge*, and secondly, the literature of *power*. The function of the first is to *teach;* the function of the second is to *move;* the first is a rudder, the second an oar or a sail. The first speaks to the mere discursive understanding; the second speaks ultimately, it may happen, to the higher understanding or reason, but always through affections of pleasure and sympathy. Remotely, it may travel towards an object seated in what Lord Bacon calls "dry light"; but proximately it does and must operate—else it ceases to be a literature of power—on and through that *humid* light which clothes itself in the mists and glittering iris of human passions, desires, and genial emotions. Men have so little reflected on the higher functions of literature as to find it a paradox if one should describe it as a mean or subordinate purpose of books to give information. But this is a paradox only in the sense which makes it honourable to be paradoxical. Whenever we talk in ordinary language of seeking information or gaining knowledge, we understand the words as connected with something of absolute novelty. But it is the grandeur of all truth which can occupy a very high place in human interests that it is never absolutely novel to the meanest of minds; it exists eternally by way of germ or latent principle in the lowest as in the highest, needing to be developed, but never to be planted. To be capable of transplantation is the immediate criterion of a truth that ranges on a lower scale. Besides which, there is a rarer thing than truth,—namely *power*, or deep sympathy with truth. What is the effect, for instance, upon society of children? By the pity, by the tenderness, and by the peculiar modes of admiration which connect themselves with the helplessness, with the innocence, and with the simplicity of children, not only are the primal affections strengthened and continually renewed, but the qualities which are dearest in the sight of heaven—the frailty, for instance, which appeals to forbearance, the innocence which symbolizes the heavenly, and the symplicity which is most alien from the worldly—are kept up in perpetual remembrance, and their ideals are continually refreshed. A purpose of the same nature is answered by the higher literature, viz. the literature of power. What do you learn from *Paradise Lost?* Nothing at all. What do you learn from a cookery-book? Something new, something that you did not know before, in every paragraph. But would you therefore put the wretched cookery-book on a higher level of estimation than the divine poem? What you owe to Milton is not any knowledge, of which a million separate items are still but a million of advancing steps on the same earthly level; what you owe is *power*,—that is, exercise and expansion to your own latent capacity of sympathy with the infinite, where every pulse and each separate influx is a step upwards, a step ascending as upon a Jacob's ladder from earth to mysterious altitudes above the earth. All the steps of knowledge, from first to last, carry you further on the same plane, but could never raise you one foot above your ancient level of earth; whereas the very first step in power is a flight—is an ascending movement into another element where earth is forgotten.

Were it not that human sensibilities are ventilated and continually called out into exercise by the great phenomena of infancy, or of real life as it moves through chance and change, or of literature as it recombines these elements in the mimicries of poetry, romance, etc., it is certain that, like any animal power or muscular energy falling into disuse, all such sensibilities would gradually droop and dwindle. It is in relation to these great *moral* capacities of man that the literature of power, as contradistinguished from that of knowledge, lives and has its field of action. It is concerned with what is highest in man; for the Scriptures themselves never condescended to deal by suggestion or coöperation with the mere discursive understanding: when speaking of man in his intellectual capacity, the Scriptures speak not of the understanding, but of "the understanding heart,"—making the heart, i.e., the great *intuitive* (or non-discursive) organ, to be the interchangeable formula for man in his highest state of capacity for the infinite. Tragedy, romance, fairy tale, or epopee, all alike restore to man's mind the ideals of justice, of hope, of truth, of mercy, of retribution, which else (left to the support of daily life in its realities) would languish for want of sufficient illustration.

What is meant, for instance, by *poetic justice?* It does not mean a justice that differs by its object from the ordinary justice of human jurisprudence, for then it must be confessedly a very bad kind of justice; but it means a justice that differs from common forensic justice by the degree in which it attains its object,—a justice that is more omnipotent over its own ends, as dealing, not with the refractory elements of earthly life, but with the elements of its own creation, and with materials flexible to its own purest preconceptions. It is certain that, were it not for the literature of power, these ideals would often remain amongst us as mere arid notional forms; whereas, by the creative forces of man put forth in literature, they gain a vernal life of restoration, and germinate into vital activities. The commonest novel, by moving in alliance with human fears and hopes, with human instincts of wrong and right, sustains and quickens those affections. Calling them into action, it rescues them from torpor. And hence the preëminency over all authors that merely *teach,* of the meanest that *moves,* or that teaches, if at all, indirectly by moving. The very highest work that has ever existed in the literature of knowledge is but a provisional work,—a book upon trial and sufferance, and *quamdiu bene se gesserit*.[1] Let its teaching be even partially revised, let it be but expanded,—nay, even let its teaching be but placed in a better order,—and instantly it is superseded. Whereas the feeblest works in the literature of power, surviving at all, survive as finished and unalterable amongst men. For instance, the *Principia* of Sir Isaac Newton was a book militant on earth from the first. In all stages of its progress it would have to fight for its existence: first, as regards absolute truth; secondly, when that combat was over, as regards its form or mode of presenting the truth. And as soon as a Laplace, or anybody else, builds higher upon the foundations laid by this book, effectually he throws it out of the sunshine into decay and darkness; by weapons won from this book he superannuates and destroys this book, so that soon the name of Newton remains as a mere *nominis umbra*,[2] but his book, as a living power, has transmigrated into other forms. Now, on the contrary, the *Iliad*, the *Prometheus* of Æschylus, the *Othello* or *King Lear*, the *Hamlet* or *Macbeth*, and the *Paradise Lost*, are not militant, but triumphant for ever, as long as the languages exist in which they speak or can be taught to speak. They never *can* transmigrate into new incarnations. To reproduce these in new forms, or variations, even if in some things they should be improved, would be to plagiarize. A good steam-engine is properly superseded by a better. But one lovely pastoral valley is not superseded by another, nor a statue of Praxiteles by a statue of Michael Angelo. These are separated not by imparity, but by disparity. They are not thought of as unequal under the same standard, but as different in *kind*, and, if otherwise equal, as equal under a different standard. Human works of immortal beauty and works of nature in one respect stand on the same footing: they never absolutely repeat each other, never approach so near as not to differ, and they differ not as better and worse, or simply by more and less,—they differ by un-

---

[1] During good behavior.
[2] Shadow of a name.

decipherable and incommunicable differences, that cannot be
caught by mimicries, that cannot be reflected in the mirror of
copies, that cannot become ponderable in the scales of vulgar
comparison. . . . At this hour, five hundred years since their
creation, the tales of Chaucer, never equalled on this earth for
their tenderness and for life of picturesqueness, are read
familiarly by many in the charming language of their natal day,
and by others in the modernizations of Dryden, of Pope, and
Wordsworth. At this hour, one thousand eight hundred years
since their creation, the pagan tales of Ovid, never equalled on
this earth for the gaiety of their movement and the capricious
graces of their narrative, are read by all Christendom. This
man's people and their monuments are dust, but *he* is alive;
he has survived them, as he told us that he had it in his commission to do, by a thousand years, "and shall a thousand more."

All the literature of knowledge builds only ground-nests,
that are swept away by floods, or confounded by the plough;
but the literature of power builds nests in aërial altitudes of
temples sacred from violation, or of forests inaccessible to
fraud. This is a great prerogative of the *power* literature, and
it is a greater which lies in the mode of its influence. The
knowledge literature, like the fashion of this world, passeth
away. An encyclopædia is its abstract; and, in this respect, it
may be taken for its speaking symbol,—that before one
generation has passed an encyclopædia is superannuated; for it
speaks through the dead memory and unimpassioned understanding, which have not the repose of higher faculties, but
are continually enlarging and varying their phylacteries. But
all literature properly so called—literature κατ' ἐξοχην[3]—for the
very reason that it is so much more durable than the literature
of knowledge, is (and by the very same proportion it is) more
intense and electrically searching in its impressions. The
directions in which the tragedy of this planet has trained our
human feelings to play, and the combinations into which the
poetry of this planet has thrown our human passions of love
and hatred, of admiration and contempt, exercise a power for

---

[3] Par excellence.

bad or good over human life that cannot be contemplated, when stretching through many generations, without a sentiment allied to awe. And of this let every one be assured—that he owes to the impassioned books which he has read many a thousand more of emotions than he can consciously trace back to them. Dim by their origination, these emotions yet arise in him, and mould him through life, like forgotten incidents of his childhood. . . .

THE DARK MIRROR

JOHN RUSKIN (1819-1900)

From *Modern Painters,* Vol. V., Pt. IX, Ch. 1, 1860. Ruskin never doubted that art was linked to morality and religion. He believed that art without human sympathy was meaningless and that human emotion, in turn, was a reflection of the Divine. Those who believe in art for art's sake will find here a counter theory.

———————

The essential connection of the power of landscape with human emotion is not less certain, because in many impressive pictures the link is slight or local. That the connection should exist at a single point is all that we need. The comparison with the dress of the body may be carried out into the extremest parallelism. It may often happen that no part of the figure wearing the dress is discernible, nevertheless, the perceivable fact that the drapery is worn by a figure makes all the difference. In one of the most sublime figures in the world this is actually so: one of the fainting Marys in Tintoret's *Crucifixion* has cast her mantle over her head, and her face is lost in its shade, and her whole figure veiled in folds of gray. But what the difference is between that gray woof, that gathers round her as she falls, and the same folds cast in a heap upon the ground, that difference, and more, exists between the power of Nature through which humanity is seen, and her power in the desert. Desert—

whether of leaf or sand—true desertness is not in the want of
leaves, but of life. Where humanity is not, and was not, the
best natural beauty is more than vain. It is even terrible; not
as the dress cast aside from the body but as an embroidered
shroud hiding a skeleton.

And on each side of a right feeling in this matter there lie,
as usual, two opposite errors.

The first, that of caring for man only; and for the rest of
the universe, little, or not at all, which, in a measure, was the
error of the Greeks and Florentines; the other, that of caring
for the universe only; for man, not at all, which, in a measure,
is the error of modern science, and of the Art connecting itself
with such science.

The degree of power which any man may ultimately possess
in landscape-painting will depend finally on his perception of
this influence. If he has to paint the desert, its awfulness—if
the garden, its gladsomeness—will arise simply and only from
his sensibility to the story of life. Without this he is nothing
but a scientific mechanist; this, though it cannot make him yet
a painter, raises him to the sphere in which he may become one.
Nay, the mere shadow and semblance of this have given
dangerous power to works in all other respects unnoticeable;
and the least degree of its true presence has given value to work
in all other respects vain.

The true presence, observe, of sympathy with the spirit of
man. Where this is not, sympathy with any higher spirit is
impossible.

For the directest manifestation of Deity to man is in His
own image, that is, in man.

"In his own image. After his likeness." *Ad imaginem et
similitudinem Suam.* I do not know what people in general
understand by those words. I suppose they ought to be understood. The truth they contain seems to lie at the foundation of
our knowledge both of God and man; yet do we not usually
pass the sentence by, in dull reverence, attaching no definite
sense to it at all? For all practical purpose, might it not as well
be out of the text?

I have no time, nor much desire, to examine the vague

expressions of belief with which the verse has been encumbered. Let us try to find its only possible plain significance.

It cannot be supposed that the bodily shape of man resembles, or resembled, any bodily shape in Deity. The likeness must therefore be, or have been, in the soul. Had it wholly passed away, and the Divine soul been altered into a soul brutal or diabolic, I suppose we should have been told of the change. But we are told nothing of the kind. The verse still stands as if for our use and trust. It was only death which was to be our punishment. Not *change*. So far as we live, the image is still there; defiled, if you will; broken, if you will; all but effaced, if you will, by death and the shadow of it. But not changed. We are not made now in any other image than God's. There are, indeed, the two states of this image—the earthly and heavenly, but both Adamite, both human, both the same likeness; only one defiled, and one pure. So that the soul of man is still a mirror, wherein may be seen, darkly, the image of the mind of God.

These may seem daring words. I am sorry that they do; but I am helpless to soften them. Discover any other meaning of the text if you are able;—but be sure that it *is* a meaning —a meaning in your head and heart;—not a subtle gloss, nor a shifting of one verbal expression into another, both idea-less. I repeat, that, to me, the verse has, and can have, no other signification than this—that the soul of man is a mirror of the mind of God. A mirror dark, distorted, broken, use what blameful words you please of its state; yet in the main, a true mirror, out of which alone, and by which alone, we can know anything of God at all.

"How?" the reader, perhaps, answers indignantly. "I know the nature of God by revelation, not by looking into myself."

Revelation to what? To a nature incapable of receiving truth? That cannot be; for only to a nature capable of truth, desirous of it, distinguishing it, feeding upon it, revelation is possible. To a being undesirous of it, and hating it, revelation is impossible. There can be none to a brute, or fiend. In so far, therefore, as you love truth, and live therein, in so far revelation can exist for you;—and in so far, your mind is the image of God's.

But consider farther, not only *to* what, but *by* what, is the revelation. By sight? or word? If by sight, then to eyes which see justly. Otherwise, no sight would be revelation. So far, then, as your sight is just, it is the image of God's sight.

If by words—how do you know their meanings? Here is a short piece of precious word revelation, for instance. "God is love."

Love! yes. But what *is that?* The revelation does not tell you that, I think. Look into the mirror, and you will see. Out of your own heart you may know what love is. In no other possible way—by no other help or sign. All the words and sounds ever uttered, all the revelations of cloud, or flame, or crystal, are utterly powerless. They cannot tell you, in the smallest point, what love means. Only the broken mirror can.

Here is more revelation. "God is just!" Just! What is that? The revelation cannot help you to discover. You say it is dealing equitably or equally. But how do you discern the equality? Not by inequality of mind; not by a mind incapable of weighing, judging, or distributing. If the lengths seem unequal in the broken mirror, for you they are unequal; but if they seem equal, then the mirror is true. So far as you recognize equality, and your conscience tells you what is just, so far your mind is the image of God's: and so far as you do *not* discern this nature of justice or equality, the words "God is just" bring no revelation to you.

"But his thoughts are not as our thoughts." No: the sea is not as the standing pool by the wayside. Yet when the breeze crisps the pool, you may see the image of the breakers, and a likeness of the foam. Nay, in some sort, the same foam. If the sea is for ever invisible to you, something you may learn of it from the pool. Nothing, assuredly, any otherwise.

"But this poor miserable Me! Is *this*, then, all the book I have got to read about God in?" Yes, truly so. No other book, nor fragment of book, than that, will you ever find;—no velvet-bound missal, nor frankincensed manuscript;—nothing hieroglyphic nor cuneiform; papyrus and pyramid are alike silent on this matter;—nothing in the clouds above, nor in the earth beneath. That flesh-bound volume is the only revelation that is, that was, or that can be. In that is the image of God painted; in that is the law of God written; in that is the promise of God revealed. Know thyself; for through thyself only thou canst know God.

Through the glass, darkly. But, except through the glass, in nowise.

A tremulous crystal, waved as water, poured out upon the ground;—you may defile it, despise it, pollute it at your pleasure, and at your peril; for on the peace of those weak waves must all the heaven you shall ever gain be first seen; and through such purity as you can win for those dark waves, must all the light of the risen Sun of righteousness be bent down, by faint refraction. Cleanse them, and calm them, as you love your life.

Therefore it is that all the power of nature depends on subjection to the human soul. Man is the sun of the world; more than the real sun. The fire of his wonderful heart is the only light and heat worth gauge or measure. Where he is, are the tropics; here he is not, the ice-world.

LIFE WITHOUT PRINCIPLE[1]

HENRY DAVID THOREAU (1817-1862)

From the *Atlantic Monthly*, 1863. Thoreau would rather go to jail or live alone in the woods than truckle to conventions which undermined the integrity of his individual self. A one-man revolution is frequently ill advised, but not so for Thoreau.

––––––––––

At a lyceum, not long since, I felt that the lecturer had chosen a theme too foreign to himself, and so failed to interest

[1] Used with the courtesy of Houghton Mifflin Co., the authorized publishers.

me as much as he might have done. He described things not
in or near to his heart, but toward his extremities and super-
ficies. There was, in this sense, no truly central or centraliz-
ing thought in the lecture. I would have had him deal with
his privatest experience, as the poet does. The greatest compliment that was ever paid me was when one asked me what *I
thought,* and attended to my answer. I am surprised, as well
as delighted, when this happens, it is such a rare use he would
make of me, as if he were acquainted with the tool. Commonly,
if men want anything of me, it is only to know how many
acres I make of their land,—since I am a surveyor,—or, at
most, what trivial news I have burdened myself with. They
never will go to law for my meat; they prefer the shell. A man
once came a considerable distance to ask me to lecture on
Slavery; but on conversing with him, I found that he and his
clique expected seven eighths of the lecture to be theirs, and
only one eighth mine; so I declined. I take it for granted, when
I am invited to lecture anywhere,—for I have had a little experience in that business,—that there is a desire to hear what *I
think* on some subject, though I may be the greatest fool in
the country,—and not that I should say pleasant things merely,
or such as the audience will assent to; and I resolve, accordingly,
that I will give them a strong dose of myself. They have sent
for me, and engaged to pay for me, and I am determined that
they shall have me, though I bore them beyond all precedent.

So now I would say something similar to you, my readers.
Since *you* are my readers, and I have not been much of a
traveller, I will not talk about people a thousand miles off but
come as near home as I can. As the time is short, I will leave
out all the flattery, and retain all the criticism.

Let us consider the way in which we spend our lives.

This world is a place of business. What an infinite bustle!
I am awaked almost every night by the panting of the locomo-
tive. It interrupts my dreams. There is no sabbath. It would be
glorious to see mankind at leisure for once. It is nothing but
work, work, work. I cannot easily buy a blank-book to
write thoughts in; they are commonly ruled for dollars and
cents. An Irishman, seeing me making a minute in the fields,

took it for granted that I was calculating my wages. If a man was tossed out of a window when an infant, and so made a cripple for life, or scared out of his wits by the Indians, it is regretted chiefly because he was thus incapacitated for—business! I think that there is nothing, not even crime, more opposed to poetry, to philosophy, ay, to life itself, than this incessant business.

There is a coarse and boisterous money-making fellow in the outskirts of our town, who is going to build a bank-wall under the hill along the edge of his meadow. The powers have put this into his head to keep him out of mischief, and he wishes me to spend three weeks digging there with him. The result will be that he will perhaps get some more money to hoard, and leave for his heirs to spend foolishly. If I do this, most will commend me as an industrious and hard-working man; but if I choose to devote myself to certain labors which yield more real profit, though but little money, they may be inclined to look on me as an idler. Nevertheless, as I do not need the police of meaningless labor to regulate me, and do not see anything absolutely praiseworthy in this fellow's undertaking any more than in many an enterprise of our own or foreign governments, however amusing it may be to him or them, I prefer to finish my education at a different school.

If a man walk in the woods for love of them half of each day, he is in danger of being regarded as a loafer; but if he spends his whole day as a speculator, shearing off those woods and making earth bald before her time, he is esteemed an industrious and enterprising citizen. As if a town had no interest in its forests but to cut them down!

Most men would feel insulted if it were proposed to employ them in throwing stones over a wall, and then in throwing them back, merely that they might earn their wages. But many are no more worthily employed now. For instance: just after sunrise one summer morning I noticed one of my neighbors walking beside his team, which was slowly drawing a heavy hewn stone swung under the axle, surrounded by an atmosphere of industry—his day's work begun, his brow commenced

to sweat, a reproach to all sluggards and idlers—pausing abreast
the shoulders of his oxen, and half turning round with a flourish
of his merciful whip, while they gained their length on him.
And I thought, Such is the labor which the American Congress
exists to protect,—honest, manly toil,—honest as the day is
long,—that makes his bread taste sweet, and keeps society
sweet,—which all men respect and have consecrated; one of
the sacred band, doing the needful, but irksome drudgery.
Indeed, I felt a slight reproach, because I observed this from
the window, and was not abroad and stirring about a similar
business. The day went by, and at evening I passed the yard
of another neighbor, who keeps many servants, and spends
much money foolishly, while he adds nothing to the common
stock, and there I saw the stone of the morning lying beside a
whimsical structure intended to adorn this Lord Timothy
Dexter's premises, and the dignity forthwith departed from
the teamster's labor, in my eyes. In my opinion, the sun was
made to light worthier toil than this. I may add that his employer has since run off, in debt to a good part of the town,
and, after passing through Chancery, has settled somewhere
else, there to become once more a patron of the arts.

The ways by which you may get money almost without
exception lead downward. To have done anything by which
you earned money *merely* is to have been truly idle or worse.
If the laborer gets no more than the wages which his employer
pays him, he is cheated, he cheats himself. If you would get
money as a writer or a lecturer, you must be popular, which
is to go down perpendicularly. Those services which the community will most readily pay for it is most disagreeable to
render. You are paid for being something less than a man. The
State does not commonly reward a genius any more wisely.
Even the poet-laureate would rather not have to celebrate the
accidents of royalty. He must be bribed with a pipe of wine;
and perhaps another poet is called away from his muse to gauge
that very pipe. As for my own business, even that kind of
surveying which I could do with most satisfaction my em-
ployers do not want. They would prefer that I should do my

work coarsely and not too well, ay, not well enough. When I observe that there are different ways of surveying, my employer commonly asks which will give him the most land, not which is most correct. I once invented a rule for measuring cordwood, and tried to introduce it in Boston; but the measurer there told me that the sellers did not wish to have their wood measured correctly,—that he was already too accurate for them, and therefore they commonly got their wood measured in Charlestown before crossing the bridge.

The aim of the laborer should be, not to get his living, to get "a good job," but to perform well a certain work; and, even in a pecuniary sense, it would be economy for a town to pay its laborers so well that they would not feel that they were working for low ends, as for a livelihood merely, but for scientific, or even moral ends. Do not hire a man who does your work for money, but him who does it for love of it.

It is remarkable that there are few men so well employed, so much to their minds, but that a little money or fame would commonly buy them off from their present pursuit. I see advertisements for *active* young men, as if activity were the whole of a young man's capital. Yet I have been surprised when one has with confidence proposed to me, a grown man, to embark in some enterprise of his, as if I had absolutely nothing to do, my life having been a complete failure hitherto. What a doubtful compliment this to pay me! As if he had met me halfway across the ocean beating up against the wind, but bound nowhere, and proposed to me to go along with him! If I did, what do you think the underwriters would say? No, no! I am not without employment at this stage of the voyage. To tell the truth, I saw an advertisement for ablebodied seamen, when I was a boy, sauntering in my native port, and as soon as I became of age I embarked.

The community has no bribe that will tempt a wise man. You may raise money enough to tunnel a mountain, but you cannot raise money enough to hire a man who is minding *his own* business. An efficient and valuable man does what he can, whether the community pay him for it or not. The inefficient

offer their inefficiency to the highest bidder, and are forever
expecting to be put into office. One would suppose that they
were rarely disappointed.

Perhaps I am more than usually jealous with respect to my
freedom. I feel that my connection with and obligation to
society are still very slight and transient. Those slight labors
which afford me a livelihood, and by which it is allowed that
I am to some extent serviceable to my contemporaries, are as
yet commonly a pleasure to me, and I am not often reminded
that they are a necessity. So far I am successful. But I foresee,
that, if my wants should be much increased, the labor required
to supply them would become a drudgery. If I should sell both
my forenoons and afternoons to society, as most appear to do,
I am sure that, for me, there would be nothing left worth living for. I trust that I shall never thus sell my birthright for
a mess of pottage. I wish to suggest that a man may be very
industrious, and yet not spend his time well. There is no more
fatal blunderer than he who consumes the greater part of his
life getting his living. All great enterprises are self-supporting.
The poet, for instance, must sustain his body by his poetry,
as a steam planing-mill feeds its boilers with the shavings it
makes. You must get your living by loving. But as it is said of
the merchants that ninety-seven in a hundred fail, so the life
of men generally, tried by this standard, is a failure, and
bankruptcy may be surely prophesied.

Merely to come into the world the heir of a fortune is not
to be born, but to be stillborn, rather. To be supported by the
charity of friends, or a government-pension,—provided you
continue to breathe,—by whatever fine synonyms you describe
these relations, is to go into the almshouse. On Sundays the
poor debtor goes to church to take an account of stock, and
finds, of course, that his outgoes have been greater than his
income. In the Catholic Church, especially, they go into
chancery, make a clean confession, give up all, and think to
start again. Thus men will lie on their backs, talking about the
fall of man, and never make an effort to get up.

As for the comparative demand which men make on life,

it is an important difference between the two, that the one is satisfied with a level success, that his marks can all be hit by point-blank shots, but the other, however low and unsuccessful his life may be, constantly elevates his aim, though at a very slight angle to the horizon. I should much rather be the last man,—though, as the Orientals say, "Greatness doth not approach him who is forever looking down; and all those who are looking high are growing poor."

It is remarkable that there is little or nothing to be remembered written on the subject of getting a living; how to make getting a living not merely honest and honorable, but altogether inviting and glorious; for if *getting* a living is not so, then living is not. One would think, from looking at literature, that this question had never disturbed a solitary individual's musings. Is it that men are too much disgusted with their experience to speak of it? The lesson of value which money teaches, which the Author of the Universe has taken so much pains to teach us, we are inclined to skip altogether. As for the means of living, it is wonderful how indifferent men of all classes are about it, even reformers, so called,—whether they inherit, or earn, or steal it. I think that Society has done nothing for us in this respect, or at least has undone what she has done. Cold and hunger seem more friendly to my nature than those methods which men have adopted and advise to ward them off.

The title *wise* is, for the most part, falsely applied. How can one be a wise man, if he does not know any better how to live than other men?—if he is only more cunning and intellectually subtle? Does Wisdom work in a treadmill? or does she teach how to succeed *by her example?* Is there any such thing as wisdom not applied to life? Is she merely the miller who grinds the finest logic? It is pertinent to ask if Plato got his *living* in a better way or more successfully than his contemporaries,—or did he succumb to the difficulties of life like other men? Did he seem to prevail over some of them merely by indifference, or by assuming grand airs? or find it easier to live, because his aunt remembered him in her will? The ways in which most men get their living, that is, live, are mere make-shifts, and a shirking of the real business of life,—chiefly because they do not know, but partly because they do not mean, any better.

The rush to California, for instance, and the attitude, not merely of merchants, but of philosophers and prophets, so called, in relation to it, reflect the greatest disgrace on mankind. That so many are ready to live by luck, and so get the means of commanding the labor of others less lucky, without contributing any value to society! And that is called enterprise! I know of no more startling development of the immorality of trade, and all the common modes of getting a living. The philosophy and poetry and religion of such a mankind are not worth the dust of a puff-ball. The hog that gets his living by rooting, stirring up the soil so, would be ashamed of such company. If I could command the wealth of all the worlds by lifting my finger, I would not pay *such* a price for it. . . .[2]

To speak impartially, the best men that I know are not serene, a world in themselves. For the most part, they dwell in forms, and flatter and study effect only more finely than the rest. We select granite for the underpinning of our houses and barns; we build fences of stone; but we do not ourselves rest on an underpinning of granitic truth, the lowest primitive rock. Our sills are rotten. What stuff is the man made of who is not coexistent in our thought with the purest and subtilest truth? I often accuse my finest acquaintances of an immense frivolity; for, while there are manners and compliments we do not meet, we do not teach one another the lessons of honesty and sincerity that the brutes do, or of steadiness and solidity that the rocks do. The fault is commonly mutual, however; for we do not habitually demand any more of each other.

That excitement about Kossuth,[3] consider how characteristic, but superficial, it was!—only another kind of politics or dancing. Men were making speeches to him all over the country,

---

[2] Some minor omissions do not impair the essay as a whole.

[3] Lajos Kossuth, a Hungarian patriot who was highly feted in America in 1851.

but each expressed only the thought, or the want of thought, of the multitude. No man stood on truth. They were merely banded together, as usual one leaning on another, and all together on nothing; as the Hindoos made the world rest on an elephant, the elephant on a tortoise, and the tortoise on a serpent, and had nothing to put under the serpent. For all fruit of that stir we have the Kossuth hat.

Just so hollow and ineffectual, for the most part, is our ordinary conversation. Surface meets surface. When our life ceases to be inward and private, conversation degenerates into mere gossip. We rarely meet a man who can tell us any news which he has not read in a newspaper, or been told by his neighbor; and, for the most part, the only difference between us and our fellow is that he has seen the newspaper, or been out to tea, and we have not. In proportion as our inward life fails, we go more constantly and desperately to the post-office. You may depend on it, that the poor fellow who walks away with the greatest number of letters, proud of his extensive correspondence, has not heard from himself this long while.

I do not know but it is too much to read one newspaper a week. I have tried it recently, and for so long it seems to me that I have not dwelt in my native region. The sun, the clouds, the snow, the trees say not so much to me. You cannot serve two masters. It requires more than a day's devotion to know and to possess the wealth of a day.

We may well be ashamed to tell what things we have read or heard in our day. I do not know why my news should be so trivial,—considering what one's dreams and expectations are, why the developments should be so paltry. The news we hear, for the most part, is not news to our genius. It is the stalest repetition. You are often tempted to ask why such stress is laid on a particular experience which you have had,—that, after twenty-five years, you should meet Hobbins, Registrar of Deeds, again on the sidewalk. Have you not budged an inch, then? Such is the daily news. Its facts appear to float in the atmosphere, insignificant as the sporules of fungi, and impinge on some neglected *thallus*, or surface of our minds, which affords a basis for them, and hence a parasitic growth. We should wash ourselves clean of such news. Of what consequence, though our planet explode, if there is no character involved in the explosion? In health we have not the least curiosity about such events. We do not live for idle amusement. I would not run round a corner to see the world blow up.

All summer, and far into the autumn, perchance, you unconsciously went by the newspapers and the news, and now you find it was because the morning and the evening were full of news to you. Your walks were full of incidents. You attended, not to the affairs of Europe, but to your own affairs in Massachusetts fields. If you chance to live and move and have your being in that thin stratum in which the events that make the news transpire,—thinner than the paper on which it is printed,—then these things will fill the world for you; but if you soar above or dive below that plane, you cannot remember nor be reminded of them. Really to see the sun rise or go down every day, so to relate ourselves to a universal fact, would preserve us sane forever. Nations! What are nations? Tartars, and Huns, and Chinamen! Like insects, they swarm. The historian strives in vain to make them memorable. It is for want of a man that there are so many men. It is individuals that populate the world. Any man thinking may say with the Spirit of Lodin,—

> I look down from my height on nations,
> And they become ashes before me;—
> Calm is my dwelling in the clouds;
> Pleasant are the great fields of my rest.[4]

Pray, let us live without being drawn by dogs, Esquimaux-fashion, tearing over hill and dale, and biting each other's ears.

Not without a slight shudder at the danger, I often perceive how near I had come to admitting into my mind the details of some trivial affair,—the news of the street; and I am astonished to observe how willing men are to lumber their minds with

---

[4] From James MacPherson's Ossianic poem, *Carricthura*.

such rubbish,—to permit idle rumors and incidents of the most insignificant kind to intrude on ground which should be sacred to thought. Shall the mind be a public arena, where the affairs of the street and the gossip of the tea-table chiefly are discussed? Or shall it be a quarter of heaven itself,—an hypaethral temple, consecrated to the service of the gods? I find it so difficult to dispose of the few facts which to me are significant, that I hesitate to burden my attention with those which are insignificant, which only a divine mind could illustrate. Such is, for the most part, the news in newspapers and conversation. It is important to preserve the mind's chastity in this respect. Think of admitting the details of a single case of the criminal court into our thoughts, to stalk profanely through their very *sanctum sanctorum* for an hour, ay, for many hours! to make a very bar-room of the mind's inmost apartment, as if for so long the dust of the street had occupied us,—the very street itself, with all its travel, its bustle, and filth, had passed through our thoughts' shrine! Would it not be an intellectual and moral suicide? When I have been compelled to sit spectator and auditor in a courtroom for some hours, and have seen my neighbors, who were not compelled, stealing in from time to time, and tiptoeing about with washed hands and faces, it has appeared to my mind's eye, that, when they took off their hats, their ears suddenly expanded into vast hoppers for sound, between which even their narrow heads were crowded. Like the vanes of windmills, they caught the broad but shallow stream of sound, which, after a few titillating gyrations in their coggy brains, passed out the other side. I wondered if, when they got home, they were as careful to wash their ears as before their hands and faces. It has seemed to me, at such a time, that the auditors and the witnesses, the jury and the counsel, the judge and the criminal at the bar,—if I may presume him guilty before he is convicted,—were all equally criminal, and a thunderbolt might be expected to descend and consume them all together.

By all kinds of traps and sign-boards, threatening the extreme penalty of the divine law, exclude such trespassers from the only ground which can be sacred to you. It is so hard to forget what it is worse than useless to remember! If I am to be a thoroughfare, I prefer that it be of the mountain-brooks, the Parnassian streams, and not the town-sewers. There is inspiration, that gossip which comes to the ear of the attentive mind from the courts of heaven. There is the profane and stale revelation of the bar-room and the police court. The same ear is fitted to receive both communications. Only the character of the hearer determines to which it shall be open, and to which closed. I believe that the mind can be permanently profaned by the habit of attending to trivial things, so that all our thoughts shall be tinged with triviality. Our very intellect shall be macadamized, as it were,—its foundation broken into fragments for the wheels of travel to roll over; and if you would know what will make the most durable pavement, surpassing rolled stones, spruce blocks, and asphaltum, you have only to look into some of our minds which have been subjected to this treatment so long.

If we have thus desecrated ourselves,—as who has not?— the remedy will be by wariness and devotion to reconsecrate ourselves, and make once more a fane of the mind. We should treat our minds, that is, ourselves, as innocent and ingenuous children, whose guardians we are, and be careful what objects and what subjects we thrust on their attention. Read not the Times. Read the Eternities. Conventionalities are at length as bad as impurities. Even the facts of science may dust the mind by their dryness, unless they are in a sense effaced each morning, or rather rendered fertile by the dews of fresh and living truth. Knowledge does not come to us by details, but in flashes of light from heaven. Yes, every thought that passes through the mind helps to wear and tear it, and to deepen the ruts, which, as in the streets of Pompeii, evince how much it has been used. How many things there are concerning which we might well deliberate whether we had better know them, —had better let their peddling-carts be driven, even at the slowest trot or walk, over that bridge of glorious span by which we trust to pass at last from the farthest brink of time to the nearest shore of eternity! Have we no culture, no refinement,—but skill only to live coarsely and serve the Devil?—to acquire a little worldly wealth, or fame, or liberty, and make a false show with it, as if we were all husk and shell, with no tender and living kernel to us? Shall our institutions be like those chestnut-burs which contain abortive nuts, perfect only to prick the fingers. . . .

What is called politics is comparatively something so superficial and inhuman that, practically, I have never fairly recognized that it concerns me at all. The newspapers, I perceive, devote some of their columns specially to politics or government without charge; and this, one would say, is all that saves it; but as I love literature and to some extent the truth also, I never read those columns at any rate. I do not wish to blunt my sense of right so much. I have not got to answer for having read a single President's Message. A strange age of the world this, when empires, kingdoms, and republics come a-begging to a private man's door, and utter their complaints at his elbow! I cannot take up a newspaper but I find that some wretched government or other, hard pushed, and on its last legs, is interceding with me, the reader, to vote for it,—more importunate than an Italian beggar; and if I have a mind to look at its certificate, made, perchance, by some benevolent merchant's clerk, or the skipper that brought it over, for it cannot speak a word of English itself, I shall probably read of the eruption of some Vesuvius, or the overflowing of some Po, true or forged, which brought it into this condition. I do not hesitate, in such a case, to suggest work, or the almshouse; or why not keep its castle in silence, as I do commonly? The poor President, what with preserving his popularity and doing his duty, is completely bewildered. The newspapers are the ruling power. Any other government is reduced to a few marines at Fort Independence. If a man neglects to read the Daily Times, government will go down on its knees to him, for this is the only treason in these days.

Those things which now most engage the attention of men, as politics and the daily routine, are, it is true, vital functions of human society, but should be unconsciously performed, like the corresponding functions of the physical body. They are *infra*-human, a kind of vegetation. I sometimes awake to a half-consciousness of them going on about me, as a man may become conscious of some of the processes of digestion in a morbid state, and so have the dyspepsia, as it is called. It is as if a thinker submitted himself to be rasped by the great gizzard of creation. Politics is, as it were, the gizzard of society, full of grit and gravel, and the two political parties are its two opposite halves,—sometimes split into quarters, it may be, which grind on each other. Not only individuals, but states, have thus a confirmed dyspepsia, which expresses itself, you can imagine by what sort of eloquence. Thus our life is not altogether a forgetting, but also, alas! to a great extent, a remembering, of that which we should never have been conscious of, certainly not in our waking hours. Why should we not meet, not always as dyspeptics, to tell our bad dreams, but sometimes as *eu*peptics, to congratulate each other on the ever-glorious morning? I do not make an exorbitant demand, surely.

HEBRAISM AND HELLENISM

MATTHEW ARNOLD (1822-1888)

From *Culture and Anarchy*, 1869. Arnold believed that the culture of ancient Greece should leaven that of modern times. Here he juxtaposes two disciplines, the Greek and the Hebrew, each purporting to promote human perfection. These two forces still jostle each other in the complex culture of the twentieth century.

———

This fundamental ground[1] is our preference of doing to thinking. Now this preference is a main element in our nature, and

———
[1] A reference to the close of the previous essay.

as we study it we find ourselves opening up a number of large questions on every side.

Let me go back for a moment to Bishop Wilson,[2] who says: "First, never go against the best light you have; secondly, take care that your light be not darkness." We show, as a nation, laudable energy and persistence in walking according to the best light we have, but are not quite careful enough, perhaps, to see that our light be not darkness. This is only another version of the old story that energy is our strong point and favorable characteristic, rather than intelligence. But we may give to this idea a more general form still, in which it will have a yet larger range of application. We may regard this energy driving at practice, this paramount sense of the obligation of duty, self-control, and work, this earnestness in going manfully with the best light we have, as one force. And we may regard the intelligence driving at those ideas which are, after all, the basis of right practice, the ardent sense for all the new and changing combinations of them which man's development brings with it, the indomitable impulse to know and adjust them perfectly, as another force. And these two forces we may regard as in some sense rivals,—rivals not by the necessity of their own nature, but as exhibited in man and his history,— and rivals dividing the empire of the world between them. And to give these forces names from the two races of men who have supplied the most signal and splendid manifestations of them, we may call them respectively the forces of Hebraism and Hellenism. Hebraism and Hellenism,—between these two points of influence moves our world. At one time it feels more powerfully the attraction of one of them, at another time of the other; and it ought to be, though it never is, evenly and happily balanced between them.

The final aim of both Hellenism and Hebraism, as of all great spiritual disciplines, is no doubt the same: man's perfection or salvation. The very language which they both of them use in schooling us to reach this aim is often identical. Even when their language indicates by variation,—sometimes a broad

[2] Bishop Thomas Wilson (1663-1755), author of *Maxims*.

variation, often a but slight and subtle variation,—the different courses of thought which are uppermost in each discipline, even then the unity of the final end and aim is still apparent. To employ the actual words of that discipline with which we ourselves are all of us most familiar, and the words of which, therefore, come most home to us, that final end and aim is "that we might be partakers of the divine nature." These are the words of a Hebrew apostle, but of Hellenism and Hebraism alike this is, I say, the aim. When the two are confronted, as they very often are confronted, it is nearly always with what I may call a rhetorical purpose; the speaker's whole design is to exalt and enthrone one of the two, and he uses the other only as a foil and to enable him the better to give effect to his purpose. Obviously, with us, it is usually Hellenism which is thus reduced to minister to the triumph of Hebraism. There is a sermon on Greece and the Greek spirit by a man never to be mentioned without interest and respect, Frederick Robertson,[3] in which this rhetorical use of Greece and the Greek spirit, and the inadequate exhibition of them necessarily consequent upon this, is almost ludicrous, and would be censurable if it were not to be explained by the exigencies of a sermon. On the other hand, Heinrich Heine,[4] and other writers of his sort give us the spectacle of the tables completely turned, and of Hebraism brought in just as a foil and contrast to Hellenism, and to make the superiority of Hellenism more manifest. In both these cases there is injustice and misrepresentation. The aim and end of both Hebraism and Hellenism is, as I have said, one and the same, and this aim and end is august and admirable.

Still, they pursue this aim by very different courses. The uppermost idea with Hellenism is to see things as they really are; the uppermost idea with Hebraism is conduct and obedience. Nothing can do away with this ineffaceable difference. The Greek quarrel with the body and its desires is, that they hinder right thinking; the Hebrew quarrel with them is, that they hinder right acting. "He that keepeth the law, happy is

[3] Frederick Robertson (1816-1853), an influential clergyman.
[4] Heinrich Heine (1799-1856), eminent German poet.

he"; "Blessed is the man that feareth the Eternal, that delighteth greatly in his commandments";—that is the Hebrew notion of felicity; and, pursued with passion and tenacity, this notion would not let the Hebrew rest till, as is well known, he had at last got out of the law a network of prescriptions to enwrap his whole life, to govern every moment of it, every impulse, every action. The Greek notion of felicity, on the other hand, is perfectly conveyed in these words of a great French moralist: *"C'est le bonheur des hommes,"*—when? when they abhor that which is evil?—no; when they exercise themselves in the law of the Lord day and night?—no; when they die daily? —no; when they walk about the New Jerusalem with palms in their hands?—no; but when they think aright, when their thought hits: *"quand ils pensent juste."* At the bottom of both the Greek and the Hebrew notion is the desire, native in man, for reason and the will of God, the feeling after the universal order,—in a word, the love of God. But, while Hebraism seizes upon certain plain, capital intimations of the universal order, and rivets itself, one may say, with unequalled grandeur of earnestness and intensity on the study and observance of them, the bent of Hellenism is to follow, with flexible activity, the whole play of the universal order, to be apprehensive of missing any part of it, of sacrificing one part to another, to slip away from resting in this or that intimation of it, however capital. An unclouded clearness of mind, an unimpeded play of thought, is what this bent drives at. The governing idea of Hellenism is *spontaneity of consciousness;* that of Hebraism, *strictness of conscience.*

Christianity changed nothing in this essential bent of Hebraism to set doing above knowing. Self-conquest, self-devotion, the following not our own individual will, but the will of God, *obedience*, is the fundamental idea of this form, also, of the discipline to which we have attached the general name of Hebraism. Only, as the old law and the network of prescriptions with which it enveloped human life were evidently a motive-power not driving and searching enough to produce the result aimed at,—patient continuance in well-doing, self-conquest,—Christianity substituted for them boundless devotion to that inspiring and affecting pattern of self-conquest offered by Jesus Christ; and by the new motive-power, of which the essence was this, though the love and admiration of Christian churches have for centuries been employed in varying, amplifying, and adorning the plain description of it. Christianity, as St. Paul truly says, "establishes the law," and in the strength of the ampler power which she has thus supplied to fulfill it, has accomplished the miracles, which we all see, of her history.

So long as we do not forget that both Hellenism and Hebraism are profound and admirable manifestations of man's life, tendencies, and powers, and that both of them aim at a like final result, we can hardly insist too strongly on the divergence of line and of operation with which they proceed. It is a divergence so great that it most truly, as the prophet Zechariah says, "has raised up thy sons, O Zion, against thy sons, O Greece!" The difference whether it is by doing or by knowing that we set most store, and the practical consequences which follow from this difference, leave their mark on all the history of our race and of its development. . . .

Both Hellenism and Hebraism arise out of the wants of human nature, and address themselves to satisfying those wants. But their methods are so different, they lay stress on such different points, and call into being by their respective disciplines such different activities, that the face which human nature presents when it passes from the hands of one of them to those of the other, is no longer the same. To get rid of one's ignorance, to see things as they are, and by seeing them as they are to see them in their beauty, is the simple and attractive ideal which Hellenism holds out before human nature; and from the simplicity and charm of this ideal, Hellenism, and human life in the hands of Hellenism, is invested with a kind of aërial ease, clearness, and radiancy; they are full of what we call sweetness and light. Difficulties are kept out of view, and the beauty and rationalness of the ideal have all our thoughts. "The best man is he who most tries to perfect himself, and the happiest man is he who most feels that he *is* perfecting himself,"—this account of the matter by Socrates, the true Socrates of the *Memorabilia,* has something so simple, spontaneous, and unsophisticated about it that it seems to fill us with clearness and hope when we hear it. But there is a saying which I have heard attributed to Mr. Carlyle about Socrates,—a very happy saying, whether it is really Mr. Carlyle's or not,—which excellently marks the essential point in which Hebraism differs from Hellenism. "Socrates," this saying goes, "is terribly *at ease in Zion.*" Hebraism,—and here is the source of its wonderful strength,—has always been severely preoccupied with an awful sense of the impossibility of being at ease in Zion; of the difficulties which oppose themselves to man's pursuit or attainment of that perfection of which Socrates talks so hopefully, and, as from this point of view one might almost say, so glibly. It is all very well to talk of getting rid of one's ignorance, of seeing things in their reality, seeing them in their beauty; but how is this to be done when there is something which thwarts and spoils all our efforts?

This something is *sin;* and the space which sin fills in Hebraism, as compared with Hellenism, is indeed prodigious. This obstacle to perfection fills the whole scene, and perfection appears remote and rising away from earth, in the background. Under the name of sin, the difficulties of knowing oneself and conquering oneself which impede man's passage to perfection, become, for Hebraism, a positive, active entity hostile to man, a mysterious power which I heard Dr. Pusey[5] the other day, in one of his impressive sermons, compare to a hideous hunchback seated on our shoulders, and which it is the main business of our lives to hate and oppose. The discipline of the Old Testament may be summed up as a discipline teaching us to abhor and flee from sin; the discipline of the New Testament, as a discipline teaching us to die to it. As Hellenism speaks of thinking clearly, seeing things in their essence and beauty, as a grand and precious feat for man to achieve, so Hebraism speaks of becoming conscious of sin, of awakening to a sense of

---

[5] Edward Pusey (1800-1882), a High Church clergyman.

sin, as a feat of this kind. It is obvious to what wide divergence these differing tendencies, actively followed, must lead. As one passes and repasses from Hellenism to Hebraism, from Plato to St. Paul, one feels inclined to rub one's eyes and ask oneself whether man is indeed a gentle and simple being, showing the traces of a noble and divine nature; or an unhappy chained captive, laboring with groaning that cannot be uttered to free himself from the body of this death.

Apparently it was the Hellenic conception of human nature which was unsound, for the world could not live by it. Absolutely to call it unsound, however, is to fall into the common error of its Hebraizing enemies; but it was unsound at that particular moment of man's development, it was premature. The indispensable basis of conduct and self-control, the platform upon which alone the perfection aimed at by Greece can come into bloom, was not to be reached by our race so easily; centuries of probation and discipline were needed to bring us to it. Therefore the bright promise of Hellenism faded, and Hebraism ruled the world. Then was seen that astonishing spectacle, so well marked by the often-quoted words of the prophet Zechariah, when men of all languages and nations took hold of the skirt of him that was a Jew, saying:—"*We will go with you, for we have heard that God is with you.*" And the Hebraism which thus received and ruled a world all gone out of the way and altogether become unprofitable, was, and could not but be, the later, the more spiritual, the more attractive development of Hebraism. It was Christianity; that is to say, Hebraism aiming at self-conquest and rescue from the thrall of vile affections, not by obedience to the letter of a law, but by conformity to the image of a self-sacrificing example. To a world stricken with moral enervation Christianity offered its spectacle of an inspired self-sacrifice; to men who refused themselves nothing, it showed one who refused himself everything;—"*my Saviour banished joy!*" says George Herbert.[6] . . .

Of two disciplines laying their main stress, the one, on clear intelligence, the other, on firm obedience; the one, on com-

---

[6] George Herbert (1593-1633), English religious poet.

prehensively knowing the ground of one's duty, the other, on diligently practising it; the one, on taking all possible care (to use Bishop Wilson's words again) that the light we have be not darkness, the other, that according to the best light we have we diligently walk,—the priority naturally belongs to that discipline which braces all man's moral powers, and founds for him an indispensable basis of character. And, therefore, it is justly said of the Jewish people, who were charged with setting powerfully forth that side of the divine order to which the words *conscience* and *self-conquest* point, that they were "entrusted with the oracles of God"; as it is justly said of Christianity, which followed Judaism and which set forth this side with a much deeper effectiveness and a much wider influence, that the wisdom of the old pagan world was foolishness compared to it. No words of devotion and admiration can be too strong to render thanks to these beneficent forces which have so borne forward humanity in its appointed work of coming to the knowledge and possession of itself; above all, in those great moments when their action was the wholesomest and the most necessary.

But the evolution of these forces, separately and in themselves, is not the whole evolution of humanity,—their single history is not the whole history of man; whereas their admirers are always apt to make it stand for the whole history. Hebraism and Hellenism are, neither of them, the *law* of human development, as their admirers are prone to make them; they are, each of them, *contributions* to human development,—august contributions, invaluable contributions; and each showing itself to us more august, more invaluable, more preponderant over the other, according to the moment in which we take them, and the relation in which we stand to them. The nations of our modern world, children of that immense and salutary movement which broke up the pagan world, inevitably stand to Hellenism in a relation which dwarfs it, and to Hebraism in a relation which magnifies it. They are inevitably prone to take Hebraism as the law of human development, and not as simply a contribution to it, however precious. And yet the lesson must perforce be learned, that the human spirit is wider than the most priceless of the forces which bear it onward, and that to the whole development of man Hebraism itself is, like Hellenism, but a contribution. . . .

But meanwhile, by alternations of Hebraism and Hellenism, of a man's intellectual and moral impulses, of the effort to see things as they really are, and the effort to win peace by self-conquest, the human spirit proceeds; and each of these two forces has its appointed hours of culmination and seasons of rule. As the great movement of Christianity was a triumph of Hebraism and man's moral impulses, so the great movement which goes by the name of the Renascence was an uprising and re-instatement of men's intellectual impulses and of Hellenism. We in England, the devoted children of Protestantism, chiefly know the Renascence by its subordinate and secondary side of the Reformation. The Reformation has been often called a Hebraizing revival, a return to the ardor and sincereness of primitive Christianity. No one, however, can study the development of Protestantism and of Protestant churches without feeling that into the Reformation too,—Hebraizing child of the Renascence and offspring of its fervor, rather than its intelligence, as it undoubtedly was,—the subtle Hellenic leaven of the Renascence found its way, and that the exact respective parts, in the Reformation, of Hebraism and of Hellenism, are not easy to separate. But what we may with truth say is, that all which Protestantism was to itself clearly conscious of, all which it succeeded in clearly setting forth in words, had the characters of Hebraism rather than of Hellenism. The Reformation was strong in that it was an earnest return to the Bible and to doing from the heart the will of God as there written. It was weak, in that it never consciously grasped or applied the central idea of the Renascence,—the Hellenic idea of pursuing, in all lines of activity, the law and science, to use Plato's words, of things as they really are. . . .

In the sixteenth century, therefore, Hellenism re-entered the world, and again stood in presence of Hebraism,—a Hebraism renewed and purged. Now, it has not been enough observed, how, in the seventeenth century, a fate befell Hellenism in some respects analogous to that which befell it at the commencement of our era. The Renascence, that great reawakening of Hellenism, that irresistible return of humanity to nature and to seeing things as they are, which in art, in literature, and in physics, produced such splendid fruits, had, like the anterior Hellenism of the pagan world, a side of moral weakness and of relaxation or insensibility of the moral fibre, which in Italy showed itself with the most startling plainness, but which in France, England, and other countries was very apparent, too. Again this loss of spiritual balance, this exclusive preponderance given to man's perceiving and knowing side, this unnatural defect of his feeling and acting side, provoked a reaction. Let us trace that reaction where it most nearly concerns us.

Science has now made visible to everybody the great and pregnant elements of difference which lie in race, and in how signal a manner they make the genius and history of an Indo-European people vary from those of a Semitic people. Hellenism is of Indo-European growth, Hebraism is of Semitic growth; and we English, a nation of Indo-European stock, seem to belong naturally to the movement of Hellenism. But nothing more strongly marks the essential unity of man, than the affinities we can perceive, in this point or that, between members of one family of peoples and members of another. And no affinity of this kind is more strongly marked than that likeness in the strength and prominence of the moral fibre, which, notwithstanding immense elements of difference, knits in some special sort of genius and history of us English, and our American descendants across the Atlantic, to the genius and history of the Hebrew people. Puritanism, which has been so great a power in the English nation, and in the strongest part of the English nation, was originally the reaction in the seventeenth century of the conscience and moral sense of our race, against the moral indifference and lax rule of conduct which in the sixteenth century came in with the Renascence. It was a reaction of Hebraism against Hellenism; and it powerfully manifested itself, as was natural, in a people with much of what we call a Hebraizing turn, with a signal affinity for the bent which was the master-bent of Hebrew life. Eminently Indo-European by its humor, by the power it shows, through this gift, of imaginatively acknowledging the multiform aspects of the problem of life, and of thus getting itself unfixed from its own over-certainty, of smiling at its own over-tenacity, our race has yet (and a great part of its strength lies here), in matters of practical life and moral conduct, a strong share of the assuredness, the tenacity, the intensity of the Hebrews. This turn manifested itself in Puritanism, and has had a great part in shaping our history for the last two hundred years. Undoubtedly it checked and changed amongst us that movement of the Renascence which we see producing in the reign of Elizabeth such wonderful fruits. Undoubtedly it stopped the prominent rule and direct development of that order of ideas which we call by the name of Hellenism, and gave the first rank to a different order of ideas. Apparently, too, as we said of the former defeat of Hellenism, if Hellenism was defeated, this shows that Hellenism was imperfect, and that its ascendancy at that moment would not have been for the world's good.

Yet there is a very important difference between the defeat inflicted on Hellenism by Christianity eighteen hundred years ago, and the check given to the Renascence by Puritanism. The greatness of the difference is well measured by the difference in force, beauty, significance, and usefulness, between primitive Christianity and Protestantism. Eighteen hundred years ago it was altogether the hour of Hebraism. Primitive Christianity was legitimately and truly the ascendant force in the world at that time, and the way of mankind's progress lay through its full development. Another hour in man's development began in the fifteenth century, and the main road of his progress then lay for a time through Hellenism. Puritanism was no longer the central current of the world's progress, it was a side stream crossing the central current and checking it. The cross and the check may have been necessary and salutary, but that does not do away with the essential difference between the main stream of man's advance and a cross or side stream. For more than two hundred years the main stream of man's advance has moved towards knowing himself and the world, seeing things as they are, spontaneity of consciousness; the main impulse of a great part, and that the strongest part, of our nation has been towards strictness of conscience. They have made the secondary the principal at the wrong moment, and the principal they have at the wrong moment treated as secondary. This contravention of the natural order has produced, as such contravention always must produce, a certain confusion and false movement, of which we are now beginning to feel, in almost every direction, the inconvenience. In all directions our habitual causes of action seem to be losing efficaciousness, credit, and control, both with others and even with ourselves. Everywhere we see the beginnings of confusion, and we want a clue to some sound order and authority. This we can only get by going back upon the actual instincts and forces which rule our life, seeing them as they really are, connecting them with other instincts and forces, and enlarging our whole view and rule of life.

A LIBERAL EDUCATION; AND WHERE TO FIND IT[1]

THOMAS HENRY HUXLEY (1825-1895)

From *Lay Sermons*, 1870. What part should science play in the program of general education? Huxley shows that a liberal education can be found readily in the study of the sciences. His friend Matthew Arnold took an opposite view, and the point is still debatable.

The business which the South London Working Men's College[2] has undertaken is a great work; indeed, I might say, that

---

[1] Used with the courtesy of Appleton-Century-Crofts, Inc., the authorized publishers.

[2] This essay is part of an address delivered in 1868 to the College, of which Huxley was principal.

Education, with which that college proposes to grapple, is the greatest work of all those which lie ready to a man's hand just at present.

And, at length, this fact is becoming generally recognized. You cannot go anywhere without hearing a buzz of more or less confused and contradictory talk on this subject—nor can you fail to notice that, in one point at any rate, there is a very decided advance upon like discussions in former days. Nobody outside the agricultural interest now dares to say that education is a bad thing. If any representative of the once large and powerful party, which, in former days, proclaimed this opinion, still exists in the semifossil state, he keeps his thoughts to himself. In fact, there is a chorus of voices, almost distressing in their harmony, raised in favor of the doctrine that education is the great panacea for human troubles, and that, if the country is not shortly to go to the dogs, everybody must be educated.

The politicians tell us, "You must educate the masses because they are going to be masters." The clergy join in the cry for education, for they affirm that the people are drifting away from church and chapel into the broadest infidelity. The manufacturers and the capitalists swell the chorus lustily. They declare that ignorance makes bad workmen; that England will soon be unable to turn out cotton goods, or steam engines, cheaper than other people; and then, Ichabod! Ichabod! the glory will be departed from us. And a few voices are lifted up in favor of the doctrine that the masses should be educated because they are men and women with unlimited capacities of being, doing, and suffering, and that it is as true now, as it ever was, that the people perish for lack of knowledge.

These members of the minority, with whom I confess I have a good deal of sympathy, are doubtful whether any of the other reasons urged in favor of the education of the people are of much value—whether, indeed, some of them are based upon either wise or noble grounds of action. They question if it be wise to tell people that you will do for them, out of fear of their power, what you have left undone, so long as your only motive was compassion for their weakness and their sorrows. And, if ignorance of everything which is needful a ruler should know is likely to do so much harm in the governing classes of the future, why is it, they ask reasonably enough, that such ignorance in the governing classes of the past has not been viewed with equal horror?

Compare the average artisan and the average country squire, and it may be doubted if you will find a pin to choose between the two in point of ignorance, class feeling, or prejudice. It is true that the ignorance is of a different sort—that the class feeling is in favor of a different class—and that the prejudice has a distinct savor of wrong-headedness in each case—but it is questionable if the one is either a bit better, or a bit worse, than the other. The old protectionist theory is the doctrine of trades unions as applied by the squires, and the modern trades unionism is the doctrine of the squires applied by the artisans. Why should we be worse off under one *régime* than under the other?

Again, this skeptical minority asks the clergy to think whether it is really want of education which keeps the masses away from their ministrations—whether the most completely educated men are not as open to reproach on this score as the workmen; and whether, perchance, this may not indicate that it is not education which lies at the bottom of the matter?

Once more, these people, whom there is no pleasing, venture to doubt whether the glory which rests upon being able to undersell all the rest of the world, is a very safe kind of glory —whether we may not purchase it too dear; especially if we allow education, which ought to be directed to the making of men, to be diverted into a process of manufacturing human tools, wonderfully adroit in the exercise of some technical industry, but good for nothing else.

And, finally, these people inquire whether it is the masses alone who need a reformed and improved education. They ask whether the richest of our public schools might not well be made to supply knowledge, as well as gentlemanly habits, a strong class feeling, and eminent proficiency in cricket. They seem to think that the noble foundations of our old universities are hardly fulfilling their functions in their present posture of half-clerical seminaries, half race-courses, where men are trained to win a senior wranglership, or a double-first, as horses are trained to win a cup, with as little reference to the need of after-life in the case of the man as in that of the racer. And while as zealous for education as the rest, they affirm that if the education of the richer classes were such as to fit them to be the leaders and the governors of the poorer; and if the education of the poorer classes were such as to enable them to appreciate really wise guidance and good governance, the politicians need not fear mob-law, nor the clergy lament their want of flocks, nor the capitalists prognosticate the annihilation of the prosperity of the country.

Such is the diversity of opinion upon the why and the wherefore of education. And my hearers will be prepared to expect that the practical recommendations which are put forward are not less discordant. There is a loud cry for compulsory education. We English, in spite of constant experience to the contrary, preserve a touching faith in the efficacy of acts of parliament; and I believe we should have compulsory education in the course of next session if there were the least probability that half a dozen leading statesmen of different parties would agree what that education should be.

Some hold that education without theology is worse than none. Others maintain, quite as strongly, that education with theology is in the same predicament. But this is certain, that those who hold the first opinion can by no means agree what theology should be taught; and that those who maintain the second are in a small minority.

At any rate "make people learn to read, write, and cipher," say a great many; and the advice is undoubtedly sensible as far as it goes. But, as has happened to me in former days, those who, in despair of getting anything better, advocate this measure, are met with the objection that it is very like making a child practise the use of a knife, fork, and spoon, without giving it a particle of meat. I really don't know what reply is to be made to such an objection.

But it would be unprofitable to spend more time in disentangling, or rather in showing up the knots in, the ravelled skeins of our neighbors. Much more to the purpose is it to ask if we possess any clue of our own which may guide us among these entanglements. And by way of a beginning, let us ask ourselves—What is education? Above all things, what is our ideal of a thoroughly liberal education?—of that education which, if we could begin life again, we would give ourselves—of that education which, if we could mold the fates to our own will, we would give our children? Well, I know not what may be your conceptions upon this matter, but I will tell you mine, and I hope I shall find that our views are not very discrepant.

Suppose it were perfectly certain that the life and fortune of every one of us would, one day or other, depend upon his winning or losing a game at chess. Don't you think that we should all consider it to be a primary duty to learn at least the names and the moves of the pieces; to have a notion of a gambit, and a keen eye for all the means of giving and getting out of check? Do you not think that we should look with a disapprobation amounting to scorn, upon the father who allowed his son, or the state which allowed its members, to grow up without knowing a pawn from a knight?

Yet it is a very plain and elementary truth, that the life, the fortune, and the happiness of every one of us, and, more or less, of those who are connected with us, do depend upon our knowing something of the rules of a game infinitely more difficult and complicated than chess. It is a game which has been played for untold ages, every man and woman of us being one of the two players in a game of his or her own. The chessboard is the world, the pieces are the phenomena of the universe, the rules of the game are what we call the laws of Nature. The player on the other side is hidden from us. We know that his play is always fair, just, and patient. But also we know, to our cost, that he never overlooks a mistake, or makes the smallest allowance for ignorance. To the man who plays well, the highest stakes are paid, with that sort of overflowing generosity with which the strong shows delight in strength. And one who plays ill is checkmated—without haste, but without remorse.

My metaphor will remind some of you of the famous picture in which Retzsch[3] has depicted Satan playing at chess with man for his soul. Substitute for the mocking fiend in that picture a calm, strong angel who is playing for love, as we say, and would rather lose than win—and I should accept it as an image of human life.

Well, what I mean by Education is learning the rules of this mighty game. In other words, education is the instruction of the intellect in the laws of Nature, under which name I include not merely things and their forces, but men and their ways; and the fashioning of the affections and of the will into an earnest and loving desire to move in harmony with those laws. For me, education means neither more nor less than this. Anything which professes to call itself education must be tried by this standard, and if it fails to stand the test, I will not call it education, whatever may be the force of authority, or of numbers, upon the other side.

It is important to remember that, in strictness, there is no such thing as an uneducated man. Take an extreme case. Suppose that an adult man, in the full vigour of his faculties, could be suddenly placed in the world, as Adam is said to have been, and then left to do as he best might. How long would he be left uneducated? Not five minutes. Nature would begin to teach him, through the eye, the ear, the touch, the properties of objects. Pain and pleasure would be at his elbow telling him to do this and avoid that; and by slow degrees the man would receive an education which, if narrow, would be

_____

[3] A nineteenth-century German painter.

thorough, real, and adequate to his circumstances, though there would be no extras and very few accomplishments.

And if to this solitary man entered a second Adam, or, better still, an Eve, a new and greater world, that of social and moral phenomena, would be revealed. Joys and woes, compared with which all others might seem but faint shadows, would spring from the new relations. Happiness and sorrow would take the place of the coarser monitors, pleasure and pain; but conduct would still be shaped by the observation of the natural consequences of actions; or, in other words, by the laws of the nature of man.

To every one of us the world was once as fresh and new as to Adam. And then, long before we were susceptible of any other mode of instruction, Nature took us in hand, and every minute of waking life brought its educational influence, shaping our actions into rough accordance with Nature's laws, so that we might not be ended untimely by too gross disobedience. Nor should I speak of this process of education as past for any one, be he as old as he may. For every man the world is as fresh as it was at the first day, and as full of untold novelties for him who has the eyes to see them. And Nature is still continuing her patient education of us in that great university, the universe, of which we are all members—Nature having no Test-Acts.

Those who take honors in Nature's university, who learn the laws which govern men and things and obey them, are the really great and successful men in this world. The great mass of mankind are the "Poll," who pick up just enough to get through without much discredit. Those who won't learn at all are plucked; and then you can't come up again. Nature's pluck means extermination.

Thus the question of compulsory education is settled so far as Nature is concerned. Her bill on that question was framed and passed long ago. But, like all compulsory legislation, that of Nature is harsh and wasteful in its operation. Ignorance is visited as sharply as wilful disobedience—incapacity meets with the same punishment as crime. Nature's discipline is not even a word and a blow, and the blow first; but the blow without the word. It is left to you to find out why your ears are boxed.

The object of what we commonly call education—that education in which man intervenes and which I shall distinguish as artificial education—is to make good these defects in Nature's methods; to prepare the child to receive Nature's education, neither incapably nor ignorantly, nor with wilful disobedience; and to understand the preliminary symptoms of her pleasure, without waiting for the box on the ear. In short, all artificial education ought to be an anticipation of natural education. And a liberal education is an artificial education which has not only prepared a man to escape the great evils of disobedience to natural laws, but has trained him to appreciate and to seize upon the rewards, which Nature scatters with as free a hand as her penalties.

That man, I think, has had a liberal education who has been so trained in youth that his body is the ready servant of his will, and does with ease and pleasure all the work that, as a mechanism, it is capable of; whose intellect is a clear, cold, logic engine, with all its parts of equal strength, and in smooth working order; ready, like a steam engine, to be turned to any kind of work, and spin the gossamers as well as forge the anchors of the mind; whose mind is stored with a knowledge of the great and fundamental truths of Nature and of the laws of her operations; one who, no stunted ascetic, is full of life and fire, but whose passions are trained to come to heel by a vigorous will, the servant of a tender conscience; who has learned to love all beauty, whether of Nature or of art, to hate all vileness, and to respect others as himself.

Such an one and no other, I conceive, has had a liberal education; for he is, as completely as a man can be, in harmony with Nature. He will make the best of her, and she of him. They will get on together rarely; she as his ever beneficent mother; he as her mouthpiece, her conscious self, her minister and interpreter. . . ,

PULVIS ET UMBRA[1]

ROBERT LOUIS STEVENSON (1850-1894)

From *Scribner's Magazine*, 1888. In his smooth and fluid style Stevenson questions what there is in man to cause him to rise from disheartening failure and continue valiantly to strive. Some regard this essay as pessimistic; others as optimistic. Much depends on one's own point of view. The title means "Dust and a Shade."

––––––––

We look for some reward of our endeavours and are disappointed; not success, not happiness, not even peace of conscience, crowns our ineffectual efforts to do well. Our frailties are invincible, our virtues barren; the battle goes sore against us to the going down of the sun. The canting moralist tells us of right and wrong; and we look abroad, even on the face of our small earth, and find them change with every climate, and no country where some action is not honoured for a virtue and none where it is not branded for a vice; and we look in our experience, and find no vital congruity in the wisest rules, but at the best a municipal fitness. It is not strange if we are tempted to despair of good. We ask too much. Our religions and moralities have been trimmed to flatter us, till they are all emasculate and sentimentalised, and only please and weaken. Truth is of a rougher strain. In the harsh face of life, faith can read a bracing gospel. The human race is a thing more ancient than the ten commandments; and the bones and revolutions of the Kosmos, in whose joints we are but moss and fungus, more ancient still.

–––––––

[1] Used with the courtesy of Charles Scribner's Sons, the authorized publishers.

I

Of the Kosmos in the last resort, science reports many doubtful things and all of them appalling. There seems no substance to this solid globe on which we stamp: nothing but symbols and ratios. Symbols and ratios carry us and bring us forth and beat us down; gravity that swings the incommensurable suns and worlds through space, is but a figment varying inversely as the squares of distances; and the suns and worlds themselves, imponderable figures of abstraction, NH_3 and H_2O. Consideration dares not dwell upon this view; that way madness lies; science carries us into zones of speculation, where there is no habitable city for the mind of man.

But take the Kosmos with a grosser faith, as our senses give it us. We behold space sown with rotatory islands, suns and worlds and the shards and wrecks of systems: some, like the sun, still blazing; some rotting, like the earth; others, like the moon, stable in desolation. All of these we take to be made of something we call matter: a thing which no analysis can help us to conceive; to whose incredible properties no familiarities can reconcile our minds. This stuff, when not purified by the lustration of fire, rots uncleanly into something we call life; seized through all its atoms with a pediculous malady; swelling in tumours that become independent, sometimes even (by an abhorrent prodigy) locomotory; one splitting into millions, millions cohering into one, as the malady proceeds through varying stages. This vital putrescence of the dust, used as we are to it, yet strikes us with occasional disgust, and the profusion of worms in a piece of ancient turf, or the air of a marsh darkened with insects, will sometimes check our breathing so that we aspire for cleaner places. But none is clean: the moving sand is infected with lice; the pure spring, where it bursts out of the mountain, is a mere issue of worms; even in the hard rock the crystal is forming.

In two main shapes this eruption covers the countenance of the earth: the animal and the vegetable: one in some degree the inversion of the other: the second rooted to the spot; the first coming detached out of its natal mud, and scurrying abroad with the myriad feet of insects, or towering into the heavens on the wings of birds,—a thing so incomprehensible that, if it be well considered, the heart stops. To what passes with the anchored vermin, we have little clue: doubtless they have their joys and sorrows, their delights and killing agonies,—it appears not how. But of the locomotory, to which we ourselves belong, we can tell more. These share with us a thousand miracles: the miracles of sight, of hearing, of the projection of sound, things that bridge space; the miracles of memory and reason, by which the present is conceived, and when it is gone its image kept living in the brains of man and brute; the miracle of reproduction, with its imperious desires and staggering consequences. And to put the last touch upon this mountain mass of the revolting and the inconceivable, all these prey upon each other, lives tearing other lives in pieces, cramming them inside themselves, and by that summary process growing fat: the vegetarian, the whale, perhaps the tree, not less than the lion of the desert,—for the vegetarian is only the eater of the dumb.

Meanwhile our rotatory island loaded with predatory life, and more drenched with blood, both animal and vegetable, than ever mutinied ship, scuds through space with unimaginable speed, and turns alternate cheeks to the reverberation of a blazing world ninety million miles away.

II

What a monstrous spectre is this man, the disease of the agglutinated dust, lifting alternate feet or lying drugged with slumber; killing, feeding, growing, bringing forth small copies of himself; grown upon with hair like grass, fitted with eyes that move and glitter in his face; a thing to set children screaming;—and yet looked at nearlier, known as his fellows know him, how surprising are his attributes! Poor soul, here for so little, cast among so many hardships, filled with desires so incommensurate and so inconsistent, savagely surrounded, savagely descended, irremediably condemned to prey upon his fellow lives: who should have blamed him had he been of a piece with his destiny and a being merely barbarous? And we look and behold him instead filled with imperfect virtues: infinitely childish, often admirably valiant, often touchingly kind; sitting down, amidst his momentary life, to debate of right and wrong and the attributes of the deity; rising up to do battle for an egg or die for an idea; singling out his friends and his mate with cordial affection; bringing forth in pain, rearing with long-suffering solicitude, his young. To touch the heart of his mystery, we find in him one thought, strange to the point of lunacy: the thought of duty; the thought of something owing to himself, to his neighbour, to his God: an ideal of decency, to which he would rise if it were possible; a limit of shame, below which, if it be possible, he will not stoop. The design in most men is one of conformity; here and there, in picked natures, it transcends itself and soars on the other side, arming martyrs with independence; but in all, in their degrees, it is a bosom thought:—not in man alone, for we trace it in dogs and cats whom we know fairly well, and doubtless some similar point of honour sways the elephant, the oyster, and the louse, of whom we know so little:—but in man, at least, it sways with so complete an empire that merely selfish things come second, even with the selfish; that appetites are starved, fears are conquered, pains supported; that almost the dullest shrinks from the reproof of a glance, although it were a child's; and all but the most cowardly stand amid the risks of war; and the more noble, having strongly conceived an act as due to their ideal, affront and embrace death. Strange enough if, with their singular origin and perverted practice, they think they are to be rewarded in some future life; stranger still, if they are persuaded of the contrary, and think this blow which they solicit will strike them senseless for eternity. I shall be reminded what a tragedy of misconception and misconduct man at large presents,—of organized injustice, cowardly violence, and treacherous crime, and of the damning imperfections of the best. They cannot be too darkly drawn. Man is indeed marked for failure in his efforts to do right. But where the best consistently miscarry, how tenfold more remarkable that all should continue to strive; and surely we should find it both touching and inspiriting, that in a field from which success is banished, our race should not cease to labour.

If the first view of this creature, stalking in his rotatory isle, be a thing to shake the courage of the stoutest, on this nearer sight he startles us with an admiring wonder. It matters not where we look, under what climate we observe him, in what state of society, in what depth of ignorance, burthened with what erroneous morality; by camp-fires in Assiniboia, the snow powdering his shoulders, the wind plucking his blanket, as he sits, passing the ceremonial calumet and uttering his grave opinions like a Roman senator; in ships at sea, a man inured to hardship and vile pleasures, his brightest hope a fiddle in a tavern and a bedizened trull who sells herself to rob him, and he for all that simple, innocent, cheerful, kindly like a child, constant to toil, brave to drown, for others; in the slums of cities, moving among indifferent millions to mechanical employment, without hope of change in the future, with scarce a pleasure in the present, and yet true to his virtues, honest up to his lights, kind to his neighbours, tempted perhaps in vain by the bright gin-palace, perhaps long-suffering with a drunken wife that ruins him; in India (a woman this time) kneeling with broken cries and streaming tears, as she drowns her child in the sacred river; in the brothel, the discard of society, living mainly on strong drink, fed with affronts, a fool, a thief, the comrade of thieves, and even here keeping the point of honour and the touch of pity, often repaying the world's scorn with service, often standing firm upon a scruple, and at a certain cost, rejecting riches:— everywhere some virtue cherished or affected, everywhere some decency of thought and carriage, everywhere the ensign of man's ineffectual goodness:—ah! if I could show you this! If I could show you these men and women, all the world over, in every stage of history, under every abuse of error, under every circumstance of failure, without hope, without help, without thanks, still obscurely fighting the lost fight of virtue, still clinging, in the brothel or on the scaffold, to some rag of honour, the poor jewel of their souls! They may seek to escape, and yet they cannot; it is not alone their privilege and glory, but their doom; they are condemned to some nobility; all their lives long, the desire of good is at their heels, the implacable hunter.

Of all earth's meteors, here at least is the most strange and consoling: That this ennobled lemur, this hair-crowned bubble of the dust, this inheritor of a few years and sorrows, should yet deny himself his rare delights, and add to his frequent pains, and live for an ideal, however misconceived. Nor can we stop with man. A new doctrine, received with screams a little while ago by canting moralists, and still not properly worked into the body of our thoughts, lights us a step farther into the heart of this rough but noble universe. For nowadays the pride of man denies in vain his kinship with the original dust. He stands no longer like a thing apart. Close at his heels we see the dog, prince of another genus: and in him too, we see dumbly testified the same cultus of an unattainable ideal, the same constancy in failure. Does it stop with the dog? We look at our feet where the ground is blackened with the swarming ant; a creature so small, so far from us in the hierarchy of brutes, that we can scarce trace and scarce comprehend his doings; and here also, in his ordered polities and rigorous justice, we see confessed the law of duty and the fact of individual sin. Does it stop, then, with the ant? Rather this desire of well-doing and this doom of frailty run through all the grades of life: rather is this earth, from the frosty top of Everest to the next margin of the internal fire, one stage of ineffectual virtues and one temple of pious tears and perseverance. The whole creation groaneth and travaileth together. It is the common and the god-like law of life. The browsers, the biters, the barkers, the hairy coats of field and forest, the squirrel in the oak, the thousand-footed creeper in the dust, as they share with us the gift of life, share with us the love of an ideal; strive like us—like us are tempted to grow weary of the struggle—to do well; like us receive at times unmerited refreshment, visitings of support, returns of courage; and are condemned like us to be crucified between that double law of the members and the will. Are they like us, I wonder, in the timid hope of some reward, some sugar with the drug? do they, too, stand aghast at unrewarded virtues, at the sufferings of those whom, in our partiality, we take to be just, and the prosperity of such as in our blindness we call wicked? It may be, and yet God knows what they should look for. Even while they look, even while they repent, the foot of man treads them by thousands in the dust, the yelping hounds burst upon their trail, the bullet speeds, the knives are heating in the den of the vivisectionist; or the dew falls, and the generation of a day is blotted out. For these are creatures compared with whom our weakness is strength, our ignorance wisdom, our brief span eternity.

And as we dwell, we living things, in our isle of terror and under the imminent hand of death, God forbid it should be man the erected, the reasoner, the wise in his own eyes —God forbid it should be man that wearies in well-doing, that despairs of unrewarded effort, or utters the language of complaint. Let it be enough for faith, that the whole creation groans in mortal frailty, strives with unconquerable constancy: surely not all in vain.

QUALITY[1]

JOHN GALSWORTHY (1867-1933)

From *The Inn of Tranquility*, 1912. Galsworthy uses the narrative technique to sharpen the conflict between the artisan and mass production.

---

[1] Reprinted from *The Inn of Tranquility* by John Galsworthy; copyright 1912 by Charles Scribner's Sons, 1940 by Ada Galsworthy; used in the United States by permission of Charles Scribner's Sons, in Canada by permission of William Heinemann, Ltd.

There is pathos in the passing of the perfectionist. Is there no room for him at all in modern society?

I knew him from the days of my extreme youth, because he made my father's boots; inhabiting with his elder brother two little shops let into one, in a small by-street—now no more, but then most fashionably placed in the West End.

That tenement had a certain quiet distinction; there was no sign upon its face that he made for any of the Royal Family—merely his own German name of Gessler Brothers; and in the window a few pairs of boots. I remember that it always troubled me to account for those unvarying boots in the window, for he made only what was ordered, reaching nothing down, and it seemed so inconceivable that what he made could ever have failed to fit. Had he bought them to put there? That, too, seemed inconceivable. He would never have tolerated in his house leather on which he had not worked himself. Besides, they were too beautiful—the pair of pumps, so inexpressibly slim, the patent leathers with cloth tops, making water come into one's mouth, the tall brown riding boots with marvellous sooty glow, as if, though new, they had been worn a hundred years. Those pairs could only have been made by one who saw before him the Soul of Boot—so truly were they prototypes incarnating the very spirit of all foot-gear. These thoughts, of course, came to me later, though even when I was promoted to him, at the age of perhaps fourteen, some inkling haunted me of the dignity of himself and brother. For to make boots—such boots as he made—seemed to me then, and still seems to me, mysterious and wonderful.

I remember well my shy remark, one day, while stretching out to him my youthful foot:

"Isn't it awfully hard to do, Mr. Gessler?"

And his answer, given with a sudden smile from out of the sardonic redness of his beard: "Id is an Ardt!"

Himself, he was a little as if made from leather, with his yellow crinkly face, and crinkly reddish hair and beard, and neat folds slanting down his cheeks to the corners of his mouth, and his guttural and one-toned voice; for leather is a sardonic substance, and stiff and slow of purpose. And that was the character of his face, save that his eyes, which were gray-blue, had in them the simple gravity of one secretly possessed by the Ideal. His elder brother was so very like him—though watery, paler in every way, with a great industry—that sometimes in early days I was not quite sure of him until the interview was over. Then I knew that it was he, if the words, "I will ask my brudder," had not been spoken; and, that, if they had, it was his elder brother.

When one grew old and wild and ran up bills, one somehow never ran them up with Gessler Brothers. It would not have seemed becoming to go in there and stretch out one's foot to that blue iron-spectacled glance, owing him for more than— say—two pairs, just the comfortable reassurance that one was still his client.

For it was not possible to go to him very often—his boots lasted terribly, having something beyond the temporary— some, as it were, essence of boot stitched into them.

One went in, not as into most shops, in the mood of: "Please serve me, and let me go!" but restfully, as one enters a church; and, sitting on the single wooden chair, waited— for there was never anybody there. Soon, over the top edge of that sort of well—rather dark, and smelling soothingly of leather—which formed the shop, there would be seen his face, or that of his elder brother, peering down. A guttural sound, and the tip-tap of bast slippers beating the narrow wooden stairs, and he would stand before one without coat, a little bent, in leather apron, with sleeves turned back, blinking —as if awakened from some dream of boots, or like an owl surprised in daylight and annoyed at this interruption.

And I would say: "How do you do, Mr. Gessler? Could you make me a pair of Russia leather boots?"

Without a word he would leave me, retiring whence he came, or into the other portion of the shop, and I could continue to rest in the wooden chair, inhaling the incense of his trade. Soon he would come back, holding in his thin, veined hand a piece of gold-brown leather. With eyes fixed on it, he would remark: "What a beaudiful biece!" When I, too, had admired it, he would speak again. "When do you wand dem?" And I would answer: "Oh! As soon as you conveniently can." And he would say: "To-morrow ford-nighd?" Or if he were his elder brother: "I will ask my brudder!"

Then I would murmur: "Thank you! Good-morning, Mr. Gessler." "Goot-morning!" he would reply, still looking at the leather in his hand. And as I moved to the door, I would hear the tip-tap of his bast slippers restoring him, up the stairs, to his dream of boots. But if it were some new kind of footgear that he had not yet made me, then indeed he would observe ceremony—divesting me of my boot and holding it long in his hand, looking at it with eyes at once critical and loving, as if recalling the glow with which he had created it, and rebuking the way in which one had disorganized this masterpiece. Then, placing my foot on a piece of paper, he would two or three times tickle the outer edges with a pencil and pass his nervous fingers over my toes, feeling himself into the heart of my requirements.

I cannot forget that day on which I had occasion to say to him: "Mr. Gessler; that last pair of town walking-boots creaked, you know."

He looked at me for a time without replying, as if expecting me to withdraw or qualify the statement, then said:

"Id shouldn'd 'ave greaked."

"It did, I'm afraid."

"You goddem wed before dey found demselves?"

"I don't think so."

At that he lowered his eyes, as if hunting for memory of those boots, and I felt sorry I had mentioned this grave thing.

"Zend dem back!" he said; "I will look at dem."

A feeling of compassion for my creaking boots surged up in me, so well could I imagine the sorrowful long curiosity of regard which he would bend on them.

"Zome boods," he said slowly, "are bad from birdt. If I can do noding wid dem, I dake dem off your bill."

Once (once only) I went absent-mindedly into his shop in a pair of boots bought in an emergency at some large firm's. He took my order without showing me any leather, and I could feel his eyes penetrating the inferior integument of my foot. At last he said:

"Dose are nod by boods."

The tone was not one of anger, nor of sorrow, not even of contempt, but there was in it something quiet that froze the blood. He put his hand down and pressed a finger on the place where the left boot, endeavoring to be fashionable, was not quite comfortable.

"Id 'urds you dere," he said. "Dose big virms 'ave no self-respect. Drash!" And then, as if something had given way within him, he spoke long and bitterly. It was the only time I ever heard him discuss the conditions and hardships of his trade.

"Dey get id all," he said, "dey get id by adverdisement, nod by work. Dey dake it away from us, who lofe our boods. Id gomes to this—bresently I haf no work. Every year id gets less—you will see." And looking at his lined face I saw things I had never noticed before, bitter things and bitter struggle—and what a lot of gray hairs there seemed suddenly in his red beard!

As best I could, I explained the circumstances of the purchase of those ill-omened boots. But his face and voice made so deep impression that during the next few minutes I ordered many pairs. Nemesis fell! They lasted more terribly than ever. And I was not able conscientiously to go to him for nearly two years.

When at last I went I was surprised to find that outside one of the two little windows of his shop another name was painted, also that of a bootmaker—making, of course, for the Royal Family. The old familiar boots, no longer in dignified isolation, were huddled in the single window. Inside, the now contracted well of the one little shop was more scented and

darker than ever. And it was longer than usual, too, before a
face peered down, and the tip-tap of the bast slippers began.
At last he stood before me, and, gazing through those rusty
iron spectacles, said:

"Mr. ——, isn'd it?"

"Ah! Mr. Gessler," I stammered, "but your boots are really
too good, you know! See, these are quite decent still!" And I
stretched out to him my foot. He looked at it.

"Yes," he said, "beople do nod wand good boods, id seems."

To get away from his reproachful eyes and voice I hastily
remarked: "What have you done to your shop?"

He answered quietly: "Id was too exbensif. Do you wand
some boods?"

I ordered three pairs, though I had only wanted two, and
quickly left. I had, I do not know quite what feeling of being
part, in his mind, of a conspiracy against him; or not perhaps
so much against him as against his idea of boot. One does not,
I suppose, care to feel like that; for it was again many months
before my next visit to his shop, paid, I remember, with the
feeling: "Oh! well, I can't leave the old boy—so here goes! Perhaps it'll be his elder brother!"

For his elder brother, I knew, had not character enough
to reproach me, even dumbly.

And, to my relief, in the shop there did appear to be his
elder brother, handling a piece of leather.

"Well, Mr. Gessler," I said, "how are you?"

He came close, and peered at me.

"I am breddy well," he said slowly; "but my elder brudder
is dead."

And I saw that it was indeed himself—but how aged and
wan! And never before had I heard him mention his brother.
Much shocked, I murmured: "Oh! I am sorry!"

"Yes," he answered, "he was a good man, he made a
good bood; but he is dead." And he touched the top of his
head, where the hair had suddenly gone as thin as it had been
on that of his poor brother, to indicate, I suppose, the cause of
death. "He could nod ged over losing de oder shop. Do you

wand any boods?" And he held up the leather in his hand: "Id's a beaudiful biece."

I ordered several pairs. It was very long before they came— but they were better than ever. One simply could not wear them out. And soon after that I went abroad.

It was over a year before I was again in London. And the first shop I went to was my old friend's. I had left a man of sixty, I came back to one of seventy-five, pinched and worn and tremulous, who genuinely, this time, did not at first know me.

"Oh! Mr. Gessler," I said, sick at heart; "how splendid your boots are! See, I've been wearing this pair nearly all the time I've been abroad; and they're not half worn out, are they?"

He looked long at my boots—a pair of Russia leather, and his face seemed to regain steadiness. Putting his hand on my instep, he said:

"Do dey vid you here? I 'ad drouble wid dat bair, I re-member."

I assured him that they had fitted beautifully.

"Do you wand any boods?" he said. "I can make dem quickly; id is a slack dime."

I answered: "Please, please! I want boots all round—every kind!"

"I will make a vresh model. Your food must be bigger." And with utter slowness, he traced round my foot, and felt my toes, only once looking up to say:

"Did I dell you my brudder was dead?"

To watch him was painful, so feeble had he grown; I was glad to get away.

I had given those boots up, when one evening they came. Opening the parcel, I set the four pairs in a row. Then one by one I tried them on. There was no doubt about it. In shape and fit, in finish and quality of leather, they were the best he had ever made me. And in the mouth of one of the Town walking-boots I found his bill. The amount was the same as usual, but it gave me quite a shock. He had never before sent it in till quarter day. I flew down-stairs, and wrote a cheque, and posted it at once with my own hand.

A week later, passing the little street, I thought I would go in and tell him how splendidly the new boots fitted. But when I came to where his shop had been, his name was gone. Still there, in the window, were the slim pumps, the patent leathers with cloth tops, the sooty riding boots.

I went in, very much disturbed. In the two little shops —again made into one—was a young man with an English face.

"Mr. Gessler in?" I said.

He gave me a strange, ingratiating look.

"No, sir," he said, "no. But we can attend to anything with pleasure. We've taken the shop over. You've seen our name, no doubt, next door. We make for some very good people."

"Yes, yes," I said; "but Mr. Gessler?"

"Oh!" he answered; "dead."

"Dead! But I only received these boots from him last Wednesday week."

"Ah!" he said; "a shockin' go. Poor old man starved 'imself."

"Good God!"

"Slow starvation, the doctor called it! You see he went to work in such a way! Would keep the shop on; wouldn't have a soul touch his boots except himself. When he got an order, it took him such a time. People won't wait. He lost everybody. And there he'd sit, goin' on and on—I will say that for him— not a man in London made a better boot! But look at the competition! He never advertised! Would 'ave the best leather, too, and do it all 'imself. Well, there it is. What could you expect with his ideas?"

"But starvation——!"

"That may be a bit flowery, as the sayin' is—but I know myself he was sittin' over his boots day and night, to the very last. You see I used to watch him. Never gave 'imself time to eat; never had a penny in the house. All went in rent and leather. How he lived so long I don't know. He regular let his fire go out. He was a character. But he made good boots."

"Yes," I said, "he made good boots."

And I turned and went out quickly, for I did not want that youth to know that I could hardly see.

PRUE[1]

ALICE MEYNELL (1850-1922)

From *Essays*, 1914. From meager evidence Mrs. Meynell, with her usual unpretentious charm, re-creates the character of Mrs. Dick Steele and makes her live. Nevertheless, only so much is there as to prod the imagination to complete the portrait.

———————

Through the long history of human relations, which is the history of the life of our race, there sounds at intervals the clamour of a single voice which has not the tone of oratory, but asks, answers, interrupts itself, interrupts—what else? Whatever else it interrupts is silence; there are pauses, but no answers. There is the jest without the laugh, and again the laugh without the jest. And this is because the letters written by Madame de Sévigné were all saved, and not many written to her; because Swift burnt the letters that were the dearest things in life to him, while "MD" [2] both made a treasury of his; and because Prue kept all the letters which Steele wrote to her from their marriage-day onwards, and Steele kept none of hers.

In Swift's case the silence is full of echoes; that is to say, his letters repeat the phrases of Stella's and Dingley's, to play with them, flout them, and toss them back against the two silenced voices. He never lets the word of these two women fall to the ground; and when they have but blundered with it, and aimed it wide, and sent it weakly, he will catch it, and play you twenty delicate and expert juggling pranks with it as he sends it back into their innocent faces. So we have something of MD's letters in the "Journal," and this in the only

———————

[1] Used with courtesy of Charles Scribner's Sons, the authorized publishers.

[2] My dears—Swift's symbol for Stella Johnson and her companion, Mrs Dingley.

form in which we desire them, to tell the truth; for when Swift gravely saves us some specimens of Stella's wit, after her death, as she spoke them, and not as he mimicked them, they make a sorry show.

In many correspondences, where one voice remains and the other is gone, the retort is enough for two. It is as when, the other day, the half of a pretty quarrel between nurse and child came down from an upper floor to the ears of a mother who decided that she need not interfere. The voice of the undaunted child it was that was audible alone, and it replied, "I'm not; *you* are"; and anon, "I'll tell *yours*." Nothing was really missing there.

But Steele's letters to Prue, his wife, are no such simple matter. The turn we shall give them depends upon the un-heard tone whereto they reply. And there is room for con-jecture. It has pleased the more modern of the many spirits of banter to supply Prue's eternal silence with the voice of a scold. It is painful to me to complain of Thackeray; but see what a figure he makes of Prue in "Esmond." It is, says the nineteenth-century humourist, in defence against the pursuit of a jealous, exacting, neglected, or evaded wife that poor Dick Steele sends those little notes of excuse: "Dearest Being on earth, pardon me if you do not see me till eleven o'clock, having met a schoolfellow from India"; "My dear, dear wife, I write to let you know I do not come home to dinner, being obliged to attend some business abroad, of which I shall give you an account (when I see you in the evening), as becomes your dutiful and obedient husband"; "Dear Prue, I cannot come home to dinner. I languish for your welfare"; "I stay here in order to get Tonson to discount a bill for me, and shall dine with him to that end"; and so forth. Once only does Steele really afford the recent humourist the suggestion that is ap-parently always so welcome. It is when he writes that he is invited to supper to Mr. Boyle's, and adds: "Dear Prue, do not send after me, for I shall be ridiculous." But even this is to be read not ungracefully by a well-graced reader. Prue was young and unused to the world. Her husband, by the way, had been already married; and his greater age makes his constant deference all the more charming.

But with this one exception, Steele's little notes, kept by his wife while she lived, and treasured after her death by her daughter and his, are no record of the watchings and dodgings of a London farce. It is worth while to remember that Steele's dinner, which it was so often difficult to eat at home, was a thing of midday, and therefore of mid-business. But that is a detail. What is desirable is that a reasonable degree of sweetness should· be attributed to Prue; for it was no more than just. To her Steele wrote in a dedication: "How often has your tenderness removed pain from my aching head, how often anguish from my afflicted heart. If there are such beings as guardian angels, they are thus employed. I cannot believe one of them to be more good in inclination, or more charming in form, than my wife."

True, this was for the public; but not so were these daily notes; and these carry to her his assurance that she is "the beautifullest object in the world. I know no happiness in this life in any degree comparable to the pleasure I have in your person and society." "But indeed, though you have every perfection, you have an extravagant fault, which almost frustrates the good in you to me; and that is, that you do not love to dress, to appear, to shine out, even at my request, and to make me proud of you, or rather to indulge the pride I have that you are mine." The correction of the phrase is finely considerate.

Prue cannot have been a dull wife, for this last compliment is a reply, full of polite alacrity, to a letter from her asking for a little flattery. How assiduously, and with what a civilized absence of uncouthness, of shamefacedness, and of slang of the mind, with what simplicity, alertness, and finish, does he step out at her invitation, and perform! She wanted a compliment, though they had been long married then, and he immediately turned it. This was no dowdy Prue.

Her request, by the way, which he repeats in obeying it, is one of the few instances of the other side of the correspondence

—one of the few direct echoes of that one of the two voices which is silent.

The ceremony of the letters and the deferent method of address and signature are never dropped in this most intimate of letter-writing. It is not a little depressing to think that in this very form and state is supposed, by the modern reader, to lurk the stealthiness of the husband of farce, the "rogue." One does not like the word. Is it not clownish to apply it with intention to the husband of Prue? He did not pay, he was always in difficulties, he hid from bailiffs, he did many other things that tarnish honour, more or less, and things for which he had to beg Prue's special pardon; but yet he is not a fit subject for the unhandsome incredulity which is proud to be always at hand with an ironic commentary on such letters as his.

I have no wish to bowdlerize Sir Richard Steele, his ways and words. He wrote to Prue at night when the burgundy had been too much for him, and in the morning after. He announces that he is coming to her "within a pint of wine." One of his gayest letters—a love-letter before the marriage, addressed to "dear lovely Mrs. Scurlock"—confesses candidly that he had been pledging her too well: "I have been in very good company, where your health, under the character of the woman I loved best, has been often drunk; so that I may say that I am dead drunk for your sake, which is more than *I die for you*."

Steele obviously drank burgundy wildly, as did his "good company"; as did also the admirable Addison, who was so solitary in character and so serene in temperament. But no one has, for this fault, the right to put a railing accusation into the mouth of Prue. Every woman has a right to her own silence, whether her silence be hers of set purpose or by accident. And every creature has a right to security from the banterings peculiar to the humourists of a succeeding age. To every century its own ironies, to every century its own vulgarities. In Steele's time they had theirs. They might have rallied Prue more coarsely, but it would have been with a different rallying.

Writers of the nineteenth century went about to rob her of her grace.

She kept some four hundred of these little letters of her lord's. It was a loyal keeping. But what does Thackeray call it? His word is "thrifty." He says: "There are four hundred letters of Dick Steele's to his wife, which that thrifty woman preserved accurately."

"Thrifty" is a hard word to apply to her whom Steele styled, in the year before her death, his "charming little insolent." She was ill in Wales, and he, at home, wept upon her pillow, and "took it to be a sin to go to sleep." Thrifty they may call her, and accurate if they will; but she lies in Westminster Abbey, and Steele called her "your Prueship."

THE ART ETERNAL[1]

H. L. MENCKEN (1880-1956)

From the New York *Evening Mail*, 1918. The "sage of Baltimore" was scholar, critic, and superjournalist. His pronouncements are still startling, humorously smart, frequently iconoclastic, and sometimes charged with enough exaggeration to break the back of truth. Who but Mencken would invite one to believe that neither the president of the United States nor the Pope of Rome could qualify for office if he were truthful?

———

One of the laudable by-products of the Freudian quackery is the discovery that lying, in most cases, is involuntary and inevitable—that the liar can no more avoid it than he can avoid blinking his eyes when a light flashes or jumping when a bomb goes off behind him. At its worst, indeed, this necessity takes on a downright pathological character, and is thus as innocent

———

[1] Reprinted from *A Mencken Chrestomathy* by H. L. Mencken, by permission of Alfred A. Knopf, Inc. Copyright 1924, 1949 by Alfred A. Knopf, Inc

as sciatica. It is part of the morbid baggage of hysterics and neurasthenics: their lying is simply a symptom of their convulsive effort to adjust themselves to an environment which bears upon them too harshly for endurance. The rest of us are not quite so hard pushed, but pushed we all are. In us the thing works through the inferiority complex, which no man can escape. He who lacks it entirely is actually reckoned insane by the fact: his satisfaction with his situation in the world is indistinguishable from a delusion of grandeur. The great majority of us—all, in brief, who are normal—pass through life in constant revolt against our limitations, objective and subjective. Our conscious thought is largely devoted to plans and specifications for cutting a better figure in human society, and in our unconscious the business goes on much more steadily and powerfully. No healthy man, in his secret heart, is content with his destiny. He is tortured by dreams and images as a child is tortured by the thought of a state of existence in which it would live in a candy-store and have two stomachs.

Lying is the product of the unconscious yearning to realize such visions, and if the policeman, conscience, prevents the lie being put into plain words, then it is at least put into more or less plausible acts. We all play parts when we face our fellow-men, as even poets have noticed. No man could bring himself to reveal his true character, and, above all, his true limitations as a citizen and a Christian, his true meannesses, his true imbecilities, to his friends, or even to his wife. Honest autobiography is therefore a contradiction in terms: the moment a man considers himself, even *in petto*,[2] he tries to gild and fresco himself. Thus a man's wife, however realistic her view of him, always flatters him in the end, for the worst she sees in him is appreciably better, by the time she sees it, than what is actually there. What she sees, even at times of the most appalling domestic revelation and confidence, is not the authentic man at all, but a compound made up in part of the authentic man and in part of his projection of a gaudy ideal. The man who is most respected by his wife is the one who makes this projection most

---

[2] In his own breast or private thought.

vivid—that is, the one who is the most daring and ingratiating liar. He can never, of course, deceive her utterly, but if he is skillful he may at least deceive her enough to make her happy.

Omnis homo mendax:[3] thus the Psalmist. So far the Freudians merely parrot him. What is new in their gospel is the doctrine that lying is instinctive, normal, and unavoidable—that a man is forced into it by his very will-to-live. This doctrine purges the business of certain ancient embarrassments, and restores innocence to the heart. Think of a lie as a compulsion neurosis, and you think of it more kindly. I need not add, I hope, that this transfer of it from the department of free will to that of determinism by no means disposes of the penalty that traditionally pursues it, supposing it to be detected and resented. The proponents of free will always make the mistake of assuming that the determinists are simply evil fellows looking for a way to escape the just consequences of their transgressing. No sense is in that assumption. If I lie on the witness-stand and am detected by the judge, I am jailed for perjury forthwith, regardless of my helplessness under compulsion. Here justice refuses absolutely to distinguish between a misfortune and a tort: the overt act is all it is concerned with. But as jurisprudence grows more intelligent and more civilized it may change its tune, to the benefit of liars, which is to say, to the benefit of humanity. Science is unflinchingly deterministic, and it has begun to force its determinism into morals. On some shining tomorrow a psychoanalyst may be put into the box to prove that perjury is simply a compulsion neurosis, like beating time with the foot at a concert or counting the lampposts along the highway.

However, I have but small faith in millenniums, and do not formally predict this one. Nor do I pronounce any moral judgment, pro or con: moral judgments, as old Friedrich[4] used to say, are foreign to my nature. But let us not forget that lying, *per se*, is not forbidden by the moral code of Christendom. Holy Writ dismisses it cynically, and the statutes of all civilized

---

[3] All men are liars, from Psalm 116: 11.
[4] Friedrich Wilhelm Nietzsche (1844-1900), German philosopher.

states are silent about it. Only the Chinese, indeed, make it a penal offense. Perjury, of course, is prohibited everywhere, and also any mendacity which amounts to fraud and deprives a fellow-man of his property. But that far more common form of truth-stretching which has only the lesser aim of augmenting the liar's personal dignity and consequence is looked upon with a very charitable eye. So is that form which has the aim of helping another person in the same way. In the latter direction lying may even take on the stature of a positive virtue. The late King Edward VII, when Prince of Wales, attained to great popularity throughout Christendom by venturing into downright perjury. Summoned into a court of law to give expert testimony regarding some act of adultery, he lied like a gentleman, as the phrase goes, to protect a woman. The lie, to be sure, was intrinsically useless; no one believed that the lady was innocent. Nevertheless, every decent Christian applauded the perjurer for his good intentions, including even the judge on the bench, sworn to combat false witness by every resource of forensics. All of us, worms that we are, occasionally face the alternatives that confronted Edward. On the one hand, we may tell the truth, regardless of consequences, and on the other hand we may mellow it and sophisticate it to make it humane and tolerable.

 For the habitual truth-teller and truth-seeker, indeed, the world has very little liking. He is always unpopular, and not infrequently his unpopularity is so excessive that it endangers his life. Run your eye back over the list of martyrs, lay and clerical: nine-tenths of them, you will find, stood accused of nothing worse than honest efforts to find out and announce the truth. Even today, with the scientific passion become familiar in the world, the general view of such fellows is highly unfavorable. The typical scientist, the typical critic of institutions, the typical truth-seeker in every field is held under suspicion by the great majority of men, and variously beset by posses of relentless foes. If he tries to find out the truth about arteriosclerosis, or surgical shock, or cancer, he is denounced as a scoundrel by the Christian Scientists, the osteopaths and the anti-vivisectionists. If he tries to tell the truth about the government, its agents seek to silence him and punish him. If he turns to fiction and endeavors to depict his fellow men accurately, he has the Comstocks[5] on his hands. In no field can he count upon a friendly audience, and freedom from assault. Especially in the United States is his whole enterprise viewed with bilious eye. The men the American people admire most extravagantly are the most daring liars; the men they detest most violently are those who try to tell them the truth. A Galileo[6] could no more be elected President of the United States than he could be elected Pope of Rome. Both high posts are reserved for men favored by God with an extraordinary genius for swathing the bitter facts of life in bandages of soft illusion.

IMAGINATION[1]

GEORGE SANTAYANA (1863-1952)

From *Soliloquies in England and Later Soliloquies,* 1922. With the philosopher Santayana one finds himself in the realm of abstract thought. He shows us that imagination, vague as it may be, is an animating force without which the world indeed would prove to be a dull and stagnant place.

Men are ruled by imagination: imagination makes them into men, capable of madness and of immense labours. We work dreaming. Consider what dreams must have dominated the builders of the Pyramids—dreams geometrical, dreams funereal, dreams of resurrection, dreams of outdoing the pyramid of some other Pharoah! What dreams occupy that fat man in the street, toddling by under his shabby hat and bedraggled

---

[5] "Comstockery" was promoted by Anthony Comstock (1844-1915), a zealous prosecutor of immorality in books, papers, and pictures.

[6] Galileo, Italian astronomer (1564-1642), defended the truth of his scientific discoveries in spite of persecution from a disbelieving world.

[1] Used with the courtesy of Charles Scribner's Sons, the authorized publishers.

rain-coat? Perhaps he is in love; perhaps he is a Catholic, and
imagines that early this morning he has partaken of the body
and blood of Christ; perhaps he is a revolutionist, with the
millennium in his heart and a bomb in his pocket. The spirit
bloweth where it listesth; the wind of inspiration carries our
dreams before it and constantly refashions them like clouds.
Nothing could be madder, more irresponsible, more dangerous than this guidance of men by dreams. What saves us is
the fact that our imaginations, groundless and chimerical as
they may seem, are secretly suggested and controlled by
shrewd old instincts of our animal nature, and by continual
contact with things. The shock of sense, breaking in upon us
with a fresh irresistible image, checks wayward imagination
and sends it rebounding in a new direction, perhaps more
relevant to what is happening in the world outside.

When I speak of being governed by imagination, of course
I am indulging in a figure of speech, in an ellipsis; in reality
we are governed by that perpetual latent process within us
by which imagination itself is created. Actual imaginings—
the cloud-like thoughts drifting by—are not masters over
themselves nor over anything else. They are like the sound of
chimes in the night; they know nothing of whence they came,
how they will fall out, or how long they will ring. There is a
mechanism in the church tower; there was a theme in the composer's head; there is a beadle who has been winding the thing
up. The sound wafted to us, muffled by distance and a thousand
obstacles, is but the last lost emanation of this magical bell-
ringing. Yet in our dream it is all in all; it is what first enter-
tains and absorbs the mind. Imagination, when it chimes within
us, apparently of itself, is no less elaborately grounded; it is a
last symptom, a rolling echo, by which we detect and name
the obscure operation that occasions it; and not this echo in its
aesthetic impotence, but the whole operation whose last witness it is, receives in science the name of imagination, and may
be truly said to rule the human world.

This extension of names is inevitable although unfortunate,
because language and perception are poetical before they

become scientific, if they ever do; as Aristotle observes that the word anger is used indifferently for two different things: dialectically, or as I call it, imaginatively, for the desire for revenge, but physically for a boiling of the humours. And utterly different as these two things are in quality, no great inconvenience results from giving them the same name, because historically they are parts of the same event. Nature has many dimensions at once, and whenever we see anything happen, much else is happening there which we cannot see. Whilst dreams entertain us, the balance of our character is shifting beneath: we are growing while we sleep. The young think in one way, the drunken in another, and the dead not at all; and I imagine—for I have imagination myself—that they do not die because they stop thinking, but they stop thinking because they die. How much veering and luffing before they make that port! The brain of man, William James used to say, has a hair-trigger organization. His life is terribly experimental. He is perilously dependent on the oscillations of a living needle, imagination, that never points to the true north.

There are books in which the footnotes, or the comments scrawled by some reader's hand in the margin, are more interesting than the text. The world is one of these books. The reciprocal interference of magnetic fields (which I understand is the latest conception of matter) may compose a marvelous moving pattern; but the chief interest to us of matter lies in its fertility in producing minds and presenting recognizable phenomena to the senses; and the chief interest of any scientific notion of its intrinsic nature lies in the fact that, if not literally true, it may liberate us from more misleading conceptions. Did we have nothing but electrical physics to think of, the nightmare would soon become intolerable. But a hint of that kind, like a hasty glance into the crater of a volcano, sends a wholesome shudder through our nerves; we realize how thin is the crust we build on, how mythical and remote from the minute and gigantic scale of nature are the bright images we seem to move among, all cut out and fitted to our human stature. Yet these bright images are our natural companions, and if we do

not worship them idolatrously nor petrify them into sub-
stances, forgetting the nimble use of them in mental discourse,
which is where they belong, they need not be more misleading
to us, even for scientific purposes, than are words or any other
symbols.

It is fortunate that the material world, whatever may be
its intrinsic structure or substance, falls to our apprehension
into such charming units. There is the blue vault of heaven,
there are the twinkling constellations, there are the mountains,
trees, and rivers, and above all those fascinating unstable unities
which we call animals and persons; magnetic fields I am quite
ready to believe them, for such in a vast vague way I feel them
to be, but individual bodies they will remain to my sensuous
imagination, and dramatic personages to my moral sense. They,
too, are animate: they, too, compose a running commentary
on things and on one another, adding their salacious footnotes
to the dull black letter of the world. Many of them are hardly
aware of their own wit; knowing they are but commentators,
they are intent on fidelity and unconscious of invention. Yet
against their will they gloss everything, willy-nilly we are all
scholiasts together. Heaven forbid that I should depreciate
this prodigious tome of nature, or question in one jot or tittle
the absolute authority of its Author; but it is like an encyclopedia in an infinite number of volumes, or a directory with
the addresses of everybody that ever lived. We may dip into
it on occasion in search of some pertinent fact, but it is not
a book to read; its wealth is infinite, but so is its monotony; it
is not composed in our style nor in our language, we could not
have written one line of it. Yet the briefest text invites reflection, and we may spin a little homily out of it in the vernacu-
lar for our own edification.

In the *Mahabharata*, a learned friend tells me, a young
champion armed for the combat and about to rush forward
between the two armies drawn up in battle array, stops for
a moment to receive a word of counsel from his spiritual
adviser—and that word occupies the next eighteen books of
the epic; after which the battle is allowed to proceed. These

Indian poets had spiritual minds, they measured things by their importance to the spirit, not to the eye. They despised verisimilitude and aesthetic proportion; they despised existence, the beauties of which they felt exquisitely nevertheless, and to which their imagination made such stupendous additions. I honour their courage in bidding the sun stand still, not that they might thoroughly vanquish an earthly enemy, but that they might wholly clarify their own soul. For this better purpose the sun need not stand still materially. For the spirit, time is an elastic thing. Fancy is quick and brings the widest vistas to a focus in a single instant. After the longest interval of oblivion and death, it can light up the same image in all the greenness of youth; and if cut short, as it were at Pompeii, in the midst of a word, it can, ages after, without feeling the break, add the last syllable. Imagination changes the scale of everything, and makes a thousand patterns of the woof of nature, without disturbing a single thread. Or rather—since it is nature itself that imagines—it turns to music what was only strain; as if the universal vibration, suddenly ashamed of having been so long silent and useless, had burst into tears and laughter at its own folly, and in so doing had become wise.

THE JUNGLE SLUGGARD[1]

WILLIAM BEEBE (1877-

From *Jungle Days*, 1925. Explorer of the depths of the sea and the depths of the jungle, William Beebe comes forth with vivid descriptions of nature's wonders and oddities. After a perusal of "The Jungle Sluggard" one will never doubt the appropriateness of the creature's name.

————————

Sloths have no right to be living on the earth today; they would be fitting inhabitants of Mars, where a year is over six

————————

[1] From *Jungle Days* by William Beebe, copyright 1925, G. P. Putnam's Sons.

hundred days long. In fact they would exist more appropriately on a still more distant planet where time—as we know it—creeps and crawls instead of flies from dawn to dusk. Years ago I wrote that sloths reminded me of nothing so much as the wonderful Rath Brother athletes or of a slowed-up moving picture, and I can still think of no better similes.

Sloths live altogether in trees, but so do monkeys, and the chief difference between them would seem to be that the latter spend their time pushing against gravitation while the sloths pull against it. Botanically the two groups of animals are comparable to the flower which holds its head up to the sun, swaying on its long stem, and, on the other hand, the over-ripe fruit dangling heavily from its base. We ourselves are physically far removed from sloths—for a while we can point with pride to the daily achievement of those ambulatory athletes, floor-walkers and policemen, yet no human being can cling with his hands to a branch for more than a comparatively short time.

Like a rainbow before breakfast, a sloth is a surprise, an unexpected fellow breather of the air of our planet. No one could prophesy a sloth. If you have an imaginative friend who has never seen a sloth and ask him to describe what he thinks it ought to be like, his uncontrolled phrases will fall far short of reality. If there were no sloths, Dunsany would hesitate to put such a creature in the forests of Mluna, Marco Polo would deny having seen one, and Munchausen would whistle as he listened to a friend's description.

A scientist—even a taxonomist himself—falters when he mentions the group to which a sloth belongs. A taxonomist is the most terribly accurate person in the world, dealing with unvarying facts, and his names and descriptions of animals defy discretion, murder imagination. Nevertheless when next you see a taxonomist disengaged, approach him boldly and ask him in a tone of quarrelsome interest to what order of Mammalia sloths belong. If an honest conservative he will say, "Edentata," which, as any ancient Greek will tell you, means a toothless one. Then if you wish to enrage and nonplus the taxonomist, which I think no one should, as I am one myself, then ask him Why? or, if he has ever been bitten by any of the eighteen teeth of a sloth?

The great savant Buffon in spite of all his genius, fell into most grievous error in his estimation of a sloth. He says, "The inertia of this animal is not so much due to laziness as to wretchedness; it is the consequence of its faulty structure. Inactivity, stupidity, and even habitual suffering result from its strange and ill-constructed conformation. Having no weapons for attack or defense, no mode of refuge even by burrowing, its only safety is in flight. . . . Everything about it shows its wretchedness and proclaims it to be one of those defective monsters, those imperfect sketches, which Nature has sometimes formed, and which, having scarcely the faculty of existence, could only continue for a short time and have since been removed from the catalogue of living beings. They are the last possible term amongst creatures of flesh and blood, and any further defect would have made their existence impossible."

If we imagine the dignified French savant himself, naked, and dangling from a lofty jungle branch in the full heat of the tropic sun, without water and with the prospect of nothing but coarse leaves for breakfast, dinner and all future meals, an impartial on-looker who was ignorant of man's normal haunts and life could very truthfully apply to the unhappy scientist, Buffon's own comments. All of his terms of opprobrium would come home to roost with him.

A bridge out of place would be an absolutely inexplicable thing, as would a sloth in Paris, or a Buffon in the trees. As a matter of fact it was only when I became a temporary cripple myself that I began to appreciate the astonishing lives which sloths lead. With one of my feet injured and out of commission I found an abundance of time in six weeks to study the individuals which we caught in the jungle near by. Not until we invent a superlative of which the word "deliberate" is the positive can we define a sloth with sufficient adequateness and briefness. I dimly remember certain volumes by an authoress whose style pictured the hero walking from the door to the front gate, placing first the right, then the left foot before him as he went. With such detail and speed of action might one write the biography of a sloth.

Ever since man has ventured into this wilderness, sloths have aroused astonishment and comment. Four hundred years ago Gonzala de Oviedo sat him down and penned a most delectable account of these creatures. He says, in part: "There is another strange beast the Spaniards call the Light Dogge, which is one of the slowest beasts and so heavie and dull in mooving that it can scarsely goe fiftie pases in a whole day. Their neckes are high and streight, and all equall like the pestle of a mortar, without making any proportion of similitude of a head, or any difference except in the noddle, and in the tops of their neckes. They have little mouthes, and moove their neckes from one side to another, as though they were astonished: their chiefe desire and delight is to cleave and sticke fast unto Trees, whereunto cleaving fast, they mount up little by little, staying themselves by their long claws. Their voice is much differing from other beasts, for they sing only in the night, and that continually from time to time, singing ever six notes one higher than another. Sometimes the Christian men find these beasts, and bring them home to their houses, where also they creepe all about with their natural slownesse. I could never perceive other but that they love onely of Aire: because they ever turne their heads and mouthes toward that part where the wind blowest most, whereby may be considered that they take most pleasure in the Aire. They bite not, nor yet can bite, having very little mouthes: they are not venemous or noyous any way, but altogether brutish, and utterly unprofitable and without commoditie yet known to men."

It is difficult to find adequate comparisons for a topsy-turvy creature like a sloth, but if I had already had synthetic experience with a Golem, I would take for a formula the general appearance of an English sheep dog, giving it a face with barely distinguishable features and no expression, an inexhaustible appetite for a single kind of coarse leaf, a gamut of emotions well below the animal kingdom, and an enthusiasm for life excelled by a healthy sunflower. Suspend this from a jungle limb by a dozen strong hooks, and—you would still have to see a live sloth to appreciate its appearance.

At rest, curled up into an arboreal ball, a sloth is indistinguishable from a cluster of leaves; in action, the second hand of a watch often covers more distance. At first sight of the shapeless ball of hay, moving with hopeless inadequacy, astonishment shifts to pity, then to impatience and finally, as we sense a life of years spent thus, we feel almost disgust. At which moment the sloth reaches blindly in our direction, thinking us a barren, leafless, but perhaps climable tree, and our emotions change again, this time to sheer delight as a tiny infant sloth raises its indescribably funny face from its mother's breast and sends forth the single tone, the high, whistling squeak, which in sloth intercourse is song, shout, converse, whisper, argument and chant. Separating him from his mother is like plucking a bur from one's hair, but when freed, he contentedly hooks his small self to our clothing and creeps slowly about.

Instead of reviewing all the observations and experiments which I perpetrated upon sloths, I will touch at once the heart of their mysterious psychology, giving in a few words a conception of their strange, uncanny minds. A bird will give up its life in defending its young; an alligator will not often desert its nest in the face of danger; a male stickleback fish will intrepidly face any intruder that threatens its eggs. In fact, at the time when the young of all animals are at the age of helplessness, the senses of the parents are doubly keen, their activities and weapons are at greatest efficiency for guarding of the young and the consequent certainty of the continuance of their race.

The resistance made by a mother sloth to the abstraction of its offspring is chiefly the mechanical tangling of the young animal's tiny claws in the long maternal fur. I have taken away a young sloth and hooked it to a branch five feet away. Being hungry it began at once to utter its high, penetrating penny whistle. To no other sound, high or low, with even a half tone's difference does the sloth pay any heed, but its dim hearing is attuned to just this vibration. Slowly the mother starts off in what she thinks is the direction of the sound. It is the moment of moments in the life of the young animal. Yet I have seen her again and again on different occasions pass within two feet of the little chap, and never look to right or left, but keep straight on, stolidly and unvaryingly to the high jungle, while her baby, a few inches out of her path, called in vain. No kidnapped child hidden in mountain fastness or urban underworld was ever more completely lost to its parent than this infant, in full view and separated by only a sloth's length of space.

A gun fired close to the ear of a sloth will usually arouse not the slightest tremor; no scent of flower or acid or carrion causes any reaction; a sleeping sloth may be shaken violently without awakening, the waving of a scarlet rag, or a climbing serpent a few feet away brings no gleam of curiosity or fear to the dull eyes; an astonishingly long immersion in water produces discomfort but not death. When we think what a constant struggle life is to most creatures, even when they are equipped with the keenest of senses and powerful means of offense, it seems incredible that a sloth can hold its own in this overcrowded tropical jungle.

From birth to death it climbs slowly about the great trees, leisurely feeding, languidly loving, and almost mechanically caring for its young. On the ground a host of enemies await it, but among the higher branches it fears chiefly occasional great boas, climbing jaguars and, worst of all, the mighty talons of harpy eagles. Its means of offense is a joke—a slow, ineffective reaching forward with open jaws, a lethargic stroke of arm and claws which anything but another sloth can avoid. Yet the race of sloths persists and thrives, and in past years I have had as many as eighteen under observation at one time.

A sloth makes no nest or shelter; it even disdains the protection of dense foliage. But for all its apparent helplessness it has a *cheval-de-frise* of protection which many animals far above it in intelligence might well envy. Its outer line of defense is invisibility—and there is none better, for until you have seen your intended prey you can neither attack nor devour him. No hedgehog or armadillo ever rolled a more perfect ball of itself than does a sloth, sitting in a lofty, swaying crotch with head and feet and legs all gathered close together inside. This posture, to an onlooker, destroys all thought of a living animal, but presents a very satisfactory white ants' nest or bunch of dead leaves. If we look at the hair of a sloth we will see small, grey patches along the length of the hairs— at first sight bits of bark and débris of wood. But these minute, scattered particles are of the utmost aid to this invisiblity. They are a peculiar species of alga or lichen-like growth which is found only in this peculiar haunt, and when the rains begin and all the jungle turns a deep, glowing emerald, these tiny plants also react to the welcome moisture and become verdant —thus throwing over the sloth a protecting, misty veil of green.

Even we dull-sensed humans require neither sight nor hearing to detect the presence of an animal like the skunk; in the absolute quiet and blackness of midnight we can tell when a porcupine has crossed our path, or when there are mice in the bureau drawers. But a dozen sloths may be hanging to the trees near at hand and never the slightest whiff of odor comes from them. A baby sloth has not even a baby smell, and all this is part of the cloak of invisibility. The voice, raised so very seldom, is so ventriloquil, and possesses such a strange, un-animal-like quality that it can never be a guide to the location much less to the identity of the author. Here we have three senses, sight, hearing, smell, all operating at a distance, two of them by vibrations, and all leagued together to shelter the sloth from attack.

But in spite of this dramatic guard of invisibility the keen eyes of an eagle, the lapping tongue of a giant boa, and the amazing delicacy of a jaguar's sense of smell break through at times. The jaguar scents sign under the tree of the sloth, climbs eagerly as far as he dares and finds ready to his paw the ball of animal unconsciousness; a harpy eagle half a mile above the jungle sees a bunch of leaves reach out a sleepy arm and scratch itself—something clumps of leaves should not do. Down spirals the great bird, slowly, majestically, knowing there is no need of haste, and alights close by the mammalian sphere. Still the sloth does not move, apparently waiting for what fate may bring—waiting with the patience and resignation which comes only to those of our fellow creatures who cannot say, "I am I!" It seems as if Nature had deserted her jungle changeling, stripped now of its protecting cloak.

The sloth however has never been given credit for its powers of passive resistance, and now, with its enemy within striking distance, its death or even injury is far from a certainty. The crotch which the sloth chooses for its favorite outdoor sport, sleep, is usually high up or far out among the lesser branches, where the eight claws of the eagle or the eighteen of a jaguar find but precarious hold. In order to strike at the quiescent animal the bird has to relinquish half its foothold, the cat nearly one quarter. If the victim were a feathery bush turkey or a soft-bodied squirrel, one stroke would be sufficient, but this strange creature is something far different. In the first place it is only to be plucked from its perch by the exertion of enormous strength. No man can seize a sloth by the long hair of the back and pull it off. So strong are its muscles, so vise-like the grip of its dozen talons that either the crotch must be cut or broken off or the long claws unfastened one by one. Neither of these alternatives is possible to the attacking cat or eagle. They must depend upon crushing or penetrating power of stroke or grasp.

Here is where the sloth's second line of defense becomes operative. First, as I have mentioned, the swaying branch and dizzy height is in his favor, as well as his immovable grip. To begin with the innermost defenses, while his jungle fellows, the ring-tailed and red howling monkeys, have thirteen ribs, the sloth may have as many as twenty; in the latter animal they are, in addition, unusually broad and flat, slats rather than rods. Next comes the skin which is so thick and tough that many an Indian's arrow falls back without even scratching the hide. The skin of the unborn sloth is as tough and strong as that of a full-grown monkey. Finally we have the fur—two distinct coats, the under one fine, short and matted, the outer long, harsh and coarse. Is it any wonder that, teetering on a swaying branch, many a jaguar has had to give up after frantic attempts to strike his claws through the felted hair, the tough skin and the bony lattice-work which protect the vitals of this Edentate bur!

Having rescued our sloth from his most immediate peril let us watch him solve some of the very few problems which life presents to him. Although the cecropia tree, on the leaves of which he feeds, is scattered far and wide through the jungle, yet sloths are found almost exclusively along river banks, and, most amazingly, they not infrequently take to the water. I have caught a dozen sloths swimming rivers a mile or more in width. Judging from the speed of short distances, a sloth can swim a mile in three hours and twenty minutes. Their thick skin and fur must be a protection against crocodiles, electric eels and perai fish as well as jaguars. Why they should ever wish to swim across these wide expanses of water is as inexplicable as the migration of butterflies. One side of the river has as many comfortable crotches, as many millions of cecropia leaves and as many eligible lady sloths as the other! In this unreasonable desire for anything which is out of reach sloths come very close to a characteristic of human beings.

Even in the jungle sloths are not always the static creatures which their vegetable-like life would lead us to believe, as I was able to prove many years ago. A young male was brought in by Indians and after keeping it a few days I shaved off two patches of hair from the center of the back, and labelling it with a metal tag I turned it loose. Forty-eight days later it was captured near a small settlement of bovianders several miles farther up and across the river. During this time it must have traversed four miles of jungle and one of river.

The principal difference between the male and female three-toed sloths is the presence on the back of the male of a large, oval spot of orange-colored fur. To any creature of more active mentality such a minor distinction must often be embarrassing. In an approaching sloth, walking upside-down as usual, this mark is quite invisible, and hence every meeting of two sloths must contain much of delightful uncertainty, of ignorance whether the encounter presages courtship or merely gossip. But color or markings have no meaning in the dull eyes of these animals. Until they have sniffed and almost touched noses they show no recognition or reaction whatever.

I once invented a sloth island—a large circle of ground surrounded by a deep ditch, where sloths climbed about some saplings and ate, but principally slept, and lived for months at a time. This was within sight of my laboratory table, so I could watch what was taking place by merely raising my head. Some of the occurrences were almost too strange for creatures of this earth. I watched two courtships, each resulting in nothing more serious than my own amusement. A female was asleep in a low crotch, curled up into a perfect ball deep within which was ensconced a month-old baby. Two yards overhead was a male who had slept for nine hours without interruption. Moved by what, to a sloth, must have been a burst of uncontrollable emotion, he slowly unwound himself and clambered downward. When close to the sleeping beauty he reached out a claw and tentatively touched a shoulder. Even more deliberately she excavated her head and long neck and peered in every direction but the right one. At last she perceived her suitor and looked away as if the sight was too much for her. Again he touched her post-like neck, and now there arose all the flaming fury of a mother at the flirtatious advances of this stranger. With incredible slowness and effort she freed an arm, deliberately drew it back and then began a slow forward stroke with arm and claws. Meanwhile her gentleman friend had changed his position so the blow swept, or, more correctly passed, through empty air, the lack of impact almost throwing her out of the crotch. The disdained one left with slowness and dignity—or had he already forgotten why he had descended?—and returned to his perch and slumber, where I am sure, not even such active things as dreams came to disturb his peace.

The second courtship advanced to the stage where the

Gallant actually got his claws tangled in the lady's back hair before she awoke. When she grasped the situation she left at once and clambered to the highest branch tip followed by the male. Then she turned and climbed down and across her annoyer, leaving him stranded on the lofty branch looking eagerly about and reaching out hopefully toward a big, green iguana asleep on the next limb in mistake for his fair companion. For an hour he wandered languidly after her, then gave it up and went to sleep. Throughout these and other emotional crises no sound is ever uttered, no feature altered from its stolid repose. The head moves mechanically and the dull eyes blink slowly, as if striving to pierce the opaque veil which ever hangs between the brain of a sloth and the sights, sounds and odors of this tropical world. If the orange back spot was ever of any use in courtship, in arousing any emotion aesthetic or otherwise, it must have been in ages long past when the ancestors of sloths, contemporaries of their gigantic relatives the Mylodons, had better eyesight for escaping from sabre-toothed tigers, than there is need today.

The climax of a sloth's emotion has nothing to do with the opposite sex or with the young, but is exhibited when two females are confined in a cage together. The result is wholly unexpected. After sniffing at one another for a moment, they engage in a slowed-up moving-picture battle. Before any harm is done one or the other gives utterance to the usual piercing whistle and surrenders. She lies flat on the cage floor and offers no defense while the second female proceeds to claw her, now and then attempting, usually vainly, to bite. It is so unpleasant that I have always separated them at this stage, but there is no doubt that in every case the unnatural affray would go on until the victim was killed. In fact I have heard of several instances where this actually took place.

A far pleasanter sight is the young sloth, one of the most adorable balls of fuzzy fur imaginable. While the sense of play is all but lacking his trustfulness and helplessness are most infantile. Every person who takes him up is an accepted substitute for his mother and he will clamber slowly about one's clothing for hours in supreme contentment. One thing I can never explain is that on the ground the baby is even more helpless than his parents. While they can hitch themselves along, body dragging, limbs outspread, until they reach the nearest tree, a young sloth is wholly without power to move. Placed on a flat bit of ground it rolls and tumbles about, occasionally greatly encouraged by seizing hold of its own foot or leg under the impression that at last it has encountered a branch.

Sloths sleep about twice as much as other mammals and a baby sloth often gets tired of being confined in the heart of its mother's sleeping sphere, and creeping out under her arm will go on an exploring expedition around and around her. When over two weeks old it has strength to rise on its hind legs and sway back and forth like nothing else in the world. Its eyes are only a little keener than those of the parent and it peers up at the foliage overhead with the most pitiful interest. It is slowly weaned from a milk diet to the leaves of the cecropia which the mother at first chews up for her offspring.

I once watched a young sloth about a month old and saw it leave its mother for the first time. As the old one moved slowly back and forth, pulling down cecropia leaves and feeding on them, the youngster took firm grip on a leaf stem, mumbling at it with no success whatever. When finally it stretched around and found no soft fur within reach it set up a wail which drew the attention of the mother at once. Still clinging to her perch, she reached out a forearm to an unbelievable distance and gently hooked the great claws about the huddled infant, which at once climbed into the hollow awaiting it.

When a very young sloth is gently disentangled from its mother and hooked on to a branch something of the greatest interest happens. Instead of walking forward, one foot after the other, and upside-down as all adult sloths do, it reaches up and tries to get first one arm then the other *over* the support, and to pull itself into an upright position. This would seem to be a reversion to a time—perhaps millions of years ago—when the ancestors of sloths had not yet begun to hang inverted from the branches. After an interval of clumsy reaching and wriggling about, the baby by accident grasps its own body or limb, and, in this case, convinced that it is at last anchored safely again to its mother, it confidently lets go with all its other claws and tumbles ignominiously to the ground.

The moment a baby sloth dies and slips from its grip on the mother's fur, it ceases to exist for her. If it could call out she would reach down an arm and hook it toward her, but simply dropping silently means no more than if a disentangled bur had fallen from her coat. I have watched such a sloth carefully and have never seen any search of her own body or of the surrounding branches, or a moment's distraction from sleep or food. An imitation of the cry of the dead baby will attract her attention, but if not repeated she forgets it at once.

It is interesting to know of the lives of such beings as this —chronic pacifists, normal morons, the superlative of negative natures, yet holding their own amidst the struggle for existence. Nothing else desires to feed on such coarse fodder, no other creature disputes with it the domain of the under side of branches, hence there is no competition. From our human point of view sloths are degenerate; from another angle they are among the most exquisitely adapted of living beings. If we humans, together with our brains, fitted as well into the possibilities of our own lives we should be infinitely finer and happier,—and, besides, I should then be able to interpret more intelligently the life and the philosophy of sloths!

SCIENCE AND THE FAITH
OF THE MODERN[1]

EDWIN GRANT CONKLIN (1863-1952)

From *Scribner's Magazine*, 1925. Dr. Conklin, one of the most eminent of modern biologists, did much to bring to the understanding of the layman the recent advances in science and the ultimate interdependence

---

[1] Used with the kind permission of the author, Edwin Grant Conklin.

of all knowledge. See how in this essay he deftly employs evolution to reconcile issues which to some minds seem contradictory.

A book was published in this country bearing the striking title, *Science Remaking the World*. Fourteen well-known scholars contributed chapters on subjects ranging all the way from electrons to evolution, from industries to food, medicine, and public health, all showing how man is gaining control over his environment. But science is remaking the world in much more fundamental ways than in these practical and material respects. It is remaking not only the outer world in which we live, but also the inner world of our thoughts and ideals. It has brought about the greatest intellectual revolution in human history, a revolution that concerns the origin, nature, and destiny of man himself—and thoughtful men everywhere are inquiring what the results are likely to be.

Many distinguished authors, scientists, philosophers, and theologians have attempted recently to analyze present tendencies and to forecast the future, with the results that range all the way from ecstatic visions of optimists to the dismal lucubrations of pessimists. Apostles of sweetness and light and eternal progress have been more than matched by the "Gloomy Dean"; Haldane and Thomson have been answered by Russell and Schiller. Ancient mythologies have been revived in the titles of modern Sibylline Books that set forth the future of mankind as symbolized by Daedalus, Icarus, Tantalus, and Prometheus.

Many advocates of the old philosophy and theology of supernaturalism and tradition attribute the present disturbed state of the world to science, which they say has been undermining the old foundations of the social order, and they call upon all men everywhere to repent and to return to the old faith. On the other hand, many advocates of science and the new knowledge maintain that for persons of mature minds, the old, naïve faith of childhood and of the childhood age of the race is gone, and gone forever, and that the only hope for the progress of mankind lies in more knowledge, newer and better faith, and not in a return to old beliefs.

Let us briefly compare some aspects of the old faith and the new knowledge and then inquire what is the duty of forward-looking men in this age of intellectual, social, and religious unrest.

The old cosmogony, philosophy, and theology sought comfort, satisfaction, and inspiration rather than unwelcome truth. It magnified man by making him the climax and goal of all creation. It placed the earth, man's home, at the center of the universe. The sun, moon, and stars were created to give light to the earth. All things were made to minister to man's welfare. Man himself was created in the image of God, perfect and immortal. By his first disobedience he fell from his high estate and

Brought death into the world and all our woe.

But the promise was given that ultimately evil should perish and good should triumph. The great Drama of Humanity ran from Paradise Lost to Paradise Regained, from initial perfection to final perfection.

In this old philosophy and theology supernaturalism was universal; there was no proper conception of nature and of natural law. The earth was peopled not only with godlike men but also with manlike gods, angels, spirits, witches, demons. Some supernatural being was responsible for every phenomenon. The movements of sun and stars, the return of the seasons, wind and rain, lightning and rainbow, volcanoes and earthquakes, plagues and pestilences, were willed by some supernatural being. All nature was the expression of wills, big or little, good or bad.

The old ethics was based primarily on the will of God, supernaturally revealed in code or book, and to this certain rules were added from time to time by Church or State under divine guidance. Right was what God approved, wrong was what He forbade, and if ever doubts arose with regard to these there were not lacking those who would interpret the will of God. Man himself was a free moral agent. No bonds of heredity or necessity rested on his mind or soul. He was the architect of his own character, the arbiter of his own destiny. All good was the result of good will, all evil of evil will, and good would be rewarded and evil punished either in this life or in an eternal life of bliss or torment.

There was enormous satisfaction in this view of the universe and of man. It not only glorified man, explained evil, and promised redemption, but it was a great stimulus to efforts for betterment and a source of high ideals and aspirations, and undoubtedly its commands and sanctions worked powerfully to preserve the ethical code. Furthermore, there was admirable directness and positiveness in the old ethics regarding right and wrong, truth and error, freedom and responsibility, rewards and punishments. There was no hazy middle ground between these, no relativity of truth or right or duty to confuse the mind. Things were absolutely true or false, completely right or wrong. This old faith with its specific commandments was especially well suited to immature minds. In the childhood of the individual and of the race there is need of authority and obedience before it is possible to appeal to reason. Childhood is predominantly the age of obedience, adolescence of imitation and example, maturity of reason and judgment. The results of permitting children to grow up as their nature and judgments dictate are perilous for the children and annoying to the neighbors. One such harassed neighbor asked the mother of some children of nature how she expected them to become civilized, and she said, "Oh, we are relying on the germ plasm"; upon which the unscientific neighbor eagerly asked: "Where do you get it?"

Heredity, or the germ plasm, determines only the capacities and potentialities of any organism. In every individual there are many capacities that remain undeveloped because of the lack of stimuli suitable to call them forth. These inherited potentialities are both good and bad, social and antisocial, and it is the purpose of education to develop the former and to suppress the latter. In the heredity of every human being there are many alternative personalities. Education is chiefly habit formation, and good education consists in the formation of good habits of body, mind, and morals. It is the duty of parents and teachers to guide children in this respect, to replace un-reason by reason, selfishness by unselfishness, and antisocial habits by social ones. To trust to germ plasm is to forget that heredity furnishes capacities for evil as well as for good, and to disregard the universal experience of mankind.

Society is compelled to repress many of the primordial reactions and instincts of the natural man. Our whole culture rests upon the suppression of antisocial impulses and the culti-vation of social and moral reactions. If such reactions are to be built into character and become "second nature," they must be cultivated early, preferably in the home, and ethical teaching must be clear-cut and authoritative. The old ethics, when wisely inculcated, was admirably suited to this purpose. It did develop men and women of high moral character, and to a large extent it forms the foundation of our present social systems.

Contrast with this older philosophy, theology, and ethics the newer revelations of science. The man of scientific mind seeks truth rather than comfort or satisfaction. He would follow evidence wherever it leads, confident that even unwel-come truth is better than cherished error, that the permanent welfare of the human race depends upon "the increase and diffusion of knowledge among men," and that truth alone can make us free. Science is not an esoteric cult and scientific methods are not mysterious or magical processes. Huxley once defined science as trained and organized common sense, and scientific methods of inquiry are only the careful and accurate methods that are used by intelligent people every-where in the affairs of everyday life. These methods consist in observation, comparison, analysis, and generalization. Every sensible person uses these methods in his business or profession, and in his judgments of men, policies, and institutions. It is only in its greater accuracy that the scientific method differs from those in universal use. It is true that no scientific observation, comparison, analysis, or generalization is ever complete or perfect; it is true that in science, as well as in all affairs of life, we deal with probabilities of a higher or lower order rather than with certainties; it is true that all generalizations are theories rather than facts and that all scientific knowledge is relative and not absolute. But in spite of these limitations, no other method of inquiry has been found as reliable as the scientific method.

It would seem incredible, were it not an actual fact, that anyone should object to the use of such methods of inquiry regarding the origin and nature of man, society, government, ethics, religion, the Bible, or anything else; but, alas! there are thousands, if not millions, of people in this country, some of them educated and intelligent with respect to things with which they have had experience, who refuse to apply common-sense methods of inquiry to such subjects, who characterize those who do this as atheists, blasphemers, dishonest scoundrels, and who denounce science and scientists for laying impious hands on sacred things which must never be studied by the methods of common sense.

To those who refuse to apply scientific methods of inquiry to the study of man and society, cosmogony and theology, ethics and religion, but who base their whole conception of these upon ancient traditions or unreasoning emotions, science has no message; they neither understand the language nor appreciate the methods of science. But to the increasing number of those who recognize that man, society, and human institutions are proper subjects of scientific investigation, and who also realize that neither authority, tradition, nor prejudice is a safe guide in the search for truth, the question may well arise as to what effect the scientific study of these subjects will have on human ideals, aspirations, and conduct. Accordingly, these remarks are addressed to those only who accept the methods and results of science in their application to man but who are concerned that mankind shall grow not only wiser but also better as the ages pass.

The methods and results of science have shaken to their foundations the old cosmogony and philosophy. It is now universally recognized that the earth is not the center of the universe, but a mere dot in a mediocre solar system whirling through immeasurable space. Man is only one of some millions of species of living things on the earth, and although in mind and soul he is the paragon of animals, it is becoming increasingly certain that the traditional views regarding his supernatural creation and divine perfection are no longer tenable. On the contrary, the sciences of geology, biology, psychology, sociology, and anthropology are furnishing an ever-increasing amount of evidence that the body, mind, and society of man are products of evolution. The old philosophy of universal supernaturalism is giving place to a philosophy of universal naturalism; everything that has been scientifically analyzed is found to be natural—that is, orderly, lawful, causal —and many men of science claim that "nature is everything that is." Belief in an anthropomorphic God, a big man in the skies who made us little men in His own image, established society, ethics, and religion by His commands, and governs the world as a human autocrat, is rapidly yielding place to more idealistic conceptions.

It appears probable that the universe and man are subject to immutable natural laws; that causality is universal in the living as well as in the lifeless world; that the entire man, body, mind, and soul, develops from a germ and is the product of heredity and environment; that will itself is no exception to universal causality, since it is merely a link in the chain of cause and effect, being itself the effect of preceding causes and the cause of succeeding effects; that freedom is the result of intelligence acting as cause; that intelligence is the capacity of consciously profiting by experience; that instincts and emotions are causally related to body functions; that society, ethics, and even religion are based primarily on instincts, emotions, reaction patterns, and ductless glands.

Some of these conclusions are tentative and may be modified by further research, but there can be no doubt as to the general trend of the scientific study of man and his activities. These conclusions, or others of a similar nature, are now accepted by most of the recent investigators in human biology, psychology, and sociology. The application of science and the scientific method of observation and experiment to human behavior has revealed much concerning the physiology of mind as well as the hidden springs of action, the unconscious complexes that determine our constitutional hopes and fears, our prevailing loves and hates, our delusions and failures, and "the sin which doth so easily beset us." Recent studies indicate that there is also a physiology of ethics, and that our conceptions of right and wrong, of good and bad, are associated with particular body functions, reaction patterns, and instincts. In short, man himself, in all of his manifold complexities and activities, is a part of Nature.

These studies and conclusions have raised serious apprehensions on the part of many friends of science and violent opposition on the part of some adherents of the old order, who hold that the guesses of "science falsely so-called" are destroying the foundations of religion, ethics, and all that is most valuable in human life. On the other hand, many Christian scientists who have been convinced by the evidence of the essential truth of these new discoveries are equally certain that truth and goodness and beauty, faith and hope and love, reverence and aspirations and ideals are just as real and as desirable as they ever were, and that religion and ethics remain secure whether the old traditions stand or not.

There can be no doubt that science has given us grander conceptions of the universe than were ever dreamed of in former times. Contrast the old cosmogony with the revelations of modern astronomy, physics, and geology; the old conception of the creation of the universe in six literal days with our present conceptions of the immensity and eternity of natural processes; the old views of the special creation by a supernatural Workman of every one of a million different species of animals and plants, beasts of prey and their victims, parasites and pests, with the scientific view that animals and plants and the universe itself are the results of an immensely long process of evolution!

Even in its revelations concerning man, science is giving us not only truer but also grander views than the old ones. There is sublimity in the conception of man as the climax of vast ages of evolution, as the highest and best product of this eternal process, as the promise of something better still to be. The evolution of man from lower forms of life is not degrading but inspiring. Nature and human history love to proclaim the fact that a humble origin does not preclude a glorious destiny. "The real dignity of man consists not in his origin, but in what he is and in what he may become."

So far as the substitution of natural law for chance or caprice is concerned it has been a great gain not only in our conceptions of the world but also with regard to our inmost selves, for it means order instead of chaos, understanding in place of confusion. If all our activities are the results of natural causation, it means that the will is not absolutely free, but practical people have always known that freedom is relative and not absolute; that we are partly free and partly bound. We know that we are able to inhibit many reactions, instincts, and forms of behavior and to choose between alternatives that are offered. But this does not mean that such freedom is uncaused activity; on the contrary, science shows that it is the result of internal causes, such as physiological states, conflicting stimuli, the remembered results of past experience or education, all of which are themselves the results of preceding causes. Conscious will is not "a little deity encapsuled in the brain" but intelligence acting as cause, while intelligence in turn is the capacity of consciously profiting by experience.

But however we may explain that which we call *freedom*, it is plain that for practical purposes it exists, though in varying degrees in different persons or in the same person at different times, and that it entails a corresponding degree of *responsibility*. The universality of natural law does not destroy ethics or the basis of ethics; on the contrary, it places morality upon a natural, causal, understandable basis. Furthermore, it leads to a more rational view of human behavior and to a more sympathetic attitude toward the criminal or the offender. As long as men regarded nonethical conduct as the result of absolutely free will, or of an evil spirit within man, it was logical enough to exorcise the demon by torture and in general to "make the punishment fit the crime" rather than make it fit the criminal. But an understanding of the fact that nonethical conduct is causal rather than capricious and is the result of natural rather than supernatural causation leads society to look for and to correct these causes rather than to seek vengeance or retribution. Indeed, the only justification for punishment of any kind is the correction of the offender or the protection of society; there is no longer any place in civilized society or in a rational theology for retributive or expiatory punishment.

A study of human history and prehistory shows that there has been a wonderful development of ethics and of religion. There is no satisfactory evidence that these were handed down from heaven in perfect form, but there is abundant evidence that they, in common with all other things, have been evolving and that this process has not yet come to an end. Much of the ethics and religion of the Old Testament was condemned by Christ and would not be tolerated in civilized-society today. Some of the ethical codes and religious practices current today will probably be considered barbarous in times to come.

Variations and mutations are the materials of the evolutionary process and they occur in all possible directions; some of them are progressive, many are retrogressive, but only those that are fit survive. The present is apparently a period of great social, ethical, and religious mutation, and many of these are certainly retrogressive; but let us hope that the decent instincts and the common sense of mankind will see to it that these retrogressive mutations do not survive.

Whatever the ultimate basis of ethics may be, whether divine commands, intuitions and instincts, utility or pleasure, the content remains essentially the same: however much codes and practices may change, our ideals and instincts remain much the same from age to age. Whether written on tables of stone or on the tables of our hearts, the "cardinal virtues" are still virtues and the "deadly sins" are still sins. The deepest instincts of human nature cry out for justice, truth, beauty, sympathy. Ethics that is based on pleasures of the highest and most enduring sort, on pleasures of the rational mind, the better instincts, refined senses, is not different from the ethics of the divine command to "lay up for yourselves treasures in heaven." These are "the enduring satisfactions of life." The new ethics of science does not essentially differ in content from the old ethics of revelation, and the commandments of a God within are no less binding than those of a God without.

Nevertheless, the decline of faith in the supernatural origin of man and of ethics, the decreasing fear of hell or hope of heaven, and the increased freedom of thought and action brought about by science and education have led, in some instances, to a general weakening of the ethical code. When increasing freedom carries with it an increasing sense of responsibility and duty it never endangers progress, but when liberty degenerates into license it marks the beginning of social and moral decay. Freedom is one of the principal goals of human endeavor, but the best use man can make of his freedom is to place limitations upon it. We can be safely freed from external restraints only in so far as we replace these by internal inhibitions.

Partly as a result of this increased freedom from the old restraints, but largely as one of the terrible aftermaths of the World War, lawlessness, immorality, and selfishness seem to be more than usually evident throughout the world today. The war gave social sanction to murder, arson, and theft; it unchained the wild beasts in men that long had been restrained; it glorified acts which in times of peace would have been abhorred; and it is no wonder that we are now reaping the whirlwind. Grafters in high office and bandits in high-powered cars are preying on society. Lawlessness and selfishness are widespread. Social solidarity has diminished; races and nations are suspicious or antagonistic; many political parties, churches, labor unions, social classes are split up into warring factions. Jealousy, suspicion, intolerance, hate, and war are preached from some pulpits and from many platforms and presses. The war that we fondly hoped was to end wars has apparently only ended peace.

The new freedom which recently has come to women, and which is in the main a progressive change, has led to some bizarre views in these later days. Some of its radical advocates are demanding that it shall mean freedom from all sex distinctions and restraints, except such as are purely personal and voluntary—freedom from marriage and reproduction and the care of children; abolition of the family with its cares and responsibilities; state subsidies for such women as are willing to be mothers and state infantoria for the rearing of all children. Less extreme and therefore more dangerous tendencies are seen in the acceptance of pleasure as the sole basis of ethics and the interpretation of the ethics of pleasure as the satisfaction of animal appetites for food, drink, and sex. The reaction from undue sex repression has led to the opposite extreme of sex exploitation. Obscene literature and plays are not only tolerated but justified and patronized by many leaders of public opinion. In several universities student publications have been suppressed recently by the authorities because of indecency or blasphemy. Free love, trial marriage, easy divorce are widely preached and practiced. We vigorously condemn and forbid polygamy in Utah but easily condone worse practices nearer home. The question of the old catechism, "What is the chief end of man?" is now answered by multitudes of people: "To glorify pleasure and enjoy it while it lasts." They say frankly: "I have but one life to live and I propose to get the most pleasure possible out of it. Why should I think of social progress or of posterity? What has posterity done for me? Let us eat, drink, and be merry— for tomorrow we die." Yes, persons who live as mere animals die as the beast dieth; they deserve no immortality on earth or anywhere else. Whether we believe in religion or not, our better instincts revolt against such ethics. We are more than brutes and cannot be satisfied with the pleasures of brutes. We may not accept the old ethics of supernaturalism and tradition, but we cannot adopt the ethics of pigs and hyenas.

What is the remedy for this condition? Fundamentalists think that science in general, biology in particular, and the theory of human evolution most of all are responsible. They would, therefore, prescribe by law that the latter may not be taught in tax-supported institutions. But if state legislatures are to decide that evolution shall not be taught, they should also eliminate the teaching of all subjects which furnish evidences of the truth of evolution; they should forbid the teaching of morphology, physiology, ecology, paleontology, genetics, comparative medicine, comparative psychology, and sociology. Indeed, there are few subjects that are now studied and taught by comparative and genetic methods that should not be banned. If the farmers of Tennessee and Kentucky can decide what may be taught in biology, they can also decide what may be taught in mathematics, as indeed one sufferer from interminable decimals proposed when he introduced a bill to fix by law the ratio of the circumference to the diameter of a circle at exactly 3.

I have been assured by persons who are very orthodox in faith but very heterodox in spelling and grammar, that "Evolution is all rot"; that it is "leprocy" (*sic*); that "the heads of evolutionists are full of mud" (their own, of course, being full of "monkey"); and that "God hath chosen the fools of this world to confound the wise," leaving it in doubt as to who is which. Mr. Bryan's characterization of scientists as "dishonest scoundrels" shows the same unrestrained emotionalism as the antivivisectionists show when they call animal experimenters "inhuman fiends." Antievolution, antivivisection, antivaccination, and antiscience are all the outgrowths of extreme emotionalism, recklessness in handling facts, and an utter ignorance of the value of scientific evidence.

Fundamentalism, if logical, would demand the abolition of the teaching of all science and scientific methods, for science in general and not merely the theory of evolution is responsible for the loss of faith in the old traditions. It is folly to attempt to promote education and science and at the same time to forbid the teaching of the principal methods and results of science. The only sensible course would be to abolish altogether the teaching of science and scientific methods and return to ecclesiasticism. The Church once told scientists what they could think and teach, and now state legislatures propose to do it. Such methods of resisting change have always failed in the past and are foredoomed to failure now.

The real problem that confronts us, and it is a great problem, is how to adjust religion to science, faith to knowledge, ideality to reality, for adjustment in the reverse direction will never happen. Facts cannot be eliminated by ideals and it is too late in the history of the world to attempt to refute the findings of science by sentimental objections or supposed theological difficulties. If science makes mistakes, science must furnish the cure; it can never be done by church councils, state legislatures, nor even by popular vote.

The only possible remedy for the present deplorable condition is not less but more and better science and education; science that recognizes that the search for truth is not the whole of life, that both scientific reality and religious ideality are necessary to normal, happy, useful living. We must keep our feet on the ground of fact and science, but lift our heads into the atmosphere of ideals. "To the solid ground of Nature trusts the mind that builds for aye." Education from the earliest years must teach love rather than hate, human brotherhood rather than war, service rather than selfishness; it must develop good habits of body and mind; it must instil reverence, not only for truth but also for beauty and righteousness.

"Where there is no vision, the people perish." Man cannot live by bread alone; he must have ideals and aspirations, faith and hope and love. In short, he must have a religion. The world never needed a religion of high ideals and aspirations more than it needs it now. But the old religion of literalism and of slavish regard to the authority of church or book, while well suited to some minds, cannot serve the needs of those who have breathed the air of science. Must all such be deprived of the benefits of a religion which they need and be forced into a false position of antagonism to religion as a whole because they cannot accept all the literalism, infantilism, and incidentalism of so-called fundamentalism? The fundamentalists, rather than the scientists, are helping to make this an irreligious age.

Science has destroyed many old traditions but it has not destroyed the foundations of ethics or religion. In some respects it has contributed greatly to these foundations:

1. The universality of natural law has not destroyed faith in God, though it has modified many primitive conceptions of deity. This is a universe of ends as well as of means, of teleology as well as of mechanism. Mechanism is universal but so also is finalism. It is incredible that the system and order of nature, the evolution of matter and worlds and life, of man and consciousness and spiritual ideals are all the results of chance. The greatest exponents of evolution, such as Darwin, Huxley, Asa Gray, and Weismann, have maintained that there is evidence of some governance and plan in Nature. This is the fundamental article of all religious faith. If there is no purpose in the universe, or in evolution, or in man, then indeed there is no God and no good. But if there is purpose in nature and in human life, it is only the imperfection of our mental vision that leads us sometimes to cry in despair: "Vanitas vanitatum, all is vanity." No one can furnish scientific proof of the existence or nature of God, but atheism leads to pessimism and despair, while theism leads to faith and hope. "By their fruits ye shall know them."

2. Science leaves us faith in the worth and dignity of man. In spite of weakness and imperfection, man is the highest product of a billion years of evolution. We are still children in the morning of time, but we are attaining reason, freedom, spirituality. The ethics of mankind is not the ethics of the jungle or the barnyard. In the new dispensation men will no longer be restrained from evil by fear of hell or hope of heaven, but by their decent instincts and their high ideals. When love of truth, beauty, goodness, of wife, children,

humanity dies in us our doom will be sealed. But it will not die in all men; the long-past course of progressive evolution proves that it will live on, somewhere and somehow.

3. Science leaves us hope for the future. Present conditions often seem desperate; pessimists tell us that society is disintegrating, that there will never be a League of Nations, that wars will never cease, that the human race is degenerating, and that our civilization is going the way of ancient Egypt, Assyria, Greece, and Rome. But though nations have risen and fallen, and cultures have waxed and waned, the major movements of human history have been forward. After civilization had once been attained, it never completely disappeared from the earth. The torch of culture was handed on from Egypt to Greece and from Greece to Rome, and from all of these to us. One often hears of lost arts and civilizations of the past, but the best elements of any culture are immortal.

The test of biological variations and mutations is whether they lead to increasing fitness, and the test of all social and moral mutations and revolutions, such as those of today, is whether they lead to increasing perfection and progress. The great principle of the survival of the fit has guided evolution from amoeba to man, from tropisms and reflexes to intelligence and consciousness, from solitary individuals to social organizations, from instincts to ethics, and this great principle will not be abrogated today or tomorrow. It is the "power, not ourselves, that makes for righteousness." Man can consciously hasten or hinder this process, but he cannot permanently destroy it. He can refuse to take part in it and can choose to be eliminated, but the past course of evolution for millions of years indicates that somewhere and somehow this process will go on.

The evolutionist is an incorrigible optimist; he reviews a billion years of evolution in the past and looks forward to perhaps another billion years of evolution in the future. He knows that evolution has not always been progressive; that there have been many eddies and back currents, and that the main current has sometimes meandered in many directions; and yet he knows that, on the whole, it has moved forward.

Through all the ages evolution has been leading toward the wider intellectual horizons, the broader social outlooks, the more invigorating moral atmosphere of the great sea of truth.

What progress in body, mind, and society; what inventions, institutions, even relations with other worlds, the future may hold in store, it hath not entered into the heart of man to conceive. What does it matter if some men refuse to join this great march onward, what does it matter if even our species should become extinct if only it give place to a better species! Our deepest instincts are for growth; the joy of life is progress. Only this would make immortality endurable. Human progress depends upon the increase and diffusion among men of both knowledge and ethics, reality and ideality, science and religion. Now for the first time in the history of life on this planet, a species can consciously and rationally take part in its own evolution. To us the inestimable privilege is given to co-operate in this greatest work of time, to have part in the triumphs of future ages. What other aim is so worthy of high endeavor and great endowment?

BULLY BOTTOM[1]

J. B. PRIESTLEY (1894-

From *The English Comic Characters*, 1925. Bottom in Shakespeare's *A Midsummer Night's Dream* is a substantial citizen transformed into a high comedian. Mr. Priestley catches the comic spirit and makes one love the ebullient, irrepressible Bully[2] Bottom, ass's head and all. It would help to be familiar with his part; indeed, the essay makes one run for the play.

On any reasonable chronology of Shakespeare's plays, Bottom is the first of his great comic figures. Once we are through the

---

[1] Reprinted from *The English Comic Characters* by J. B. Priestley, by permission of Dodd, Mead & Company, New York, and of John Lane, The Bodley Head, Limited, London.

[2] Good companion, or "buddy."

door of Peter Quince's house, when all the company is assembled there, we are at last in the presence of one of the foolish Immortals; we come to celebrate a staggering feat of parturition, for here, newly created, is a droll as big as a hill. Before this, Shakespeare has shown us through a little gallery of amusing figures, but we have seen no one of the stature of "sweet bully Bottom." In *The Comedy of Errors*, the two Dromios and the rest are nothing but odd curves in a whimsical design. The comedians of *Love's Labour's Lost* are well enough in their way; the picked and spruce Don Armado, Holofernes with his "golden cadence of poesy," Sir Nathaniel and Moth, all capping one another's fantastic phrases; but they are little more than quaint shadows that caper for an hour or so on the sunlit lawns of that park in Navarre and then flit out of mind when the sun goes down. In *The Two Gentlemen of Verona*, Speed and Launce (and the dog) are not so much individual creations as lively examples of an admired formula for comic relief, the Elizabethan equivalents of our cross-talk red-nosed gentry. Bottom is neither a curve nor a shadow nor a formula, but a gigantic individual creation, the first of the really great comic figures. "Bottom," writes Dowden, magnificently professorial, "is incomparably a finer efflorescence of the absurd than any preceding character of Shakespeare's invention." And a pity it is that we cannot slip into that comic English Athens and tell Bottom to his large solemn face how fine an efflorescence of the absurd he is, if only because the very extravagance of the phrase would summon back old times to his mind, and before we knew where we were we should find ourselves with tattered play-bills of *Pyramus and Thisbe* in our hands and the whole queer story would be out. The absurd would effloresce before our very eyes.

Bottom is easily the most substantial figure in the piece. This is not saying a great deal, because *A Midsummer Night's Dream* has all the character of a dream; its action is ruled by caprice and moonlit madness; its personages appear to be under the spell of visions or to walk and talk in their sleep; its background is shadowy and shifting, sometimes breaking into absolute loveliness, purple and dark green and heavy with the night scent of flowers, but always something broken, inconsequent, suddenly glimpsed as the moon's radiance frees itself for a little space from cloud and foliage; and the whole play, with its frequent talk of visions, dreams, imagination, antique fables and fairy toys, glides past like some lovely hallucination, a masque of strange shadows and voices heard in the night. The characters are on three different levels. There are first the immortals, who have nothing earthy in their composition and are hardly to be distinguished from the quivering leaves and the mist of hyacinths, tiny creatures spun out of cobwebs and moonshine. Then there are the wandering lovers, all poetry and imagination, driven hither and thither by their passionate moods. Lastly there is Bottom (and with him, of course, his companions), who is neither a flickering elf nor a bewildered passionate lover, but a man of this world, comfortably housed in flesh, a personage of some note among the artisans of Athens and, we have no doubt, in spite of certain unmistakable signs of temperament in him, a worthy dependable householder. We suspect that he has, somewhere in the background, a shrewish wife who spends her time alternately seeing through her husband and being taken in by him, for he is essentially one of those large, heavy-faced, somewhat vain and patronizing men, not without either humour or imagination, who always induce in women alternating moods of irritation and adoration. Among his fellow artisans, Bottom is clearly the ladies' man, the gallant. He it is who shows himself sensitive to the delicacy of the sex in the matter of the killing and the lion, and we feel that his insistence upon a prologue, "a device to make all well," is only the result of his delicacy and chivalry. Snout and Starveling, who hasten to agree with him, are simply a pair of whimpering poltroons, who have really no stomach for swords and killing and raging melodrama and are afraid of the consequences if they should startle the audience. But Bottom, we feel, has true sensibility and in his own company is the champion of the sex; he knows that it is a most dreadful thing to bring in the lion, that most fearful wild-fowl, among ladies, and his sketch of the prologue has in it the true note of artful entreaty: *"Ladies, or, Fair Ladies,—I would wish you,—or, I would request you,—or, I would entreat you,—not to fear, not to tremble: my life for yours."* Such a speech points to both knowledge of the sex and long practice, and given friendly circumstances, the speaker might be a very dangerous man. We should like to see Bottom making love among his own kind; the result would have startled some of his critics. As it is, we only see him, crowned with an ass's head, suddenly transformed into the paramour of the queen of the fairies, and even in a situation so unexpected, so remote from his previous experience, he acquits himself, as we shall see, very creditably. What would happen if one of the gentlemen who call friend Bottom "gross, stupid, and ignorant," let us say the average professor of English literature, suddenly found himself in the arms of a very beautiful and very amorous fairy, even if his head were not discoverable by immediate sight but only by long acquaintance to be that of an ass? He would probably acquit himself no better than would Snout or Starveling in similar circumstances, and Shakespeare took care to wave away his Snouts and Starvelings and called the one man to that strange destiny, that "most rare vision," who was worthy of the occasion. Bottom, as Hazlitt said, is a character that has not had justice done to him: he is "the most romantic of mechanics."

Against the background of the whole play, which is only so much gossamer and moonlight, the honest weaver appears anything but romantic, a piece of humorous, bewildered flesh, gross, earthy. He is a trades-unionist among butterflies, a ratepayer in Elfland. Seen thus, he is droll precisely because he is a most prosaic soul called to a most romantic destiny. But if we view him first among his own associates, we shall see that he is the only one of them who was fit to be "translated." Puck, who was responsible for the transformation, described him as "the shallowest thickskin of that barren sort," the biggest fool in a company of fools; but Puck was no judge of character. Bottom, though he may be the biggest fool (and a big fool is no common person), is really the least shallow and thickskinned of his group, in which he shows up as the romantic, the poetical, the imaginative man, who naturally takes command. We admit that he is conceited, but he is, in some measure, an artist, and artists are notoriously conceited. The company of such tailoring and bellows-mending souls would make any man of spirit conceited. Old Quince, who obviously owes his promotion to seniority and to nothing else, is nominally in charge of the revels, but the players have scarcely met together and Quince has scarcely had time to speak a word before it is clear that Bottom, and Bottom alone, is the leader. Quince ("Good Peter Quince," as Bottom, with easy contempt and patronage, calls him) is nothing but a tool in the hands of the masterful weaver, who directs the whole proceedings, the calling of the roll of players, the description of the piece, the casting of the parts, and so forth, step by step. The other members of the company not having a glimmer of imagination, the artist among them, the man of temperament, takes charge. And he alone shows any enthusiasm for the drama itself, for the others are only concerned with pleasing the Duke; if they do badly, if they should, for example, frighten the ladies, they may be hanged, whereas if they do well, they may receive a little pension. When Bottom is missing, just before the play is due to begin, and the other players are in despair, their talk plainly shows what it is they have at heart:

SNUG. Masters, the Duke is coming from the temple, and there is two or three lords and ladies more married: if our sport had gone forward, we had all been made men.

FLUTE. O sweet bully Bottom! Thus hath he lost sixpence a-day during his life; he could not have 'scaped sixpence a-day: an the Duke had not given him sixpence a-day for playing Pyramus, I'll be hanged; he would have deserved it: sixpence a-day in Pyramus, or nothing.

The heart has gone out of the performance, left as it is to these Flutes, Snugs, and Starvelings who can dream of nothing more than sixpence a-day; but as soon as Bottom, the enthusiast, the

romantic, the artist, returns, all is changed, for the leaven of
art and imagination begins to work again:

Enter BOTTOM

BOTTOM. Where are these lads? where are these hearts?
QUINCE. Bottom!—O most courageous day! O most happy hour!
BOTTOM. Masters, I am to discourse wonders: but ask me not what;
    for, if I tell you, I am no true Athenian. I will tell you every-
    thing, right as it fell out.
QUINCE. Let us hear, sweet Bottom.
BOTTOM. Not a word of me. All that I will tell you is, that the
    Duke hath dined. Get your apparel, good strings to your
    beards, new ribbons to your pumps; meet presently at the
    palace; every man look o'er his part; for the short and the long
    is, our play is preferred. In any case, let Thisbe have clean
    linen; and let not him that plays the lion pare his nails, for
    they shall hang out for the lion's claws. And, most dear actors,
    eat no onions or garlic, for we are to utter sweet breath; and
    I do not doubt but to hear them say it is a sweet comedy. No
    more words: away! go; away!

And they and we with them are hustled off to the palace, heart-
ened and invigorated, ready to agree with Flute and Quince
that bully Bottom has the best wit and the best person of any
handicraft man in Athens.

When the players are first met together and the parts are
being given out, it is not just Bottom's conceit that makes him
want to play every part himself. Of all those present, he is
the only one who shows any passion for the drama itself, the art
of acting, the enthralling business of moving and thrilling an
audience. The others are only concerned with getting through
their several tasks in the easiest and safest manner, with one eye
on the hangman and the other on the exchequer. But the creative artist is stirring in the soul of Bottom; his imagination is
catching fire; so that no sooner is a part mentioned than he can
see himself playing it, and playing it in such a manner as to lift
the audience out of their seats. He is set down for the principal

part, that of the lover, but no sooner has he accepted it, seeing himself condoling and moving storms "That will ask some tears in the true performing of it: if I do it, let the audience look to their eyes; I will move storms, I will condole in some measure"), than he regrets that he cannot play a tyrant, for he is familiar with Ercles' vein and even shows the company how he would deal with it. Then when Thisbe is mentioned, he sees himself playing her too, speaking in a monstrous little voice. The lion is the next part of any importance, and though it consists of nothing but roaring, Bottom has no doubt that he could make a success of that too, by means of a roar that would do any man's heart good to hear it, or, failing that, if such a full-blooded performance should scare the ladies, a delicately modulated roar that would not shame either a suckling dove or a nightingale. Even when he is finally restricted to one part, that of Pyramus, he alone shows an eagerness to come to grips with the details of the part, particularly in the matter of beards, undertaking as he does "to discharge it in either your straw-colour beard, your orange-tawny beard, your purple-in-grain beard, or your French-crown-colour beard, your perfect yellow." All this shows the eagerness and the soaring imagination of the artist, and if it shows too an unusual vanity, a confidence in one's ability to play any number of parts better than any one else could play them, a confidence so gigantic that it becomes ridiculous, it must be remembered that vanity and a soaring imagination are generally inseparable. It is clear that a man cannot play every part, cannot be lover, tyrant, lady, and lion at once; but it is equally clear that every man of imagination and spirit ought to want to play every part. It is better to be vain, like Bottom, than to be dead in the spirit, like Snug or Starveling. If it is a weakness to desire to play lover, lady, and lion, it is a weakness of great men, of choice, fiery, and fantastic souls who cannot easily realize or submit to the limitations pressing about our puny mortality. The whole scene, with our friend, flushed and triumphant, the centre of it, is droll, of course, but we really find it droll because we are being allowed to survey it from a height and know that the whole matter is ridiculous and contemptible. These fellows, we can see, should never have left their benches to follow the Muses. But to the gods, the spectacle of Bottom, soaring and magnificent, trying to grasp every part, would be no more ridiculous than the spectacle of Wagner perspiring and gesticulating at Bayreuth: they are both artists, children of vanity and vision, and are both ridiculous and sublime. We can see how droll Bottom is throughout this scene because Shakespeare, having seated us among the gods, has invited us to remark the droll aspects of the situation; but to Flute and Starveling Bottom is a man to be admired and wondered at, and probably to Flute's eldest son (that promising young bellowsmender), to whom he has condescended on one or two occasions, our droll weaver is the greatest man in the world, a hero and an artist, in short, a Wagner. We have but to seat ourselves again among the gods to see that "the best in this kind are but shadows," at once droll, heroic, and pitiful, capering for a little space between darkness and darkness.

Once Bottom is metamorphosed, we no longer see him against the background of his fellow artisans but see him firmly set in the lovely moonlit world of the elves and fays, a world so delicate that honey-bags stolen from the bees serve for sweetmeats and the wings of painted butterflies pass for fans, and here among such airy creatures, Bottom, of course is first glimpsed as something monstrous, gross, earthy. It would be bad enough even if he were there in his own proper person, but he is wearing an ass's head and presents to us the figure of a kind of comic monster. Moreover, he is loved at first sight by the beautiful Titania, who, with the frankness of an immortal, does not scruple to tell him so as soon as her eyes, peering through enchantments, are open. A man may have the best wit and the best person of any handicraftsman in Athens and yet shrink from the wizardries of such a night, being compelled to wear the head of an ass, deserted by his companions, conjured into fairyland, bewilderingly promoted into the paramour of the fairy queen and made the master of such elvish and microscopic attendants as Peas-blossom and Cobweb and Moth. But Bottom, as we have said, rises to the occasion, ass's head and all; not only does he not shrink and turn tail, not only does he accept the situation, he contrives to carry it off with an air; he not only rises to the occasion, he improves it. Now that all the whimsies under the midsummer moon are let loose and wild imagination has life dancing to its tune, this is not the time for the Bottom we have already seen, the imaginative, temperamental man, to come forward and dominate the scene, or else all hold upon reality is lost; that former Bottom must be kept in check, left to wonder and perhaps to play over to himself the lover and the lion; this is the moment for that other, honest Nick Bottom the weaver, the plain man who is something of a humorist, good solid flesh among all such flimsies and whimsies, madness and moonshine. Does the newly awakened lovely creature immediately confess that she is enamoured of him, then he carries it off bravely, with a mingled touch of wit, philosophy, and masculine complacency: "Methinks, mistress, you should have little reason for that: and yet, to say the truth, reason and love keep little company together now-a-days; the more the pity that some honest, neighbors will not make them friends. Nay, I can gleek[3] upon occasion." And we can see the ass's head tilted towards the overhanging branches, as he gives a guffaw at his "gleeking" and takes a strutting turn or two before this astonishing new mistress.

But nothing takes him by surprise in this sudden advancement. His tone is humorous and condescending, that of a solid complacent male among feminine fripperies. When his strange little servitors are introduced to him, the Duke himself could not carry it off better: "I shall desire you of more acquaintance, good Master Cobweb: if I cut my finger, I shall make bold with you"—then turning regally to the next: "Your name, honest gentleman?" Good Master Mustard-seed is commiserated with because "that same cowardly, giant-like ox-beef hath devoured many a gentleman of your House"; all are noticed and dispatched with the appropriate word; it is like a parody of an official reception. In the next scene, we discover him even

_____
[3] Jest.

more at his ease than before, lolling magnificently, embraced
by his lady and surrounded by his devoted attendants, who are
being given their various duties. "Monsieur Cobweb, good
monsieur"—and indeed there was probably something very
Gallic about this Cobweb—"get your weapons in your hand,
and kill me a red-hipp'd humble-bee on the top of a thistle;
and good monsieur, bring me the honey-bag. Do not fret yourself too much in the action, monsieur; and, good monsieur, have
a care the honey-bag break not. I would be loth to have you
overflown with a honey-bag, signior." Bottom is clearly making
himself at home in Elfland; he is beginning to display a certain
fastidiousness, making delicate choice of a "red-hipp'd humble-
bee on the top of a thistle." And if Puck won the first trick
with the love philtre and the ass's head, we are not sure that
Bottom is not now winning the second, for every time he
addresses one of his attendants he is scoring off Elfland and
is proving himself a very waggish ass indeed. Even his remarks
on the subject of music ("I have a reasonable good ear in
music: let us have the tongs and the bones") and provender
("I could munch your good dry oats. Methinks I have a great
desire to a bottle of hay: good hay, sweet hay, hath no fellow")
have to our ears a certain consciously humorous smack, as if
the speaker were not quite such an ass as he seems but were enjoying the situation in his own way, carrying the inimitable, if
somewhat vulgar, manner of the great Bottom, pride of
handicraftsmen, even into the heart of Faerie.

If he shows no surprise, however, and almost contrives to
carry off the situation in the grand manner, we must remember
that he, like Titania, is only dreaming beneath the moon-
coloured honeysuckle and musk roses; the enamoured fairy
and all her attendant sprites are to him only phantoms, bright
from the playbox of the mind, there to be huddled away when
a sudden puff of wind or a falling leaf brings the little drama
to an end; and so he acts as we all act in dreams, who may ourselves be "translated" nightly by Puck and sent on the wildest
adventures in elfin woods for all we know to the contrary.
When Bottom awakes, yawning and stiff in the long grass, his

sense of wonder blossoms gigantically, and the artist in him, he who would play the tyrant, the lover, the damsel, and the lion, leaps to life: "I have had a most rare vision. I have had a dream, —past the wit of man to say what dream it was: man is but an ass, if he go about to expound this dream." So fiery and eager is that wonder and poetry in him which all the long hours at Athenian looms have not been able to wither away, as he stands crying in ecstasy in the greenwood, that we cannot be surprised that his style, which he very rightly endeavours to heighten for the occasion, should break down under the stress of it: "The eye of man hath not heard, the ear of man hath not seen, man's hand is not able to taste, his tongue to conceive, nor his heart to report, what my dream was." But no matter; the dramatic enthusiast in him now takes command: Peter Quince (whom we did not suspect of authorship) shall write a ballad of this dream, to be called Bottom's Dream, and it shall be sung, by a newly resurrected Pyramus, at the end of the coming play; and off he goes, his head humming with plans, back to the town to put heart into his lads. There he plays Pyramus as Pyramus was never played before; takes charge of the whole company, does not scruple to answer a frivolous remark of the Duke's, and finally speaks the last word we hear from the handicraftsmen. We learn nothing more of him, but perhaps when the lovers were turning to their beds and the fairies were dancing in the glimmering light, Bottom, masterful, triumphant, was at Peter Quince's with the rest, sitting over a jug or two and setting his fellow players agape with his tale of the rare vision. There was a poet somewhere in this droll weaver and so he came to a poet's destiny, finding himself wearing the head of an ass (as we all must do at such moments), the beloved of an exquisite immortal, the master of Cobwebs and Peas-blossoms, coming to an hour's enchantment while the moon climbs a hand's-breath up the sky—and then, all "stolen hence," the dream done and the dreamer left to wonder. Such is the destiny of poets, who are themselves also weavers.

It is a critical commonplace that these Athenian clowns are very English, just as the setting that frames them is exquisitely

English; and it follows very naturally that the greatest of them is the most English. There is indeed no more insular figure in all Shakespeare's wide gallery than Bottom. A superficial examination of him will reveal all those traits that unfriendly critics of England and Englishmen have remarked for centuries. Thus, he is ignorant, conceited, domineering; he takes himself and his ridiculous concerns seriously and shows no lightness of touch; knowing perhaps the least, he yet talks the most, of all his company; he cannot understand that his strutting figure is the drollest sight under the sky, never for one instant realises that he is nothing but an ignorant buffoon; the soulless vulgarity of his conduct among the fairies smells rank in the nostrils of men of taste and delicacy of mind; in short, he is indeed the "shallowest thickskin of that barren sort," lout-in-chief of a company of louts. But something more than a superficial examination will, as we have partly seen, dispose of much of this criticism, and will lead to the discovery in Bottom of traits that our friendly critics have remarked in us and that we ourselves know to be there. Bottom is very English in this, that he is something of a puzzle and an apparent contradiction. We have already marked the poetry and the artist in him, and we have only to stare at him a little longer to be in doubt about certain characteristics we took for granted. Is he entirely our butt or is he for at least part of the time solemnly taking us in and secretly laughing at us? Which of us has not visited some rural tap-room and found there, wedged in a corner, a large, round-faced, wide-mouthed fellow, the local oracle; and, having listened to some of his pronouncements, have laughed in our sleeves at his ignorance, dogmatism, and conceit; and yet, after staying a little longer and staring at the creature's large, solemn face, a face perilously close to vacuity, have noticed in it certain momentary twinkles and creases that have suddenly left us a little dubious about our hasty conclusions? And then it has dawned upon us that the fellow is, in his own way, which is not ours nor one to which we are accustomed, a humorist, and that somewhere behind that immobile and almost vacuous front, he has been enjoying us, laughing at us, just as we have been enjoying him and laughing at him. It is an experience that should make us pause before we pass judgment upon Bottom, who is the first cousin of all such queer characters, rich and ripe personages who are to be found, chiefly in hostelries but now and then carrying a bag of tools or flourishing a paint-brush, in almost every corner of this England, which is itself brimmed with puzzling contradictions, a strange mixture of the heavy butt and the conscious humorist. Bottom is worlds away from the fully conscious humour of a Falstaff, but we cannot have followed him from Peter Quince's house to the arms of Titania and seen him in Bank Holiday humour with his Cobwebs and Mustard-seeds, without noticing that he is something more than a rustic target. He is English, and he is conceited, ignorant, dogmatic, and asinine, but there stirs within him, as there does within his fellow workmen even now, a poet and humorist, waiting for the midsummer moon. And lastly, he is not dead, he has not left us, for I saw him myself, some years ago, and he had the rank of corporal and was gloriously at ease in a tumble-down estaminet near Amiens, and there he was playing the tyrant, the lover, and the lion all at once, and Sergeant Quince and Privates Snug and Starveling were there with him. They were paying for his beer and I suspect that they were waiting, though obviously waiting in vain, to hear him cry once more: "Enough; hold or cut bow-strings." [4]

BEETHOVEN'S CENTENARY [1]

GEORGE BERNARD SHAW (1856-1950)

From *Radio Times*, March 18, 1927. Shaw may not have been, as someone has said, "the best music critic who ever lived," but he did break down conventional clichés and wrote honestly and fearlessly of London music. Instead of critical claptrap, music is the thing! Here is an evaluation in

---

[4] Keep your promise, no matter what.
[1] Used with the kind permission of The Public Trustee and The Society of Authors, London, England.

retrospect of one of the world's greatest musicians. Shaw's hand is sure.
One can all but hear the music.

A hundred years ago a crusty old bachelor of fifty-seven, so
deaf that he could not hear his own music played by a full
orchestra, yet still able to hear thunder, shook his fist at the
roaring heavens for the last time, and died as he had lived, chal-
lenging God and defying the universe. He was Defiance Incar-
nate: he could not even meet a Grand Duke and his court in the
street without jamming his hat tight down on his head and strid-
ing through the very middle of them. He had the manners of a
disobliging steamroller (most steamrollers are abjectly obliging
and conciliatory); and he was rather less particular about his
dress than a scarecrow: in fact he was once arrested as a tramp
because the police refused to believe that such a tatterdemalion
could be a famous composer, much less a temple of the most
turbulent spirit that ever found expression in pure sound. It was
indeed a mighty spirit; but if I had written the mightiest, which
would mean mightier than the spirit of Handel, Beethoven himself would have rebuked me; and what mortal man could
pretend to a spirit mightier than Bach's? But that Beethoven's
spirit was the most turbulent is beyond all question. The im-
petuous fury of his strength, which he could quite easily contain and control, but often would not, and the uproariousness
of his fun, go beyond anything of the kind to be found in
the works of other composers. Greenhorns write of syncopation
now as if it were a new way of giving the utmost impetus to a
musical measure; but the rowdiest jazz sounds like The
Maiden's Prayer after Beethoven's third Leonora overture; and
certainly no negro corobbery that I ever heard could inspire
the blackest dancer with such *diable au corps* as the last movement of the Seventh Symphony. And no other composer has
ever melted his hearers into complete sentimentality by the
tender beauty of his music, and then suddenly turned on them
and mocked them with derisive trumpet blasts for being such

fools. Nobody but Beethoven could govern Beethoven; and when, as happened when the fit was on him, he deliberately refused to govern himself, he was ungovernable.

It was this turbulence, this deliberate disorder, this mockery, this reckless and triumphant disregard of conventional manners, that set Beethoven apart from the musical geniuses of the ceremonious seventeenth and eighteenth centuries. He was a giant wave in that storm of the human spirit which produced the French Revolution. He called no man master. Mozart, his greatest predecessor in his own department, had from his childhood been washed, combed, splendidly dressed, and beautifully behaved in the presence of royal personages and peers. His childish outburst at the Pompadour, "Who is this woman who does not kiss me? The Queen kisses me," would be incredible of Beethoven, who was still an unlicked cub even when he had grown into a very grizzly bear. Mozart had the refinement of convention and society as well as the refinement of nature and of the solitudes of the soul. Mozart and Gluck are refined as the court of Louis XIV was refined: Hayden is refined as the most cultivated country gentlemen of his day were refined: compared to them socially Beethoven was an obstreperous Bohemian: a man of the people. Hayden, so superior to envy that he declared his junior, Mozart, to be the greatest composer that ever lived, could not stand Beethoven: Mozart, more farseeing, listened to his playing, and said "You will hear of him some day"; but the two would never have hit it off together had Mozart lived long enough to try. Beethoven had a moral horror of Mozart, who in Don Giovanni had thrown a halo of enchantment round an aristocratic blackguard, and then, with the unscrupulous moral versatility of a born dramatist, turned round to cast a halo of divinity round Sarastro, setting his words to the only music yet written that would not sound out of place in the mouth of God.

Beethoven was no dramatist: moral versatility was to him revolting cynicism. Mozart was still to him the master of masters (this is not an empty eulogistic superlative: it means literally that Mozart is a composer's composer much more than he has ever been a really popular composer); but he was a court flunkey in breeches whilst Beethoven was a Sansculotte;[2] and Haydn also was a flunkey in the old livery: the Revolution stood between them as it stood between the eighteenth and nineteenth centuries. But to Beethoven Mozart was worse than Haydn because he trifled with morality by setting vice to music as magically as virtue. The Puritan who is in every true Sansculotte rose up against him in Beethoven, though Mozart had shewn him all the possibilities of nineteenth-century music. So Beethoven cast back for a hero to Handel, another crusty old bachelor of own kidney, who despised Mozart's hero Gluck, though the pastoral symphony in The Messiah is the nearest thing in music to the scenes in which Gluck, in his Orfeo, opened to us the plains of Heaven.

Thanks to broadcasting, millions of musical novices will hear the music of Beethoven this anniversary year for the first time with their expectations raised to an extraordinary pitch by hundreds of newspaper articles piling up all the conventional eulogies that are applied indiscriminately to all the great composers. And like his contemporaries they will be puzzled by getting from him not merely a music that they did not expect, but often an orchestral hurlyburly that they may not recognize as what they call music at all, though they can appreciate Gluck and Haydn and Mozart quite well. The explanation is simple enough. The music of the eighteenth century is all dance music. A dance is a symmetrical pattern of steps that are pleasant to move to; and its music is a symmetrical pattern of sound that is pleasant to listen to even when you are not dancing to it. Consequently the sound patterns, though they begin by being as simple as chessboards, get lengthened and elaborated and enriched with harmonies until they are more like Persian carpets; and the composers who design these patterns no longer expect people to dance to them. Only a whirling Dervish could dance a Mozart symphony: indeed, I have reduced two young and practised dancers to exhaustion by

* Literally, without breeches; a name given to the revolutionists in France.

making them dance a Mozart overture. The very names of the dances are dropped: instead of suites consisting of sarabands, pavanes, gavottes, and jigs, the designs are presented as sonatas and symphonies consisting of sections called simply movements, and labelled according to their speed (in Italian) as allegros, adagios, scherzos, and prestos. But all the time, from Bach's preludes to Mozart's Jupiter Symphony, the music makes a symmetrical sound pattern, and gives us the dancer's pleasure always as the form and foundation of the piece.

Music, however, can do more than make beautiful sound patterns. It can express emotion. You can look at a Persian carpet and listen to a Bach prelude with a delicious admiration that goes no further than itself; but you cannot listen to the overture to Don Giovanni without being thrown into a complicated mood which prepares you for a tragedy of some terrible doom over-shadowing an exquisite but Satanic gaiety. If you listen to the last movement of Mozart's Jupiter Symphony, you hear that it is as much a riotous corobbery as the last movement of Beethoven's Seventh Symphony: it is an orgy of ranting drumming tow-row-row, made poignant by an opening strain of strange and painful beauty which is woven through the pattern all through. And yet the movement is a masterpiece of pattern designing all the time.

Now what Beethoven did, and what made some of his greatest contemporaries give him up as a madman with lucid intervals of clowning and bad taste, was that he used music altogether as a means of expressing moods, and completely threw over pattern designing as an end in itself. It is true that he used the old patterns all his life with dogged conservatism (another Sansculotte characteristic, by the way); but he imposed on them such an overwhelming charge of human energy and passion, including that highest passion which accompanies thought, and reduces the passion of the physical appetites to mere animalism, that he not only played Old Harry with their symmetry but often made it impossible to notice that there was any pattern at all beneath the storm of emotion. The Eroica Symphony begins by a pattern (borrowed from an

overture which Mozart wrote when he was a boy), followed
by a couple more very pretty patterns; but they are tremen-
dously energized, and in the middle of the movement the
patterns are torn up savagely; and Beethoven, from the point
of view of the mere pattern musician, goes raving mad, hurling
out terrible chords in which all the notes of the scale are
sounded simultaneously, just because he feels like that, and
wants you to feel like it.

And there you have the whole secret of Beethoven. He
could design patterns with the best of them; he could write
music whose beauty will last you all your life; he could take
the driest sticks of themes and work them up so interestingly
that you find something new in them at the hundredth hearing:
in short, you can say of him all that you can say of the greatest
pattern composers; but his diagnostic, the thing that marks
him out from all the others, is his disturbing quality, his power
of unsettling us and imposing his giant moods on us. Berlioz
was very angry with an old French composer who expressed
the discomfort Beethoven gave him by saying "*J'aime la
musique qui me berce,*" "I like music that lulls me." Beethoven's
is music that wakes you up; and the one mood in which you
shrink from it is the mood in which you want to be let alone.

When you understand this you will advance beyond the
eighteenth century and the old-fashioned dance band (jazz, by
the way, is the old dance band Beethovenized), and understand
not only Beethoven's music, but what is deepest in post-Bee-
thoven music as well.

COMFORT [1]

ALDOUS HUXLEY (1894-

From *Proper Studies,* 1927. "The proper study of mankind is man,"
quotes Aldous Huxley as the subtitle of his book, and the quotation might

[1] Reprinted from *Proper Studies,* copyright, 1927, 1955, by Aldous
Huxley, and published by Harper and Brothers. Used with the permission
of the author and the publisher.

appropriately be applied to nearly all of his writing. "Comfort" is a study
in behavior. "Don't loll if you want to study," is the old saying. Is it true?

NOVELTY OF THE PHENOMENON

French hotel-keepers call it *Le confort moderne*, and they are
right. For comfort is a thing of recent growth, younger than
steam, a child when telegraphy was born, only a generation
older than radio. The invention of the means of being comfortable and the pursuit of comfort as a desirable end—one
of the most desirable that human beings can propose to themselves—are modern phenomena, unparalleled in history since
the time of the Romans. Like all phenomena with which we
are extremely familiar, we take them for granted, as a fish takes
the water in which it lives, not realizing the oddity and novelty
of them, not bothering to consider their significance. The
padded chair, the well-sprung bed, the sofa, central heating,
and the regular hot bath—these and a host of other comforts
enter into the daily lives of even the most moderately pros-
perous of the Anglo-Saxon bourgeoisie. Three hundred years
ago they were unknown to the greatest kings. This is a curious
fact which deserves to be examined and analyzed.

The first thing that strikes one about the discomfort in
which our ancestors lived is that it was mainly voluntary.
Some of the apparatus of modern comfort is of purely modern
invention; people could not put rubber tyres on their carriages
before the discovery of South America and the rubber plant.
But for the most part there is nothing new about the material
basis of our comfort. Men could have made sofas and smoking-
room chairs, could have installed bathrooms and central heating
and sanitary plumbing any time during the last three or four
thousand years. And as a matter of fact, at certain periods they
did indulge themselves in these comforts. Two thousand years
before Christ, the inhabitants of Cnossos were familiar with
sanitary plumbing. The Romans had invented an elaborate
system of hot-air heating, and the bathing facilities in a smart

Roman villa were luxurious and complete beyond the dreams of the modern man. There were sweating-rooms, massage-rooms, cold plunges, tepid drying-rooms with (if we may believe Sidonius Apollinaris) improper frescoes on the walls and comfortable couches where you could lie and get dry and talk to your friends. As for the public baths they were almost inconceivably luxurious. 'To such a height of luxury have we reached,' said Seneca, 'that we are dissatisfied if, in our baths, we do not tread on gems.' The size and completeness of the thermae was proportionable to their splendour. A single room of the baths of Diocletian has been transformed into a large church.

It would be possible to adduce many other examples showing what could be done with the limited means at our ancestors' disposal in the way of making life comfortable. They show sufficiently clearly that if the men of the Middle Ages and early modern epoch lived in filth and discomfort, it was not for any lack or ability to change their mode of life; it was because they chose to live in this way, because filth and discomfort fitted in with their principles and prejudices, political, moral, and religious.

COMFORT AND THE SPIRITUAL LIFE

What have comfort and cleanliness to do with politics, morals, and religion? At a first glance one would say that there was and could be no causal connection between armchairs and democracies, sofas and the relaxation of the family system, hot baths and the decay of Christian orthodoxy. But look more closely and you will discover that there exists the closest connection between the recent growth of comfort and the recent history of ideas. I hope in this essay to make that connection manifest, to show why it was not possible (not materially, but psychologically impossible) for the Italian princes of the quattrocento, for the Elizabethan, even for Louis xiv. to live in what the Romans would have called common cleanliness and decency, or enjoy what would be to us indispensable comforts.

Let us begin with the consideration of armchairs and central heating. These, I propose to show, only became possible with the breakdown of monarchical and feudal power and the decay of the old family and social hierarchies. Smoking-room chairs and sofas exist to be lolled in. In a well-made modern armchair you cannot do anything but loll. Now, lolling is neither dignified nor respectful. When we wish to appear impressive, when we have to administer a rebuke to an inferior, we do not lie in a deep chair with our feet on the mantel-piece; we sit up and try to look majestical. Similarly, when we wish to be polite to a lady or show respect to the old or eminent, we cease to loll; we stand, or at least we straighten ourselves up. Now, in the past human society was a hierarchy in which every man was always engaged in being impressive towards his inferiors or respectful to those above him. Lolling in such societies was utterly impossible. It was as much out of the question for Louis xiv. to loll in the presence of his courtiers as it was for them to loll in the presence of their king. It was only when he attended a session of the Parlement that the King of France ever lolled in public. On these occasions he reclined in the Bed of Justice, while princes sat, the great officers of the crown stood, and the smaller fry knelt. Comfort was proclaimed as the appanage of royalty. Only the king might stretch his legs. We may feel sure, however, that he stretched them in a very majestic manner. The lolling was purely ceremonial and accompanied by no loss of dignity. At ordinary times the king was seated, it is true, but seated in a dignified and upright position; the appearance of majesty had to be kept up. (For, after all, majesty is mainly a question of majestical appearance.) The courtiers, meanwhile, kept up the appearances of deference, either standing, or else, if their rank was very high and their blood peculiarly blue, sitting, even in the royal presence, on stools. What was true of the king's court was true of the nobleman's household; and the squire was to his dependants, the merchant was to his apprentices and servants, what the monarch was to his courtiers. In all cases the superior had to express his superiority by being dignified, the inferior his inferiority by being deferential; there could be no lolling. Even in the intimacies of family life it was the same: the parents ruled like popes and princes, by divine right; the children were their subjects. Our fathers took the fifth commandment very seriously—how seriously may be judged from the fact that during the great Calvin's theocratic rule of Geneva a child was publicly decapitated for having ventured to strike its parents. Lolling on the part of children, though not perhaps a capital offence, would have been regarded as an act of the grossest disrespect, punishable by much flagellation, starving, and confinement. For a slighter insult—neglect to touch his cap—Vespasiano Gonzaga kicked his only son to death; one shudders to think what he might have been provoked to do if the boy had lolled. If the children might not loll in the presence of their parents, neither might the parents loll in the presence of their children, for fear of demeaning themselves in the eyes of those whose duty it was to honour them. Thus we see that in the European society of two or three hundred years ago it was impossible for any one—from the Holy Roman Emperor and the King of France down to the poorest beggar, from the bearded patriarch to the baby—to loll in the presence of any one else. Old furniture reflects the physical habits of the hierarchical society for which it was made. It was in the power of mediaeval and renaissance craftsmen to create armchairs and sofas that might have rivalled in comfort those of to-day. But society being what, in fact, it was, they did nothing of the kind. It was not, indeed, until the sixteenth century that chairs became at all common. Before that time a chair was a symbol of authority. Committee-men now loll, Members of Parliament are comfortably seated, but authority still belongs to a Chairman, still issues from a symbolical Chair. In the Middle Ages only the great had chairs. When a great man travelled, he took his chair with him, so that he might never be seen detached from the outward and visible sign of his authority. To this day the Throne no less than the Crown is the symbol of royalty. In mediaeval times the vulgar sat, whenever it was permissible for them to sit, on benches, stools, and settles. With the rise, during the Renaissance period, of a rich and independent bourgeoisie, chairs began to be more freely used. Those who could afford chairs sat in them, but sat with dignity and discomfort; for the chairs of the sixteenth century were still very throne-like, and imposed upon those who sat in them a painfully majestic attitude. It was only in the eighteenth century, when the old hierarchies were seriously breaking up, that furniture began to be comfortable. And even then there was no real lolling. Armchairs and sofas on which men (and, later, women) might indecorously sprawl, were not made until democracy was firmly established, the middle classes enlarged to gigantic proportions, good manners lost from out of the world, women emancipated, and family restraints dissolved.

CENTRAL HEATING AND THE FEUDAL SYSTEM

Another essential component of modern comfort—the adequate heating of houses—was made impossible, at least for the great ones of the earth, by the political structure of ancient societies. Plebeians were more fortunate in this respect than nobles. Living in small houses, they were able to keep warm. But the nobleman, the prince, the king, and the cardinal inhabited palaces of a grandeur corresponding with their social position. In order to prove that they were greater than other men, they had to live in surroundings considerably more than life-size. They received their guests in vast halls like roller-skating rinks; they marched in solemn processions along galleries as long and as draughty as Alpine tunnels, up and down triumphal staircases that looked like the cataracts of the Nile frozen into marble. Being what he was, a great man in those days had to spend a great deal of his time in performing solemn symbolical charades and pompous ballets—performances which required a lot of room to accommodate the numerous actors and spectators. This explains the enormous dimensions of royal and princely palaces, even of the houses of ordinary landed gentlemen. They owed it to their position to live, as though they were giants, in rooms a hundred feet long and thirty high. How splendid, how magnificent! But oh, how bleak! In our

days the self-made great are not expected to keep up their
position in the splendid style of those who were great by divine
right. Sacrificing grandiosity to comfort, they live in rooms
small enough to be heated. (And so, when they were off duty,
did the great in the past; most old palaces contain a series of
tiny apartments to which their owners retired when the charades of state were over. But the charades were long-drawn
affairs, and the unhappy princes of old days had to spend a
great deal of time being magnificent in icy audience-chambers
and among the whistling draughts of interminable galleries.)
Driving in the environs of Chicago, I was shown the house of
a man who was reputed to be one of the richest and most
influential of the city. It was a medium-sized house of perhaps fifteen or twenty smallish rooms. I looked at it in astonishment, thinking of the vast palaces in which I myself have
lived in Italy (for considerably less rent than one would have
to pay for garaging a Ford in Chicago). I remembered the rows
of bedrooms as big as ordinary ballrooms, the drawing-rooms
like railway stations, the staircase on which you could drive a
couple of limousines abreast. Noble *palazzi*, where one has
room to feel oneself a superman! But remembering also those
terrible winds that blow in February from the Apennines, I
was inclined to think that the rich man of Chicago had done
well in sacrificing the magnificences on which his counterpart
in another age and country would have spent his riches.

BATHS AND MORALS

It is to the decay of monarchy, aristocracy, and ancient social
hierarchy that we owe the two components of modern comfort hitherto discussed; the third great component—the bath—
must, I think, be attributed, at any rate in part, to the decay of
Christian morals. There are still on the continent of Europe,
and for all I know, elsewhere, convent schools in which young
ladies are brought up to believe that human bodies are objects
of so impure and obscene a character that it is sinful for them
to see, not merely other people's nakedness, but even their own.
Baths, when they are permitted to take them (every alternate

Saturday) must be taken in a chemise descending well below
the knees. And they are even taught a special technique of
dressing which guarantees them from catching so much as a
glimpse of their own skin. These schools are now, happily, ex-
ceptional, but there was a time, not so long ago, when they were
the rule. Theirs is the great Christian ascetic tradition which
has flowed on in majestic continuity from the time of St. Anthony and the unwashed, underfed, sex-starved monks of the
Thebaid, through the centuries, almost to the present day. It is
to the weakening of that tradition that women at any rate owe
the luxury of frequent bathing.

The early Christians were by no means enthusiastic bathers;
but it is fair to point out that Christian ascetic tradition has not
at all times been hostile to baths as such. That the Early Fathers
should have found the promiscuity of Roman bathing shocking
is only natural. But the more moderate of them were prepared
to allow a limited amount of washing, provided that the business was done with decency. The final decay of the great
Roman baths was as much due to the destructiveness of the
Barbarians as to Christian ascetic objections. During the Ages
of Faith there was actually a revival of bathing. The Crusaders
came back from the East, bringing with them the oriental
vapour bath, which seems to have had a considerable popularity all over Europe. For reasons which it is difficult to understand, its popularity gradually waned, and the men and women
of the late sixteenth and early seventeenth centuries seem to
have been almost as dirty as their barbarous ancestors. Medical
theory and court fashions may have had something to do with
these fluctuations.

The ascetic tradition was always strongest where women
were concerned. The Goncourts record in their diary the
opinion, which seems to have been current in respectable circles
during the Second Empire, that female immodesty and immorality had increased with the growth of the bath habit.
"Girls should wash less," was the obvious corollary. Young
ladies who enjoy their bath owe a debt of gratitude to Voltaire
for his mockeries, to the nineteenth-century scientists for their

materialism. If these men had never lived to undermine the convent school tradition, our girls might still be as modest and as dirty as their ancestresses.

COMFORT AND MEDICINE

It is, however, to the doctors that the bath-lovers owe their greatest debt. The discovery of microbic infection has put a premium on cleanliness. We wash now with religious fervour, like the Hindus. Our baths have become something like magic rites to protect us from the powers of evil, embodied in the dirt-loving germ. We may venture to prophesy that this medical religion will go still further in undermining the Christian ascetic tradition. Since the discovery of the beneficial effects of sunlight, too much clothing has become, medically speaking, a sin. Immodesty is now a virtue. It is quite likely that the doctors, whose prestige among us is almost equal to that of the medicine men among their savages, will have us stark naked before very long. That will be the last stage in the process of making clothes more comfortable. It is a process which has been going on for some time—first among men, later among women—and among its determining causes are the decay of hierarchic formalism and of Christian morality. In his lively little pamphlet describing Gladstone's visit to Oxford shortly before his death, Mr. Fletcher has recorded the Grand Old Man's comments on the dress of the undergraduates. Mr. Gladstone, it appears, was distressed by the informality and the cheapness of the students' clothes. In his day, he said, young men went about with a hundred pounds worth of clothes and jewellery on their persons, and every self-respecting youth had at least one pair of trousers in which he never sat down for fear of spoiling its shape. Mr. Gladstone visited Oxford at a time when undergraduates still wore very high starched collars and bowler hats. One wonders what he would have said of the open shirts, the gaudily coloured sweaters, the loose flannel trousers of the present generation. Dignified appearances have never been less assiduously kept up than they are at present; informality has reached an unprecedented pitch. On all but the most solemn occasions a man, whatever his rank or position, may wear what he finds comfortable.

The obstacles in the way of women's comforts were moral as well as political. Women were compelled not merely to keep up social appearances, but also to conform to a tradition of Christian ascetic morality. Long after men had abandoned their uncomfortable formal clothes, women were still submitting to extraordinary inconveniences in the name of modesty. It was the war which liberated them from their bondage. When women began to do war work, they found that the traditional modesty in dress was not compatible with efficiency. They preferred to be efficient. Having discovered the advantages of immodesty, they have remained immodest ever since, to the great improvement of their health and increase of their personal comfort. Modern fashions are the most comfortable that women have ever worn. Even the ancient Greeks were probably less comfortable. Their under-tunic, it is true, was as rational a garment as you could wish for; but their outer robe was simply a piece of stuff wound round the body like an Indian *sari*, and fastened with safety-pins. No woman whose appearance depended on safety-pins can ever have felt really comfortable.

COMFORT AS AN END IN ITSELF

Made possible by changes in the traditional philosophy of life, comfort is now one of the causes of its own further spread. For comfort has now become a physical habit, a fashion, an ideal to be pursued for its own sake. The more comfort is brought into the world, the more it is likely to be valued. To those who have known comfort, discomfort is a real torture. And the fashion which now decrees the worship of comfort is quite as imperious as any other fashion. Moreover, enormous material interests are bound up with the supply of the means of comfort. The manufacturers of furniture, of heating apparatus, of plumbing fixtures, cannot afford to let the love of comfort die. In modern advertisement they have means for compelling it to live and grow.

Having now briefly traced the spiritual origins of modern comfort, I must say a few words about its effects. One can never have something for nothing, and the achievement of comfort has been accompanied by a compensating loss of other equally, or perhaps more, valuable things. A man of means who builds a house to-day is in general concerned primarily with the comfort of his future residence. He will spend a great deal of money (for comfort is very expensive: in America they talk of giving away the house with the plumbing) on bathrooms, heating apparatus, padded furnishings, and the like; and having spent it, he will regard his house as perfect. His counterpart in an earlier age would have been primarily concerned with the impressiveness and magnificence of his dwelling—with beauty, in a word, rather than comfort. The money our contemporary would spend on baths and central heating would have been spent in the past on marble staircases, a grand façade, frescoes, huge suites of gilded rooms, pictures, statues. Sixteenth-century popes lived in a discomfort that a modern bank manager would consider unbearable; but they had Raphael's frescoes, they had the Sistine chapel, they had their galleries of ancient sculpture. Must we pity them for the absence from the Vatican of bathrooms, central heating, and smoking-room chairs? I am inclined to think that our present passion for comfort is a little exaggerated. Though I personally enjoy comfort, I have lived very happily in houses devoid of almost everything that Anglo-Saxons deem indispensable. Orientals and even South Europeans, who know not comfort and live very much as our ancestors lived centuries ago, seem to get on very well without our elaborate and costly apparatus of padded luxury. I am old-fashioned enough to believe in higher and lower things, and can see no point in material progress except in so far as it subserves thought. I like labour-saving devices, because they economize time and energy which may be devoted to mental labour. (But then I enjoy mental labour; there are plenty of people who detest it, and who feel as much enthusiasm for thought-saving devices as for automatic dishwashers and sewing-machines.) I like rapid and easy transport, because by enlarging the world in which men can live it enlarges their minds. Comfort for me has a similar justification: it facilitates mental life. Discomfort handicaps thought; it is difficult when the body is cold and aching to use the mind. Comfort is a means to an end. The modern world seems to regard it as an end in itself, an absolute good. One day, perhaps, the earth will have been turned into one vast feather-bed, with man's body dozing on top of it and his mind underneath, like Desdemona, smothered.

ON NOT BEING A PHILOSOPHER [1]

ROBERT LYND (1879-1949)

From *It's a Fine World*, 1930. The essays of Robert Lynd have a charm and simplicity which invite. In this friendly essay he weighs theories which are accepted by logic against practices which are followed by inclination. For everyone there is a point where the practical subdues the ideal. Just where that point is is worth a moment's thought.

"Have you read Epictetus lately?" "No, not lately." "Oh, you ought to read him. Tommy's been reading him for the first time, and is fearfully excited." I caught this scrap of dialogue from the next table in the lounge of an hotel. I became interested, curious, for I had never read Epictetus, though I had often looked at his works on the shelf—perhaps I had even quoted him—and I wondered if here at last was the book of wisdom that I had been looking for at intervals ever since I was at school. Never have I lost my early faith that wisdom is to be found somewhere in a book—to be picked up as easily as a shell from the sand. I desire wisdom as keenly as Solomon did, but it must be wisdom that can be obtained with very little effort—wisdom that can be caught almost by infection. I have

[1] Used with the kind permission of Methuen and Co., Ltd. of London, England.

no time or energy for the laborious quest of philosophy. I wish the philosophers to perform the laborious quest and, at the end of it, to feed me with the fruits of their labours; just as I get eggs from the farmer, apples from the fruit-grower, medicines from the chemist, so do I expect the philosopher to provide me with wisdom at the cost of a few shillings. That is why at one time I read Emerson and, at another, Marcus Aurelius. To read them, I hoped, was to become wise by reading. But I did not become wise. I agreed with them while I read them, but, when I had finished reading, I was still much the same man that I had been before, incapable of concentrating on the things on which they said I should concentrate or of not being indifferent to the things to which they said I should not be indifferent. Still, I have never lost faith in books, believing that somewhere printed matter exists from which I shall be able to absorb philosophy and strength of character while smoking in an arm-chair. It was in this mood that I took down Epictetus after hearing the conversation in the hotel lounge.

I read him, I confess, with considerable excitement. He is the kind of philosopher I like, not treating life as if at its finest it were an argument conducted in difficult jargon, but discussing, among other things, how men should behave in the affairs of ordinary life. Also, I agreed with nearly everything he said. Indifference to pain, death, poverty—yes, that is eminently desirable. Not to be troubled about anything over which one has no control, whether the oppression of tyrants or the peril of earthquakes—on the necessity of this also, Epictetus and I are as one. Yet, close as is the resemblance between our opinions, I could not help feeling, as I read, that Epictetus was wise in holding his opinions and that I, though holding the same opinions, was far from wise. For, indeed, though I held the same opinions for purposes of theory, I could not enter-tain them for a moment for purposes of conduct. Death, pain, and poverty are to me very real evils, except when I am in an armchair reading a book by a philosopher. If an earthquake happened while I was reading a book of philosophy, I should forget the book of philosophy and think only of the earthquake and how to avoid tumbling walls and chimneys. This, though I am the staunchest possible admirer of Socrates, Pliny, and people of that sort. Sound though I am as an armchair philosopher, at a crisis I find that both the spirit and the flesh are weak.

Even in the small things of life I cannot comfort myself like a philosopher of the school of Epictetus. Thus, for example, when he advises us how to "eat acceptably to the gods" and bids us to this end to be patient even under the most incompetent service at our meals, he commends a spiritual attitude of which my nature is incapable. "When you have asked for warm water," he says, "and the slave does not heed you; or if he does heed you but brings tepid water; or if he is not even to be found in the house, then to refrain from anger and not to explode, is not this acceptable to the gods? . . . Do you not remember over whom you rule—that they are kinsmen, that they are brothers by nature, and they are the offspring of Zeus?" That is all perfectly true, and I should like very much to be a man who could sit in a restaurant, smiling patiently and philosophically while the waiter brought all the wrong things or forgot to bring anything at all. But in point of fact bad waiting irritates me. I dislike having to ask three times for the wine-list. I am annoyed when, after a quarter of an hour's delay, I am told that there is no celery. It is true that I do not make a scene on such occasions. I have not enough courage for that. I am as sparing of objurgations as a philosopher, but I suspect that the scowling spirit within me must show itself in my features. Certainly, I do not think of telling myself: "This waiter is my kinsman; he is the offspring of Zeus." Besides, even if he were, why should the offspring of Zeus wait so badly? Epictetus never dined at the —— Restaurant. And yet his patience might have served him even there. If so, what a difference between Epictetus and me! And, if I cannot achieve his imperturbability in so small affairs as I have mentioned, what hope is there of my being able to play the philosopher in presence of tyrants and earthquakes?

Again, when Epictetus expresses his opinions on material possessions and counsels us to be so indifferent to them that we should not object to their being stolen, I agree with him in theory and yet in practice I know I should be unable to obey him. There is nothing more certain than that a man whose happiness depends on his possessions is not happy. I am sure a wise man can be happy on a pittance. Not that happiness should be the aim of life, according to Epictetus or myself. But Epictetus at least holds up an ideal of imperturbability, and he assures us that we shall achieve this if we care so little for material things that it does not matter to us whether somebody steals them or not. "Stop admiring your clothes," he bids us, "and you are not angry at the man who steals them." And he goes on persuasively concerning the thief: "*He* does not know wherein the true good of man consists, but fancies that it consists in having fine clothes, the very same fancy that you also entertain. Shall he not come, then, and carry them off?" Yes, logically I suppose he should, and yet I cannot feel so at the moment at which I find that a guest at a party has taken my new hat and left his old one in its place. It gives me no comfort to say to myself: "*He* does not know wherein the true good of man consists, but fancies that it consists in having my hat." Nor should I dream of attempting to console a guest at a party in my own house with such philosophy in similar circumstances. It is very irritating to lose a new hat. It is very irritating to lose anything at all, especially if one thinks it has been taken on purpose. I feel that I could imitate Epictetus if I lived in a world in which nothing happened. But in a world in which things disappear through loss, theft, and "pinching," and in which bad meals are served by bad waiters in many of the restaurants, and a thousand other disagreeable things happen, an ordinary man might as well set out to climb the Himalayas in walking shoes as attempt to live the life of a philosopher at all hours.

In spite of this, however, most of us cannot help believing that the philosophers were right—right when they proclaimed, amid all their differences, that most of the things we bother about are not worth bothering about. It is easier to believe that oneself is a fool than that Socrates was a fool, and yet, if he was not right, he must have been the greatest fool who ever lived. The truth is, nearly everybody is agreed that such men as

Socrates and Epictetus were right in their indifference to external things. Even men earning £10,000 a year and working for
more would admit this. Yet, while admitting it, most of us
would be alarmed if one of our dearest friends began to put
the philosophy of Epictetus into practice too literally. What
we regard as wisdom in Epictetus we should look on as insanity
in an acquaintance. Or, perhaps, not in an acquaintance, but
at least in a near relation. I am sure that if I became as indifferent to money and comfort and all external things as Epictetus,
and reasoned in his fashion with a happy smile about property
and thieves, my relations would become more perturbed than
if I became a successful company promoter with the most mate-
rialistic philosophy conceivable. Think, for example, of the
reasoning of Epictetus over the thief who stole his iron lamp:

He bought a lamp for a very high price; for a lamp he became
a thief, for a lamp he became faithless, for a lamp he became bestial.
This is what seemed to him to be profitable!

The reasoning is sound, yet neither individually nor as a
society do we live in that contempt of property on which
it is based. A few saints do, but even they are at first a cause
of great concern to their friends. When the world is normally
cheerful and comfortable, we hold the paradoxical belief that
the philosophers were wise men, but that we should be fools to
imitate them. We are convinced that, while philosophers are
worth reading, material things are worth bothering about. It is
as though we enjoyed wisdom as a spectacle—a delightful spectacle on a stage which it would be unseemly for the audience to
attempt to invade. Were the Greeks and the Romans made
differently? Did the admirers of Socrates and Epictetus really
attempt to become philosophers, or were they like ourselves,
hopeful of achieving wisdom, not by practice but through a
magic potion administered by a wiser man than they? To become wise without effort—by listening to a voice, by reading a
book—it is at once the most exciting and the most soothing of
dreams. In such a dream I took down Epictetus. And, behold,
it was only a dream.

ONCE MORE TO THE LAKE[1]

E. B. WHITE (1899-

Written August, 1941. From *One Man's Meat*, 1941. With Mr. White it is informality at its best. *One Man's Meat* consists of a miscellany of reflections redolent of rural Maine, whimsical to be sure but much more than that. Time marches on in Maine, but Mr. White is able to link the march with the universal falling of the sands.

———

One summer, along about 1904, my father rented a camp on a lake in Maine and took us all there for the month of August. We all got ringworm from some kittens and had to rub Pond's Extract on our arms and legs night and morning, and my father rolled over in a canoe with all his clothes on; but outside of that the vacation was a success and from then on none of us ever thought there was any place in the world like that lake in Maine. We returned summer after summer—always on August 1st for one month. I have since become a salt-water man, but sometimes in summer there are days when the restlessness of the tides and the fearful cold of the sea water and the incessant wind which blows across the afternoon and into the evening make me wish for the placidity of a lake in the woods. A few weeks ago this feeling got so strong I bought myself a couple of bass hooks and a spinner and returned to the lake where we used to go, for a week's fishing and to revisit old haunts.

I took along my son, who had never had any fresh water up his nose and who had seen lily pads only from train windows. On the journey over to the lake I began to wonder what it would be like. I wondered how time would have marred this unique, this holy spot—the coves and streams, the hills that the sun set behind, the camps and the paths behind the camps. I was sure that the tarred road would have found it out and I wondered in what other ways it would be desolated. It is strange how much you can remember about places like that once you allow your mind to return into the grooves which lead back. You remember one thing, and that suddenly reminds you of another thing. I guess I remembered clearest of all the early mornings, when the lake was cool and motionless, remembered how the bedroom smelled of the lumber it was made of and of the wet woods whose scent entered through the screen. The partitions in the camp were thin and did not extend clear to the top of the rooms, and as I was always the first up I would dress softly so as not to wake the others, and sneak out into the sweet outdoors and start out in the canoe, keeping close along the shore in the long shadows of the pines. I remembered being very careful never to rub my paddle against the gunwale for fear of disturbing the stillness of the cathedral.

The lake had never been what you would call a wild lake. There were cottages sprinkled around the shores, and it was in farming country although the shores of the lake were quite heavily wooded. Some of the cottages were owned by nearby farmers, and you would live at the shore and eat your meals at the farmhouse. That's what our family did. But although it wasn't wild, it was a fairly large and undisturbed lake and there were places in it which, to a child at least, seemed infinitely remote and primeval.

I was right about the tar: it led to within half a mile of the shore. But when I got back there, with my boy, and we settled into a camp near a farmhouse and into the kind of summertime I had known, I could tell that it was going to be pretty much the same as it had been before—I knew it, lying in bed the first morning, smelling the bedroom, and hearing the boy sneak quietly out and go off along the shore in a boat. I began to sustain the illusion that he was I, and therefore, by simple transposition, that I was my father. This sensation persisted, kept cropping up all the time we were there. It was not an entirely new feeling, but in this setting it grew much stronger. I seemed to be living a dual existence. I would be in the middle of some simple act, I would be picking up a bait box or laying down a table fork, or I would be saying something, and suddenly it would be not I but my father who was saying the words or making the gesture. It gave me a creepy sensation.

We went fishing the first morning. I felt the same damp moss covering the worms in the bait can, and saw the dragonfly alight on the tip of my rod as it hovered a few inches from the surface of the water. It was the arrival of this fly that convinced me beyond any doubt that everything was as it always had been, that the years were a mirage and there had been no years. The small waves were the same, chucking the rowboat under the chin as we fished at anchor, and the boat was the same boat, the same color green and the ribs broken in the same places, and under the floor-boards the same fresh-water leavings and débris —the dead helgramite, the wisps of moss, the rusty discarded fishhook, the dried blood from yesterday's catch. We stared silently at the tips of our rods, at the dragonflies that came and went. I lowered the tip of mine into the water, tentatively, pensively dislodging the fly, which darted two feet away, poised, darted two feet back, and came to rest again a little farther up the rod. There had been no years between the ducking of this dragonfly and the other one—the one that was part of memory. I looked at the boy, who was silently watching his fly, and it was my hands that held his rod, my eyes watching. I felt dizzy and didn't know which rod I was at the end of.

We caught two bass, hauling them in briskly as though they were mackerel, pulling them over the side of the boat in a businesslike manner without any landing net, and stunning them with a blow on the back of the head. When we got back for a swim before lunch, the lake was exactly where we had left it, the same number of inches from the dock, and there was only the merest suggestion of a breeze. This seemed an utterly enchanted sea, this lake you could leave to its own devices for a few hours and come back to, and find that it had not stirred, this constant and trustworthy body of water. In the shallows, the dark, water-soaked sticks and twigs, smooth and old, were undulating in clusters on the bottom against the clean ribbed sand, and the track of the mussel was plain. A school of minnows swam by, each minnow with its small individual shadow, doubling the attendance, so clear and sharp in the sunlight. Some of the other campers were in swimming, along the shore, one of them with a cake of soap, and the water felt thin and clear and unsubstantial. Over the years there had been this person with the cake of soap, this cultist, and here he was. There had been no years.

Up to the farmhouse to dinner through the teeming, dusty field, the road under our sneakers was only a two-track road. The middle track was missing, the one with the marks of the hooves and the splotches of dried, flaky manure. There had always been three tracks to choose from in choosing which track to walk in; now the choice was narrowed down to two. For a moment I missed terribly the middle alternative. But the way led past the tennis court, and something about the way it lay there in the sun reassured me; the tape had loosened along the backline, the alleys were green with plantains and other weeds, and the net (installed in June and removed in September) sagged in the dry noon, and the whole place steamed with midday heat and hunger and emptiness. There was a choice of pie for dessert, and one was blueberry and one was apple, and the waitresses were the same country girls, there having been no passage of time, only the illusion of it as in a dropped curtain—the waitresses were still fifteen; their hair had been washed, that was the only difference—they had been to the movies and seen the pretty girls with the clean hair.

Summertime, oh summertime, pattern of life indelible, the fadeproof lake, the woods unshatterable, the pasture with the sweetfern and the juniper forever and ever, summer without end; this was the background, and the life along the shore was the design, the cottagers with their innocent and tranquil design, their tiny docks with the flagpole and the American flag floating against the white clouds in the blue sky, the little paths over the roots of the trees leading from camp to camp and the paths leading back to the outhouses and the can of lime for sprinkling, and at the souvenir counters at the store the miniature birch-bark canoes and the post cards that showed things looking a little better than they looked. This was the American family at play, escaping the city heat, wondering whether the newcomers in the camp at the head of the cove were "common" or "nice," wondering whether it was true that the people who drove up for Sunday dinner at the farmhouse were turned away because there wasn't enough chicken.

It seemed to me, as I kept remembering all this, that those times and those summers had been infinitely precious and worth saving. There had been jollity and peace and goodness. The arriving (at the beginning of August) had been so big a business in itself, at the railway station the farm wagon drawn up, the first smell of the pine-laden air, the first glimpse of the smiling farmer, and the great importance of the trunks and your father's enormous authority in such matters, and the feel of the wagon under you for the long ten-mile haul, and at the top of the last long hill catching the first view of the lake after eleven months of not seeing this cherished body of water. The shouts and cries of the other campers when they saw you, and the trunks to be unpacked, to give up their rich burden. (Arriving was less exciting nowadays, when you sneaked up in your car and parked it under a tree near the camp and took out the bags and in five minutes it was all over, no fuss, no loud wonderful fuss about trunks.)

Peace and goodness and jollity. The only thing that was wrong now, really, was the sound of the place, an unfamiliar nervous sound of the outboard motors. This was the note that jarred, the one thing that would sometimes break the illusion and set the years moving. In those other summertimes all motors were inboard; and when they were at a little distance, the noise they made was a sedative, an ingredient of summer sleep. They were one-cylinder and two-cylinder engines, and some were make-and-break and some were jump-spark, but they all made a sleepy sound across the lake. The one-lungers throbbed and fluttered, and the twin-cylinder ones purred and purred, and that was a quiet sound too. But now the campers all had outboards. In the daytime, in the hot mornings, these motors made a petulant, irritable sound; at night, in the still evening when the afterglow lit the water, they whined about one's ears like mosquitoes. My boy loved our rented outboard, and his great desire was to achieve singlehanded mastery over it, and authority, and he soon learned the trick of choking it a little (but not too much), and the adjustment of the needle valve. Watching him I would remember the things you could do with the old one-cylinder engine with the heavy flywheel, how you could have it eating out of your hand if you got really close to it spiritually. Motor boats in those days didn't have clutches, and you would make a landing by shutting off the motor at the proper time and coasting in with a dead rudder. But there was a way of reversing them, if you learned the trick, by cutting the switch and putting it on again exactly on the final dying revolution of the flywheel, so that it would kick back against compression and begin reversing. Approaching a dock in a strong following breeze, it was difficult to slow up sufficiently by the ordinary coasting method, and if a boy felt he had complete mastery over his motor, he was tempted to keep it running beyond its time and then reverse it a few feet from the dock. It took a cool nerve, because if you threw the switch a twentieth of a second too soon you would catch the flywheel when it still had speed enough to go up past center, and the boat would leap ahead, charging bull-fashion at the dock.

We had a good week at the camp. The bass were biting well and the sun shone endlessly, day after day. We would be tired at night and lie down in the accumulated heat of the little bedrooms after the long hot day and the breeze would stir almost imperceptibly outside and the smell of the swamp drift in through the rusty screens. Sleep would come easily and in the morning the red squirrel would be on the roof, tapping out his gay routine. I kept remembering everything, lying in bed in the mornings—the small steamboat that had a long rounded stern like the lip of a Ubangi, and how quietly she ran on the moonlight sails, when the older boys played their mandolins and the girls sang and we ate doughnuts dipped in sugar, and how sweet the music was on the water in the shining night, and what it had felt like to think about girls then. After breakfast we would go up to the store and the things were in the same place—the minnows in a bottle, the plugs and spinners disarranged and pawed over by the youngsters from the boys'

camp, the fig newtons and the Beeman's gum. Outside, the
road was tarred and cars stood in front of the store. Inside, all
was just as it had always been, except there was more Coca-
Cola and not so much Moxie and root beer and birch beer and
sarsaparilla. We would walk out with a bottle of pop apiece
and sometimes the pop would backfire up our noses and hurt.
We explored the streams, quietly, where the turtles slid off
the sunny logs and dug their way into the soft bottom; and we
lay on the town wharf and fed worms to the tame bass. Everywhere we went I had trouble making out which was I, the one
walking at my side, the one walking in my pants.

One afternoon while we were there at that lake a thunder-
storm came up. It was like the revival of an old melodrama that
I had seen long ago with childish awe. The second-act climax
of the drama of the electrical disturbance over a lake in
America had not changed in any important respect. This was
the big scene, still the big scene. The whole thing was so
familiar, the first feeling of oppression and heat and a general
air around camp of not wanting to go very far away. In mid-
afternoon (it was all the same) a curious darkening of the sky,
and a lull in everything that had made life tick; and then the
way the boats suddenly swung the other way at their moorings
with the coming of a breeze out of the new quarter, and the
premonitory rumble. Then the kettle drum, then the snare,
then the bass drum and cymbals, then crackling light against
the dark, and the gods grinning and licking their chops in the
hills. Afterward the calm, the rain steadily rustling in the calm
lake, the return of light and hope and spirits, and the campers
running out in joy and relief to go swimming in the rain, their
bright cries perpetuating the deathless joke about how they
were getting simply drenched, and the children screaming with
delight at the new sensation of bathing in the rain, and the joke
about getting drenched linking the generations in a strong in-
destructible chain. And the comedian who waded in carrying an
umbrella.

When the others went swimming my son said he was going
in too. He pulled his dripping trunks from the line where they
had hung all through the shower, and wrung them out.

Languidly, and with no thought of going in, I watched him, his hard little body, skinny and bare, saw him wince slightly as he pulled up around his vitals the small, soggy, icy garment. As he buckled the swollen belt suddenly my groin felt the chill of death.

OUR NATION OF HIGHBROWS[1]

JACQUES BARZUN (1907-

From *Teacher in America*, 1945. No one has a better right to criticize what is taught than a teacher. Barzun accuses the citizenry of the United States of accumulating facts and cherishing them like dollars. There is some justification for this arraignment when it is considered that nearly all collegiate tests measure facts rather than knowledge. The essay suggests distortions and misapplied emphases.

All generous minds have a horror of what are commonly called "facts." They are the brute beasts of the intellectual domain. . . . I allow no "facts" at this table.—The Autocrat of the Breakfast Table

Presumably all this vast machine, this teaching and course taking, this examining and graduating in all kinds, works towards some great end. Above the social need to read and write, above the skillful doing of technical tasks, above even self-fulfillment, there must be a result—conscious or unconscious—affecting the country as a whole. I can only think that this ceaseless activity answers the need of every nation to have a head, that is to say, a portion of itself devoting all its energy to leadership in intellectual matters—science and art and government and literature and education.

Do I mean a group set apart and known as intellectuals? No, that is a loaded word, at once too contemptuous and not inclusive enough. A top layer of highbrows? Well, that is the

---

[1] Reprinted from *Teacher in America* by Jacques Barzun, by permission of Little, Brown and Co. Copyright 1944, 1945, by Jacques Barzun.

common term, but in my opinion a bad one, because it suggests that the body of the nation is composed of lowbrows, whereas the truth is that highbrow and lowbrow are by nature one person, and that person is every American, more or less. The two words "high" and "low" simply denote two phases, like the alternating light and dark of a blinker; and I very much fear that some of our teaching and learning encourages not only this lack of steady glow, but the bad emotions that go with it. Always beware of a man who begins: "I'm only a lowbrow, of course, but I want to tell you that—" Nine times out of ten, what he will tell you is fact, or prejudice passing for fact, of which he is intensely proud and for which he claims your admiration. That is, he is a highbrow, or in older parlance, a pedant. Only, being a partial and not a thorough pedant, he also exhibits the other character of lowbrow and belongs to the huge class I should like to call the "high-lows."

There is no snob under heaven to equal this type, and its characteristics are by no means new. "Who does not know fellows," asks Holmes the Autocrat, "that always have an ill-conditioned fact or two which they lead after them into decent company like so many bulldogs . . . ? The men of facts wait their turn in grim silence, with that slight tension about the nostrils which the consciousness of carrying a 'settler' in the form of a fact or a revolver gives the individual thus armed. . . . What! Because bread is good and wholesome and nourishing, shall you thrust a crumb into my windpipe while I am talking?"

This is uncompromising enough, but for a teacher and a scientist to disallow facts and condemn "men of facts" calls for explanation, particularly if, as I hinted, some national issue hangs upon it. To many good people, our American zeal for acquiring and storing facts is praiseworthy, and I am ready to concede that once in a while the presence of factual minds in our midst is an asset. In a vast housekeeping operation such as war, the men of facts can be mustered out and pumped dry for the good of the state, their scattered drops of particular knowledge being caused to flow together into a great reservoir.

But even in war this is useful only if the scarcer and more valuable type of man is available, the man of ideas, with a mind accustomed not merely to holding facts in solution but to crystallizing them for use. And the making of such men in sufficient numbers and varieties ought to be the great end of all our teaching.

The highbrow or man of facts is a mere container. His mind is a sponge, which takes up so much and gives it out again on a little squeezing. You will recognize him in the character of Howard Littlefield in Sinclair Lewis's *Babbitt*. His conversation, you remember, is made up of facts about the various derivatives of coal tar and the gross income of some corporation or other in Zenith. The trouble with him is not that he knows these things, or even that he repeats them, but that they are idle possessions of which he is proud and for which he is alternately hated and admired by his friends.

Now I contend that he and his kind are a drag on the nation's intelligence, that his view of things and men is part of a false ideal mistaken for practical wisdom, and that its corrupting influence in our culture argues a recurrent fault in our scheme of instruction, from the primary grades to the highest reaches of scholarship.

Perhaps the proposition I must chiefly document is that we are a nation of highbrows, for we affect to scorn the species and boast of our unspoiled simplicity of mind. Yet we can see the young highbrow, like the silkworm on its mulberry leaf, develop from earliest reading days upon the sports page of the newspaper. It is there that every boy begins to lay in his stock of facts—batting averages, names and records—which he prides himself on knowing and for which "the fellows" admire him. At school, as we know, the teaching of history, literature, or general science encourages the same habit, even when the boy disdains the school's less exciting collection of facts. The good pupil, the grind, is simply the boy who sops up the facts of American history instead of baseball history.[2]

---

[2] Proved by the kind of tests in American history used to show up our ignorance of the subject. See *New York Times*, April 1943, *passim*. [Author's note.]

Grown to man's estate, the American boy goes on acquiring facts—tons of them in his professional school, cartloads more in the course of his career—not working facts used in business, but honorific facts hoarded from pride and to fill a vacancy. The lawyer learns market quotations, and the Railroad Traffic Manager the serial number of freight cars. Most of the printed matter which our representative man buys or receives deals with facts. His favorite magazines boil them down so that he can take in more. On his suburban train, he reads advertisements which, when they are not simply erotic, give out facts— the pedigree of the sheep at the basis of somebody's blankets, or the mileage of steel cable used in the latest suspension bridge.

The fiction our citizen enjoys must have a solid ballast of correct information; else he writes to the editor about the discrepancies, and the editor thanks him in the same mail as he reprimands the storyteller. As for his hobby, it reveals another facet of his cubic intellect. He probably "loves the woods" and thinks of himself as an amateur botanist or ornithologist, but he is really a mere collector of facts about leaves, bark, birds, and ferns. He does not know how often he lectures, and it is you—the author, the teacher, the scientist—whom he vaguely disapproves of for doing it professionally. You, being in the minority with respect to his kind, exist on sufferance and should be correspondingly shamefaced. See how the newspaper betrays this expectation:—

Months before the invasion [of Normandy] parties of civilian scientists landed . . . and obtained samples of sandsoil so when the tanks and trucks bustled ashore the drivers would be prepared. . . .

The dramatic story . . . which began in musty libraries, shifted to laboratories, and ended on shell-swept beaches, was told today by a mild-mannered professor in baggy clothes.[3]

The tone of this report is friendly but the condescension is plain. The "musty" libraries—unlike the airy tanks—and the

---

[3] *New York Times*, June 10, 1944. See also the attack on Freudian psychoanalysis for its reliance on "words" and "ideas" to cure mental ills as against the "factual" use of insulin. *World-Telegram*, January 4, 1943. [Author's note.]

mild-mannered professor—unlike the fierce truck drivers—establish the superiority of the lowbrow over the man of knowledge. Yet at the same time, it is the remarkable feat of knowingness that we are asked almost pruriently to admire.

This double standard is reflected in our best sellers (fiction apart), most of which are bulky recitals of fact—sometimes little more than compilations of newspaper clippings seasoned with backstairs gossip—yet professing to supply an understanding. Books of reference, anthologies of the best this and that, works of the "Quick, Watson, some culture" type, and fashionable popularizations—all feed the same insatiable appetite without perceptibly lessening ignorance, prejudice, or dullness. Impressive by their mass and reassuring by their factuality, these books escape the odium of being highbrow because they do not call for reflection but only for absorption. Built on the "and" principle—"this is true *and* this is true, *and* also this, *and* yet again this other thing"—they follow naturally in the worst textbook tradition, blandly ignoring how one fact is subordinated to another, or the whole set of facts to things outside the covers of the book. Summaries there may be, but no principles. For publishing experience does show that faced with an idea, no matter how simply expressed or illustrated, the layman is shocked into resistance. Automatically, his brow wrinkles in self-defense and shortens its span from natural high to affected low.

This seesawing between high and low is unquestionably a national tradition. Whereas the brain trust was a joke before anyone knew the men who belonged to it, the country has again and again given itself over to factual pedantry with great enthusiasm and no sense of ridicule. As Mr. Henry Morton Robinson has pointed out, "while naval petroleum reserves were being looted [in the 20's] American citizens were furrowing their brows over 'a drupaceous fruit beginning with "g." ' " [4] Then followed the "Ask me Another" craze—encouraged by the All-American sage, Thomas A. Edison—which in

---

[4] *Fantastic Interim*, p. 71. [Author's note.] The reference is to the crossword puzzle fad.

turn was followed by its modern embodiment, the "Information, Please" radio program and related quizzlings. Not once but many times, I have heard the chief fact-givers in these shows credited with supreme intellect and culture—which they may indeed possess, but which they surely have no opportunity of displaying under the rules of the game.

Perhaps this misjudgment by people who should know better is the best illustration of my belief, that facts drive out true culture in the same way that cheap money drives out gold. When everyone is talking fact, who has ears for opinion? Who observes the distinction? The pleasure that should normally be aroused by a question, a hypothesis, a difficulty, a paradox, an unexpected point of view, becomes attached to a statement of fact; and conversely, the boredom that properly belongs to the recital of bare fact comes to be associated with the discussion of principles. Hence the dreary exchange of affidavits which passes for conversation. Nothing follows upon anything else. The doctor tells medical anecdotes which do not mesh in with the stories of bank loans and legal misadventure, while the emptiest mind present interposes locker-room stories with a "that reminds me"—which becomes the falsest phrase in the language.

Why am I so bent on conversation? For pleasure first, pure selfishness, but also because conversation is a school for thinkers and should be a school for democrats. When one finds supposedly educated people arguing heatedly over matters of fact and shying away from matters of opinion; when one sees one's hosts getting nervous at a difference of views regarding politics or the latest play; when one is formally entertained with information games or queries cut out of the paper about the number of geese in a gaggle; when the dictionary and the encyclopedia are regarded as final arbiters of judgment and not as fallible repositories of fact; when intelligent youth is advised not to go against the accepted belief in any circle because it will startle, shock, and offend—it is time to recognize, first, that the temper of democratic culture is tested at every dinner table and in every living room—just as much as at school, in the pulpit, or on the platform; and second, that by this test and despite our boasted freedom of opinion, we lack men and women whose minds have learned to move easily and fearlessly in the perilous jungle of ideas.[5]

The evil arises from a radically false relation to knowledge, which is only a step away from a radically false relation to life. Undoubtedly, no man can think without facts, and that is why teaching is of facts and about them. But if they are stored up by thoughtless habit as a squirrel stores up nuts, kept as exhibits and never stirred about to see how they mix and react, their only use is the sterile one of filling the void from which they first came. The men of fact wait in grim silence, as Holmes said, to make a throw and claim a point.

To be sure, some predicaments seem to call for pure information, as when one of my students, now a war correspondent, had to navigate a fishing boat to escape by night from the enemy. "I knew," he said, "that the stars moved, but not in what direction." Yet he "thought" his way out in the end. No one can know all the facts he might possibly need, though many students confess to having this Gargantuan appetite and try to feed it. But the scheme is unpractical: life is too short, memory balks, and worst of all, while the scholar turns himself into a human silo for grains of knowledge, thought starves in the midst of plenty.

It would only be a slight exaggeration to say that facts grow out of knowledge, and not knowledge out of facts. In any case both should remain means to the good life and never usurp the place of ends. Why does it never occur to the hardened highbrow either that you already know his facts and do not wish to have them rehearsed, or that although they are new to you, you are not seated at his festive board in order to cram, either physically or mentally? The only answer to this is that he has no notion of what life is for. He is indeed aware that although one eats food to keep alive, a certain artistic form and pleasure can be given to dining. But he fails utterly to make the parallel

---

[5] See my article on "The Literature of Ideas" in the Anniversary Number of the Saturday Review, August 5, 1944. [Author's note.]

applicable to his raw facts, and never suspects that they may all be variations of one dull dish, savorless and indigestible.

In a great passage of his *Psychology*, James gives a suggestive account of this blindness from the point of view of his science. And the real meaning of the light touch and the allusive manner is so often overlooked or denied in our day that his conclusions are worth quoting at length, with the warning that in contrasting "gentleman" and "plebeian," James is not thinking of fixed social classes but of mental types; he might as easily have said "acrobat" and "clodhopper":—

When two minds of a high order, interested in kindred subjects, come together, their conversation is chiefly remarkable for the summariness of its allusions and the rapidity of its transitions. Before one of them is half through a sentence, the other knows his meaning and replies. Such genial play with such massive materials, such an easy flashing of light over far perspectives, such careless indifference to the dust and apparatus that ordinarily surround the subject and seem to pertain to its essence, make these conversations seem true feasts for gods to a listener who is educated enough to follow them at all. His mental lungs breathe more deeply, in an atmosphere more broad and vast than is their wont. On the other hand, the excessive explicitness and short-windedness of an ordinary man are as wonderful as they are tedious to the man of genius. But we need not go so far as the ways of genius. Ordinary social intercourse will do. There the charm of conversation is in direct proportion to the possibility of abridgment and elision, and in inverse ratio to the need of explicit statement. With old friends a word stands for a whole story or set of opinions. With newcomers everything must be gone over in detail. Some persons have a real mania for completeness, they must express every step. They are the most intolerable of companions, and although their mental energy may in its way be great, they always strike us as weak and second-rate. In short, the essence of plebeianism, that which separates vulgarity from aristocracy, is perhaps less a defect than an excess, the constant need to animadvert upon matters which for the aristocratic temperament do not exist. To ignore, to disdain to consider, to overlook, are the essence of the "gentleman." . . . All this suppression of the secondary leaves the field *clear*—for higher flights, should they choose to come. But even if they never came, what thoughts there were would still manifest the aristocratic type and wear the wellbred form. . . .

I may appear to have strayed from psychological analysis into aesthetic criticism. But the principle of selection is so important that no illustrations seem redundant which may help show how great is its scope.

The analogy with art is suggestive, and neutralizes any irrelevant overtone that might come from the word "aristocratic." For it has often been remarked that many simple people who make no pretense to culture, and even less to high birth, have the ability to endow whatever they say with charm and meaning. Often this power seems to go with the practice of a handicraft or of a trade that enters into conflict with the elements. From which we might argue that a habit of shaping matter by hand, or the need to cope with nature, liberates the mind from facts by spurring the creative will to act upon them. Is not this in truth the main point of Thoreau's *Walden*, which we Americans keep reading and reprinting without taking to heart its emphatic lesson?

II

If this addiction to fact—from which none of us is wholly exempt—is indeed nationwide, it can cause no surprise to hear that even in the open city of the intellect one finds mantraps and impediments of the same sort. The observer finds that even where brows are all of a good size, some are higher than others; some kinds of facts are admired, others despised. I have already spoken of the rival faculty clans for or against science, for or against the study of history or of a foreign language. These are the most obvious rifts. Behind the monumental gates, the garment of learning is the object of a tug of war that leaves it looking like a collection of rags. A number of times I have attended informal discussion groups made up of university men; always I have found manners apologetic, susceptibilities raw, and discussion scurrying to take refuge in the shelter of a specialty. In fact, such groups do not long hold together, for there is no common ground and too much common restraint. Discrepancies of age and rank add further obstacles, and one wonders whether there ever was literal meaning in the phrase "a *company* of scholars."

The lines of snobbery do not coincide only with subject matters. A vast distance separates the college professor socially from the high school teacher, and both from the instructors in preparatory schools. Prejudice thrives in the no man's land, to the infinite harm of all concerned; for no routine scorn on the part of colleges and no complacency about doing the harder job on the part of secondary schools is going to unify the course of studies through which every able American boy must pass. It will therefore continue to be an ill-joined affair precisely at the point where students find it so difficult to keep in stride. Better understanding may come from the scheme already tried out of sending to college selected high school seniors, but surely intellectual contact between a teacher of science in the twelfth grade and his successor in the college freshman course should not wait upon innovations affecting only a few among the school population. How can there be a regular gradation of trained minds throughout our society if hairlines of difference act like the Great Wall of China?

Again, why must there be arbitrary barriers, not only among the several disciplines on a single campus—that is known to be bad and a change is in sight—but also between journalism and literature or journalism and scholarship? One would suppose the substance of these three was three different things instead of one presented in as many ways. But the prevalent attitude splits the field and generates undisguised hostility. A reporter from a large news agency—an entire stranger—once rang me up for the favor of a brief consultation. He came, bringing with him a large roll of pictures to be syndicated throughout the country. They showed important events and figures in European history, for which he had written the captions. Were they correct? Of the fifteen or twenty sizable blocks of print, perhaps three or four were right enough to pass. The others all contained one or more serious errors, not of incidental fact, but of major significance. I suggested changes, but as I half expected, my visitor argued. Was it so very wrong, he wondered, to represent Bismarck as always seeking war?

The important thing, he felt, was to have the dates right. I pointed out the relative values of fact and truth and reminded him that he was the one who came to ask my opinion. Whereupon he shifted his ground and maintained that what he had written came from a good encyclopedia. Why was I questioning it? I could not tell him that he had misread and misinterpreted, and he went away, as disgruntled, no doubt, as I was discouraged.

In such an instance we come close to the root of the whole cultural problem, the inherent weakness of all modern literacy: it is half-baked and arrogant. It trifles solemnly with the externals of things, neglecting even the surfaces or the handles by which a truth may be seized: it goes like a child for the false glint or striking triviality of detail.[6]

This vice is not limited to journalists as a group but to all "intellectuals" who trust the journalistic way of bottling and labeling information. Why does every war against Germany bring up the same old platitudes about Fichte and Hegel and Nietzsche, which later on are forgotten or disavowed by their authors? Simply because the college-educated mind is a collection of such ideas, barely scalp-deep, and all the more treacherous that they have the rounded self-sufficient appearance of "facts." If you say "Nietzsche" I think "Blond Beast of Prey"; if you say "Rousseau," I think "Noble Savage"; if you say "Emerson," I think "Self-reliance"; if you say "Darwin," I think "evolution"; if you say "Farewell Address," I think "no entangling alliances." I think no further because "I know it for a fact." Yet there would still be not one grain of accurate sense in any of these associations, though every jury in the country should acquit me of misrepresentation. Wouldn't it be far better, as Josh Billings remarked, "not to know so much as to know so many things that ain't so"?

Far better, because there is something incurable about the

---

[6] We were told by radio during the siege of Cherbourg that the fortifications of the town had been built by Vauban for Napoleon. Why? Probably because Vauban's name occurs in some article on Cherbourg and Napoleon serves as a generic name for all French rulers and conquerors. [Author's note.] Vauban, a French military engineer, lived nearly a century before Napoleon.

organ that wraps itself around such "facts." Nothing new will penetrate it or mingle with them, and since all true learning depends on fitting and refitting the new to the old in the mind, self-education stops on the near side of any catch phrase. When a student comes to college stuffed with ready-made notions, it is still possible to say to him: "You know nothing if you only know these things; forget them; pull them out one by one and go bury them." But no one can serve corresponding notice on an adult who thinks he has *finished* his education. Even when the ignorant or half-educated are humble enough to consult a genuine authority, he turns out not to be wanted—he disappoints—unless he brings a special jargon that can be laid on and shown off without compelling the inquirer to learn or change his mind.[7]

Surely this deserves to be called mental cowardice—a vice that differs from laziness and often masquerades as modesty. The man who calls himself a lowbrow is of course boasting and lying but also shirking. The educated woman's "I wouldn't know anything about that" is not modest, but defensive. "How do you know you wouldn't? Your very ignorance refutes itself. Wait and see: read to the end of the page; listen to the end of the sentence; DON'T RUN AWAY! For even if the new idea fails to enlighten, it will not hurt you. Remember that what one fool can do, another can; and by good luck and the use of a little mental courage, you *might* after a while be able to recognize a syllogism or to tell 'God Save the Weasel' from 'Pop Goes the Queen'!"

The nearer one gets to popular tastes and unstudied actions, the more widespread the signs of mental cowardice. Observe how timid and sensitive and frightened are the readers of cheap fiction: the slightest novelty, the least deviation from formula, scatters their mind in a panic; so that the art of

[7] A colleague of mine in the classics was rung up by a firm that wanted to know the Latin term for "advertising man." When he said there was no such term, he was asked to make up one, which he did, but this did not suit, because they had one of their own, which they wanted approved, namely, *Homo publicitas*. The copywriter who struck off this gem must be the same who was impelled a little later to call television "the video art." Pedantry in low places! [Author's note.]

catering for them as magazine editors consists in being in a perpetual sweat of anxiety about particular ideas, feelings, and words. Compared to them the so-called esthete is a tough character ever ready for a word and a blow, even if the blow is aimed at his solar plexus and the word is one made up of six others, scrambled together by the art of James Joyce. Not that "intellectuals" do not also huddle in cliques with a very narrow range of physical tolerance for the unfamiliar, but at least their pride is on the side of intellectual adventure.

I suppose that the frantic clutch for a mental security card has something to do with the dread of all realities and the increasing difficulty of getting at them. For most people the objection to intellect is the same as the objection to art: both are too strong, to direct, too close. So it is better to pretend that intellect is out of reach in the clouds. But the clouds are not what they are thought to be. They exist, but they are not natural to intellect. Rather they are smoke screens, which we owe to commentators, to journalism, to "literacy." The clouds come from the objectors themselves. The result is that for a man to find his way through to the real Nietzsche or Darwin is a laborious task. He must forget what he "knows" and read Nietzsche himself, not one book merely but perhaps as many as three, lending his mind to each, while comparing and assimilating. He must consult biographers and critics and sort out the chaff; and when he has done, though he has satisfied his curiosity and come to grips with the real substance behind the word "Nietzsche," he finds that he has only cut himself off from newspaper-educated opinion.

No wonder most people prefer to invest their mental energies in tasks requiring less gumption, and that these tasks acquire an unmerited worthiness. If you notice, we are all scholars now, we do research—the man of business like all the rest. But the research is of the assembling-and-packaging kind. There is a tremendous demand to "know"—to know what? To know the ratings of soap operas or the length of time it takes to read the Constitution; to know the average life of a front tire on a four-door sedan, or the five hundred best books

of the decade, classified in groups and rated in order of merit
by leading librarians.

Hundreds of study groups and fact-finding commissions,
public or private, give their members in this way the pleasant
illusion of being practical scholars and social "scientists." The
facts usually lie in surface soil—supposing they are facts at all
and not verbalisms—and they can be had for a little scratching.
The results are then published and we have another layer
of paper wadding between us and the horrors of life. Just as
there is a business concern that will remind you by telephone
that it is your wife's birthday, making you a model husband,
so "research" has now progressed to the point where our culture has been broken down into published "facts," making you
a realist. You can find a hundred specimen cases, fully charted,
of almost anything you are interested in; which should give
you the double satisfaction of quenching your own thirst for
facts, and of knowing that the preparation of the study fulfilled
a similar need in the researcher. He is proud and you admire
him, looking down—both of you—on other highbrows.

After your labors, no one need ever again open a real book—
let alone the mind's eye. All one need do is consult the Progress
Report, the Summary of Findings to Date, or the Study of
Fifty One-Armed Paperhangers. In the end, the nation may
not have a very clear head, but it has a Gallup poll.

WHAT USE IS POETRY?[1]

GILBERT HIGHET (1906-

From *A Clerk of Oxenford*, 1954. The virtue of this essay is that it is
simple, practical, and inviting. It is addressed to "everyman," to people
who unknowingly love poetry as naturally as they do singing. True, some
poetry is complex, but so are some people's feelings. It is well to start, as

[1] Reprinted from *A Clerk of Oxenford* by Gilbert Highet and used
with the permission of the Oxford University Press. Copyright 1954 by
Gilbert Highet.

Mr. Highet does, with the simple and move with steady determination toward the deeper rewards of more subtle poetic expression.

Children ask lots and lots of questions, about religion, about sex, about the stars. But there are some questions which they never ask: they leave grown-ups to ask them and to answer them. Often this means that the questions are silly: that they are questions about nonexistent problems, or questions to which the answer is obvious. Sometimes it means that the question *should* be asked, but that the answer is difficult or multiplex.

So, children never ask what is the good of music. They just like singing and dancing, and even drumming on a low note of the piano. In the same way, they never ask what is the use of poetry. They all enjoy poems and songs, and very often come to like them before they can even talk properly; but it never occurs to them that they ought to find reasons for their enjoyment. But grown-ups do inquire about the justification of poetry: they ask what is the point of putting words in a special order and extracting special sound effects from them, instead of speaking plainly and directly. And often—because they get no adequate answer, either from the poets or from the professors—they conclude that poetry is only a set of tricks like conjuring, or a complicated game like chess; and they turn away from it in discouragement . . . until, perhaps, a poetic film like *Henry V* shocks them into realizing something of its power; or, as they grow older, they find that a poem learned in childhood sticks in their mind and becomes clearer and more beautiful with age.

What is the use of poetry?

There must be a number of different answers to the question. Just as a picture can be meant to give pleasure, or to carry a puzzle, or to convey information, so poems are meant for many different things. We can begin to get some of the answers if we look at the poetry that children themselves naturally enjoy, and then see how it is connected with the most famous grown-up poems.

The first pleasure of poetry is the simplest. It is the same pleasure that we have in music—the pleasure of following a pattern of sound. Everyone loves talking, and most people like what might be called doodling in sound. So, if you look through the *Oxford Dictionary of Nursery Rhymes*, you will find several tongue-twisters, like this:

> *Peter Piper picked a peck of pickled pepper;*
> *A peck of pickled pepper Peter Piper picked;*
> *If Peter Piper picked a peck of pickled pepper,*
> *Where's the peck of pickled pepper Peter Piper picked?*

On a grown-up level, many a famous poem is little more than a pattern of sound: for instance, Shakespeare's love song:

> *It was a lover and his lass,*
> *With a hey and a ho and a hey nonino,*
> *That o'er the green cornfield did pass,*
> *In the spring time, the only pretty ring time,*
> *When birds do sing, hey ding a ding ding;*
> *Sweet lovers love the spring.*

Much of the best poetry of Swinburne is pattern-making in sound, with a very light core of meaning. Here are four exquisite lines which really mean very little more than the sound of spring showers:

> *When the hounds of spring are on winter's traces,*
> *The mother of months in meadow or plain*
> *Fills the shadows and windy places*
> *With lisp of leaves and ripple of rain.*

Small meaning, but lovely rhythm and melody.

Now, there is a second pleasure in poetry. This is that it is sometimes better than prose for telling a story. It even gives authority to a story which is illogical or incredible, or even gruesome. That is one reason children love the poem that tells of the tragic fate of Jack and Jill. There is an interesting variant of it: the cumulative story, in which one detail is piled up on another until the whole story has been set forth with the simple exactitude of a primitive painting: for instance, "The

House That Jack Built," and the funeral elegy, "Who Killed Cock Robin?" and the famous old Jewish rhyme, "Had Gadyo," about the kid bought for two pieces of money— which is said to symbolize a vast stretch of the history of the Jewish people. Another variant is the limerick, which is simply a funny story in verse. Many a man who would protest that he knew no poetry, and cared nothing for it, could still recite eight or ten limericks in the right company.

In serious adult poetry there are many superb stories, in- cluding the two oldest books in Western literature, the *Iliad* and the *Odyssey*. Every good collection of poems will include some of the most dramatic tales ever told, the English and Scottish ballads, which are still occasionally sung in our own southern states. One of the strangest things about the stories told as ballads is their terrible abruptness and directness. They leave out a great deal. They give only a few details, a name or two; they draw the outlines, harsh and black or blood-red, and they concentrate on the actions and the passions. Such is the ballad about an ambush in which a knight was killed by his own wife's brother. It is called "The Dowie Houms of Yarrow" (that means the sad fields beside the river Yarrow, in the Scottish borders), and it opens immediately with the quarrel, almost with the clash of swords:

> *Late at een, drinkin' the wine,*
> *And ere they paid the lawin',*
> *They set a combat them between,*
> *To fight it in the dawin'.*

Within only a few verses, the knight has been surrounded, and treacherously murdered, fighting against heavy odds; and when his widow goes out to find his body, her anguish is de- scribed in one of the most terrible stanzas in all poetry:

> *She kissed his cheek, she kamed his hair,*
> *As oft she did before, O;*
> *She drank the red blood frae him ran,*
> *On the dowie houms o' Yarrow.*

That story in poetry and a few others like "Edward, Edward"
—in which a mother persuades her son to kill his own father,
and drives him mad—are absolutely unforgettable.

But besides storytelling, poetry has another use, known all
over the world. This is mnemonic. Put words into a pattern,
and they are easier to remember. I should never have known
the lengths of the months if I had not learned:

> Thirty days hath September,
> April, June, and November;
> All the rest have thirty-one,
> Excepting February alone,
> And that has twenty-eight days clear
> And twenty-nine in each leap year.

This is certainly four hundred years old, for it occurs in an
English manuscript dated about 1555, and there is a French
poem, with the same rhyme scheme, written three hundred
years earlier. (It might be easier to change the calendar, but
mankind is by nature conservative.) On a simpler level there
are many nursery rhymes in every language which are designed
to teach children the very simplest things; for instance, counting and performing easy actions:

> One, two,
> Buckle my shoe,
> Three, four,
> Shut the door.

And even earlier, before the child can speak, he is lucky if his
mother can recite the poem that goes over his five toes or
fingers, one after another:

> This little pig went to market,
> This little pig stayed at home,

up to the comical climax when the child is meant to squeak too,
and to enjoy staying at home.

Adults also remember facts better if they are put into verse. Nearly every morning I repeat to myself:

> *Early to bed and early to rise*
> *Makes a man healthy and wealthy and wise.*

And nearly every evening I change it to Thurber's parody:

> *Early to rise and early to bed*
> *Makes a male healthy and wealthy and dead;*

or occasionally to George Ade's variant:

> *Early to bed and early to rise*
> *Will make you miss all the regular guys.*

This is the source of what they call didactic poetry, poetry meant to teach. The best-known example of it is the Book of Proverbs in the Bible, which ought to be translated into rhythmical prose, or even verse. The third oldest book in Greek literature, not much younger than Homer, is a farmer's handbook all set out in poetry, so that it could be learned off by heart and remembered: it is the *Works and Days* by Hesiod. To teach has long been one of the highest functions of the poet: great poetry can be written in order to carry a message of philosophical or practical truth—or sometimes an ironical counsel, as in this strange poem by Sir Walter Scott:

> *Look not thou on beauty's charming;*
> *Sit thou still when kings are arming;*
> *Taste not when the winecup glistens;*
> *Speak not when the people listens;*
> *Stop thine ear against the singer;*
> *From the red gold keep thy finger;*
> *Vacant heart and hand and eye,*
> *Easy live and quiet die.*

There is one peculiar variation on the poem that conveys information. This is the riddle poem, which tells you something —but only if you are smart enough to see through its disguise. There are some such riddles in the Bible: Samson created a good one, about the dead lion with a hive of wild bees inside it. Legend has it that Homer died of chagrin because he could not solve a rather sordid poetic puzzle. The nursery rhyme "Humpty Dumpty" was really a riddle to begin with (before Lewis Carroll and his illustrator gave it away). We are supposed to guess what was the mysterious person or thing which fell down, and then could not possibly be put together again, not even by all the king's horses and all the king's men, and nowadays by all the republic's scientific experts: the answer is an egg. There is a beautiful folk song made up of three such riddles: the cherry without a stone, the chicken without a bone, and the baby that does not cry. It is at least five hundred years old, and yet for four hundred years it was passed on from one singer to another, without ever being printed.

Again, there are some famous and splendid poems that deal with mystical experience in riddling terms, phrases which have two meanings, or three, or one concealed: these are also didactic, informative, and yet riddles. One such poem, by an American poet, deals with the paradox of God—the complete God, who includes all the appearances of the universe, both the appearance of good and the appearance of evil. This is Emer· son's "Brahma."

> If the red slayer think he slays,
>   Or if the slain think he is slain,
> They know not well the subtle ways
>   I keep, and pass, and turn again.
>
> Far or forgot to me is near;
>   Shadow and sunlight are the same;
> The vanished gods to me appear;
>   And one to me are shame and fame.

> *They reckon ill who leave me out;*
> *When me they fly, I am the wings;*
> *I am the doubter and the doubt,*
> *And I the hymn the Brahmin sings.*
>
> *The strong gods pine for my abode,*
> *And pine in vain the sacred Seven;*
> *But thou, meek lover of the good!*
> *Find me, and turn thy back on heaven.*

This is a riddle which is meant not for children but for adults. There are similar riddles in the Bible, sometimes equally beautiful. Such is the meditation on old age at the end of that mysterious and rather unorthodox book called *Koheleth*, or *Ecclesiastes*:

> *Remember now thy Creator in the days of thy youth,*
> *while the evil days come not,*
> *nor the years draw nigh, when thou shalt say, I have no*
> *pleasure in them;*
>
> *while the sun or the light or the moon or the stars be*
> *not darkened, nor the clouds return after the rain;*
>
> *in the day when the keepers of the house shall tremble,*
> *and the strong men shall bow themselves,*
> *and the grinders cease because they are few,*
> *and those that look out of the windows be darkened,*
> *and the doors shall be shut in the streets,*
> *when the sound of the grinding is low,*
> *and he shall rise up at the voice of the bird,*
> *and all the daughters of music shall be brought low,*
> *also when they shall be afraid of that which is high,*
> *and fears shall be in the way,*
> *and the almond tree shall flourish,*
> *and the grasshopper shall be a burden,*

and desire shall fail:
  because man goeth to his long home
  and the mourners go about the streets;

or ever the silver cord be loosed,
  or the golden bowl be broken,
  or the pitcher be broken at the fountain
  or the wheel broken at the cistern.

Then shall the dust return to the earth as it was;
  and the spirit shall return unto God who gave it.

All these enigmatic and memorable phrases are descriptions of the symptoms of the last and almost the bitterest fact in life, old age. They show that it is pathetic, and yet they make it beautiful.

Such poetry is unusual. Or rather, its manner is unusual and its subject is a fact of common experience. It is possible for poets to speak plainly and frankly about everyday life; and that is one more of the uses of poetry—one of the best known. Poetry can express general experience: can say what many men and women have thought and felt. The benefit of this is that it actually helps ordinary people, by giving them words. Most of us are not eloquent. Most of us—especially in times of intense emotion—cannot say what we feel; often we hardly know what we feel. There, in our heart, there is the turmoil, be it love or protest or exultation or despair: it stirs us, but all our gestures and words are inadequate. As the emotion departs, we know that an opportunity was somehow missed, an opportunity of realizing a great moment to the full. It is in this field that poetry comes close to religion. Religion is one of the experiences which the ordinary man finds most difficult to compass in words. Therefore he nearly always falls back on phrases which have been composed for him by someone more gifted. Many, many thousands of times, in battles and concentration camps and hospitals, beside death beds, and even on death beds, men and women have repeated a very ancient poem only six verses long, and have found comfort in it, such as no words of their own would have brought them. It begins, "The Lord is my shepherd; I shall not want."

If we look at poetry or any of the arts from this point of view, we shall gain a much greater respect for them. They are not amusements or decorations; they are aids to life. Ordinary men and women find living rather difficult. One of their chief difficulties is to apprehend their own thoughts and feelings, and to respond to them by doing the right things and saying the right sentences. It is the poets who supply the words and sentences. They too have felt as we do, but they have been able to speak, while we are dumb.

Not only that. By expressing common emotions clearly and eloquently, the poets help us to understand them in other people. It is difficult to understand—for any grown-up it is difficult to understand—what goes on in the mind of a boy or girl. Parents are often so anxious and serious that they have forgotten what it was like to be young, and vague, and romantic. It is a huge effort, rather an unpleasantly arduous effort, to think oneself back into boyhood. Yet there are several poems which will allow us to understand it, and even to enjoy the experience. One of them is a fine lyric by Longfellow, called "My Lost Youth":

> I remember the gleams and glooms that dart
>   Across the schoolboy's brain;
> The song and the silence in the heart,
> That in part are prophecies, and in part
>   Are longings wild and vain.
>   And the voice of that fitful song
>   Sings on, and is never still:
>   "A boy's will is the wind's will,
> And the thoughts of youth are long, long thoughts."
>
> There are things of which I may not speak;
>   There are dreams that cannot die;

There are thoughts that make the strong heart weak,
And bring a pallor into the cheek,
   And a mist before the eye.
      And the words of that fatal song
      Come over me like a chill:
      "A boy's will is the wind's will,
And the thoughts of youth are long, long thoughts."

If you have a young son who seems to be woolgathering half the time, and who sometimes does not even answer when he is spoken to, you should read and reflect on that poem of Longfellow.

This function of poetry is not the only one, but it is one of the most vital: to give adequate expression to important general experiences. In 1897, when Queen Victoria celebrated her Diamond Jubilee, the Poet Laureate was that completely inadequate little fellow, Alfred Austin; but the man who wrote the poem summing up the emotions most deeply felt during the Jubilee was Rudyard Kipling. It is called "Recessional." It is a splendid poem, almost a hymn—Biblical in its phrasing and deeply prophetic in its thought:

      The tumult and the shouting dies—
         The captains and the kings depart—
      Still stands Thine ancient sacrifice,
         An humble and a contrite heart.
      Lord God of Hosts, be with us yet,
      Lest we forget, lest we forget!

However, as you think over the poems you know, you will realize that many of them seem to be quite different from this. They are not even trying to do the same thing. They do not express important general experiences in universally acceptable words. On the contrary, they express strange and individual experiences in abstruse and sometimes unintelligible words. We enjoy them not because they say what we have often thought but because they say what we should never have dreamed of thinking. If a poem like Kipling's "Recessional" or Longfellow's "Lost Youth" is close to religion, then this other kind of poetry is close to magic: its words sound like spells; its subjects are often dreams, visions, and myths.

Such are the two most famous poems by Coleridge: "The Ancient Mariner" and "Kubla Khan." They are scarcely understandable. They are unbelievable. Beautiful, yes, and haunting, yes, but utterly illogical; crazy. Coleridge himself scarcely knew their sources, deep in his memory and his sub-conscious—sources on which a modern scholar has written a superb book. Both of them end with a mystical experience that none of us has ever had: "The Ancient Mariner" telling how, like the Wandering Jew, he must travel forever from country to country, telling his story with "strange power of speech"; and "Kubla Khan" with the poet himself creating a magical palace:

> *I would build that dome in air,*
> *That sunny dome! those caves of ice!*
> *And all who heard should see them there,*
> *And all should cry, Beware! Beware!*
> *His flashing eyes, his floating hair!*
> *Weave a circle round him thrice,*
> *And close your eyes with holy dread,*
> *For he on honey-dew hath fed,*
> *And drunk the milk of Paradise.*

Not long after those fantastic verses were written, young Keats was composing a lyric, almost equally weird, which is now considered one of the finest odes in the English language. It ends with the famous words which we all know, and which few of us believe:

> *Beauty is truth, truth beauty,—that is all*
> *Ye know on earth, and all ye need to know.*

It is the 'Ode on a Grecian Urn'; but how many of us have ever stood, like Keats, meditating on the paintings that sur-

round a Greek vase? and, even if we have, how many of us
have thought that

> *Heard melodies are sweet, but those unheard*
> *Are sweeter?*

It is a paradox. The entire ode is a paradox: not an expression of ordinary life, but an extreme extension of it, almost a
direct contradiction of usual experience.

Most modern poetry is like this. It tells of things almost
unknown to ordinary men and women, even to children. If it
has power over them at all, it is because it enchants them by
its strangeness. Such is the poetry of Verlaine, and Mallarmé,
and Rimbaud; of the difficult and sensitive Austrian poet Rilke;
in our own language, such is most of Auden's poetry, and Ezra
Pound's; and what could be more unusual than most of T. S.
Eliot—although he is the most famous poet writing today?
Suppose we test this. Let us take something simple. Spring.
What have the poets said about the first month of spring,
about April? Most of them say it is charming and frail:

> *April, April,*
> *Laugh thy girlish laughter;*
> *Then, the moment after,*
> *Weep thy girlish tears!*

That is Sir William Watson: turn back, and see Shakespeare
talking of
> *The uncertain glory of an April day;*

turn forward, and hear Browning cry

> *O to be in England*
> *Now that April's there!*

and then hundreds of years earlier, see Chaucer beginning his
Canterbury Tales with a handshake of welcome to 'Aprille.

with his shoures soote.' Indeed, that is what most of us feel
about April: it is sweet and delicate and youthful and hopeful. But T. S. Eliot begins *The Waste Land* with a grim statement which is far outside ordinary feelings:

> *April is the cruellest month, breeding*
> *Lilacs out of the dead land, mixing*
> *Memory and desire, stirring*
> *Dull roots with spring rain.*

And the entire poem, the best known of our generation, is a
description of several agonizing experiences which most of us
not only have never had but have not even conceived as possible. Yet there is no doubt that it is good poetry, and that it
has taken a permanent place in our literature, together with
other eccentric and individual visions.

But some of us do not admit it to be poetry—or rather claim
that, if it is so extreme and unusual, poetry is useless. This is
a mistake. The universe is so vast, the universe is so various,
that we owe it to ourselves to try to understand every kind of
experience—both the usual and the remote, both the intelligible
and the mystical. Logic is not enough. Not all the truth about
the world, or about our own lives, can be set down in straightforward prose, or even in straightforward poetry. Some important truths are too subtle even to be uttered in words. A
Japanese, by arranging a few flowers in a vase, or Rembrandt,
by drawing a dark room with an old man sitting in it, can convey meanings which no one could ever utter in speech. So also,
however extravagant a romantic poem may seem, it can tell us
something about our world which we ought to know.

It is easier for us to appreciate this nowadays than it would
have been for our grandfathers in the nineteenth century, or
for their great-grandfathers in the eighteenth century. Our
lives are far less predictable; and it is far less possible to use
logic alone in organizing and understanding them. Therefore
there are justifications, and good ones, for reading and memor-
izing not only what we might call universal poetry but also

strange and visionary poetry. We ourselves, at some time within the mysterious future, may well have to endure and to try to understand some experience absolutely outside our present scope: suffering of some unforeseen kind, a magnificent and somber duty, a splendid triumph, the development of some new power within us. We shall be better able to do so if we know what the poets (yes, and the musicians) have said about such enchantments and extensions of life. Many a man has lived happily until something came upon him which made him, for the first time, think of committing suicide. Such a man will be better able to understand himself and to rise above the thought if he knows the music that Rachmaninoff wrote when he, too, had such thoughts and conquered them, or if he reads the play of *Hamlet,* or if he travels through Dante's *Comedy,* which begins in utter despair and ends in the vision of

love, that moves the sun and the other stars.

And even if we ourselves are not called upon to endure such extremes, there may be those around us, perhaps very close to us, who are faced with situations the ordinary mind cannot assimilate: sudden wealth, the temptations of great beauty, the gift of creation, profound sorrow, unmerited guilt. The knowledge of what the poets have said about experiences beyond the frontiers of logic will help us at least to sympathize with them in these experiences. Such understanding is one of the most difficult and necessary efforts of the soul. Shelley compared the skylark, lost in the radiance of the sun, to

a Poet hidden
In the light of thought
Singing hymns unbidden,
Till the world is wrought
To sympathy with hopes and fears it heeded not.

To create such sympathy is one of the deepest functions of poetry, and one of the most bitterly needed.

The Poet can tell more in fewer words.

PROSPECTS IN THE ARTS
AND SCIENCES[1]

J. ROBERT OPPENHEIMER (1904–

Delivered at Columbia University, December 26, 1954. This essay reflects the comprehensive mind of the Director of the Institute for Advanced Study at Princeton. One cannot know all, but one is obliged to be aware of much. Note the aptness of the analogy of the superhighway and the village. There is a solidarity of knowledge, but to an individual some areas of it become close while others remain remote. Note that the scientist and the artist both live "at the edge of mystery." Each can help the other. Both can establish ties which bind human knowledge into a consummate whole.

The words "prospects in the arts and sciences" mean two quite different things to me. One is prophecy: What will the scientists discover and the painters paint, what new forms will alter music, what parts of experience will newly yield to objective description? The other meaning is that of a view: What do we see when we look at the world today and compare it with the past? I am not a prophet; and I cannot very well speak to the first subject, though in many ways I should like to. I shall try to speak to the second, because there are some features of this view which seem to me so remarkable, so new and so arresting, that it may be worth turning our eyes to them; it may even help us to create and shape the future better, though we cannot foretell it.

In the arts and in the sciences, it would be good to be a

---

[1] This was the concluding address at the Columbia University Bicentennial. Used with the kind permission of Columbia University and of Dr. Oppenheimer.

prophet. It would be a delight to know the future. I had thought for a while of my own field of physics and of those nearest to it in the natural sciences. It would not be too hard to outline the questions which natural scientists today are asking themselves and trying to answer. What, we ask in physics, is matter, what is it made of, how does it behave when it is more and more violently atomized, when we try to pound out of the stuff around us the ingredients which only violence creates and makes manifest? What, the chemists ask, are those special features of nucleic acids and proteins which make life possible and give it its characteristic endurance and mutability? What subtle chemistry, what arrangements, what reactions and controls make the cells of living organisms differentiate so that they may perform functions as oddly diverse as transmitting information throughout our nervous systems or covering our heads with hair? What happens in the brain to make a record of the past, to hide it from consciousness, to make it accessible to recall? What are the physical features which make consciousness possible?

All history teaches us that these questions that we think the pressing ones will be transmuted before they are answered, that they will be replaced by others, and that the very process of discovery will shatter the concepts that we today use to describe our puzzlement.

It is true that there are some who profess to see in matters of culture, in matters precisely of the arts and sciences, a certain macrohistorical pattern, a grand system of laws which determines the course of civilization and gives a kind of inevitable quality to the unfolding of the future. They would, for instance, see the radical, formal experimentation which characterized the music of the last half century as an inevitable consequence of the immense flowering and enrichment of natural science; they would see a necessary order in the fact that innovation in music precedes that in painting and that in turn in poetry, and point to this sequence in older cultures. They would attribute the formal experimentation of the arts to the dissolution, in an industrial and technical society, of authority,

of secular, political authority, and of the catholic authority of
the church. They are thus armed to predict the future. But this,
I fear, is not my dish.

If a prospect is not a prophecy, it is a view. What does the
world of the arts and sciences look like? There are two ways of
looking at it: One is the view of the traveler, going by horse or
foot, from village to village to town, staying in each to talk
with those who live there and to gather something of the
quality of its life. This is the intimate view, partial, somewhat
accidental, limited by the limited life and strength and curiosity
of the traveler, but intimate and human, in a human compass.
The other is the vast view, showing the earth with its fields and
towns and valleys as they appear to a camera carried in a high
altitude rocket. In one sense this prospect will be more complete; one will see all branches of knowledge, one will see all
the arts, one will see them as part of the vastness and complica-
tion of the whole of human life on earth. But one will miss a
great deal; the beauty and warmth of human life will largely
be gone from that prospect.

It is in this vast high altitude survey that one sees the general
surprising quantitative features that distinguish our time. This
is where the listings of science and endowments and laboratories and books published show up; this is where we learn
that more people are engaged in scientific research today than
ever before, that the Soviet world and the free world are running neck and neck in the training of scientists, that more books
are published per capita in England than in the United States,
that the social sciences are pursued actively in America, Scan-
dinavia, and England, that there are more people who hear the
great music of the past, and more music composed and more
paintings painted. This is where we learn that the arts and
sciences are flourishing. This great map, showing the world
from afar and almost as to a stranger, would show more: It
would show the immense diversity of culture and life, diversity
in place and tradition for the first time clearly manifest on a
world-wide scale, diversity in technique and language, separating science from science and art from art, and all of one from

all of the other. This great map, world-wide, culture-wide, remote, has some odd features. There are innumerable villages. Between the villages there appear to be almost no paths discernible from this high altitude. Here and there passing near a village, sometimes through its heart, there will be a superhighway, along which windy traffic moves at enormous speed. The superhighways seem to have little connection with villages, starting anywhere, ending anywhere, and sometimes appearing almost by design to disrupt the quiet of the village. This view gives us no sense of order or of unity. To find these we must visit the villages, the quiet, busy places, the laboratories and studies and studios. We must see the paths that are barely discernible; we must understand the superhighways, and their dangers.

In the natural sciences these are and have been and are likely to continue to be heroic days. Discovery follows discovery, each both raising and answering questions, each ending a long search, and each providing the new instruments for a new search. There are radical ways of thinking unfamiliar to common sense and connected with it by decades or centuries of increasingly specialized and unfamiliar experience. There are lessons of how limited, for all its variety, the common experience of man has been with regard to natural phenomena, and hints and analogies as to how limited may be his experience with man. Every new finding is a part of the instrument kit of the sciences for further investigation and for penetrating into new fields. Discoveries of knowledge fructify technology and the practical arts, and these in turn pay back refined techniques, new possibilities of observation and experiment.

In any science there is harmony between practitioners. A man may work as an individual, learning of what his colleagues do through reading or conversation; he may be working as a member of a group on problems whose technical equipment is too massive for individual effort. But whether he is a part of a team or solitary in his own study, he, as a professional, is a member of a community. His colleagues in his own branch of science will be grateful to him for the inventive or creative thoughts he has, will welcome his criticism. His world and work will be objectively communicable; and he will be quite sure that if there is error in it, that error will not long be undetected. In his own line of work he lives in a community where common understanding combines with common purpose and interest to bind men together both in freedom and in cooperation.

This experience will make him acutely aware of how limited, how inadequate, how precious is this condition of his life; for in his relations with a wider society, there will be neither the sense of community nor of objective understanding. He will sometimes find, in returning to practical undertakings, some sense of community with men who are not expert in his science, with other scientists whose work is remote from his, and with men of action and men of art. The frontiers of science are separated now by long years of study, by specialized vocabularies, arts, techniques, and knowledge from the common heritage even of a most civilized society; and anyone working at the frontier of such science is in that sense a very long way from home, a long way too from the practical arts that were its matrix and origin, as indeed they were of what we today call art.

The specialization of science is an inevitable accompaniment of progress; yet it is full of dangers, and it is cruelly wasteful, since so much that is beautiful and enlightening is cut off from most of the world. Thus it is proper to the role of the scientist that he not merely find new truth and communicate it to his fellows, but that he teach, that he try to bring the most honest and intelligible account of new knowledge to all who will try to learn. This is one reason—it is the decisive organic reason— why scientists belong in universities. It is one reason why the patronage of science by and through universities is its most proper form; for it is here, in teaching, in the association of scholars, and in the friendships of teachers and taught, of men who by profession must themselves be both teachers and taught, that the narrowness of scientific life can best be moderated, and that the analogies, insights, and harmonies of scientific discovery can find their way into the wider life of man.

In the situation of the artist today there are both analogies to and differences from that of the scientist; but it is the differences which are the most striking, and which raise the problems that touch most on the evil of our day. For the artist it is not enough that he communicate with others who are expert in his own art. Their fellowship, their understanding, and their appreciation may encourage him; but that is not the end of his work, nor its nature. The artist depends on a common sensibility and culture, on a common meaning of symbols, on a community of experience and common ways of describing and interpreting it. He need not write for everyone or paint or play for everyone. But his audience must be man; it must be man, and not a specialized set of experts among his fellows. Today that is very difficult. Often the artist has an aching sense of great loneliness, for the community to which he addresses himself is largely not there; the traditions and the culture, the symbols and the history, the myths and the common experience, which it is his function to illuminate, to harmonize, and to portray, have been dissolved in a changing world.

There is, it is true, an artificial audience maintained to moderate between the artist and the world for which he works: the audience of the professional critics, popularizers, and advertisers of art. But though, as does the popularizer and promoter of science, the critic fulfills a necessary present function and introduces some order and some communication between the artist and the world, he cannot add to the intimacy and the directness and the depth with which the artist addresses his fellow men.

To the artist's loneliness there is a complementary great and terrible barrenness in the lives of men. They are deprived of the illumination, the light and tenderness and insight of an intelligible interpretation, in contemporary terms, of the sorrows and wonders and gaieties and follies of man's life. This may be in part offset, and is, by the great growth of technical means for making the art of the past available. But these provide a record of past intimacies between art and life; even when they are applied to the writing and painting and composing of the day, they do not bridge the gulf between a society, too vast and too disordered, and the artist trying to give meaning and beauty to its parts.

In an important sense this world of ours is a new world, in which the unity of knowledge, the nature of human communities, the order of society, the order of ideas, the very notions of society and culture have changed and will not return to what they have been in the past. What is new is new not because it has never been there before, but because it has changed in quality. One thing that is new is the prevalence of newness, the changing scale and scope of change itself, so that the world alters as we walk in it, so that the years of man's life measure not some small growth or rearrangement or moderation of what he learned in childhood, but a great upheaval. What is new is that in one generation our knowledge of the natural world engulfs, upsets, and complements all knowledge of the natural world before. The techniques, among and by which we live, multiply and ramify, so that the whole world is bound together by communication, blocked here and there by the immense synapses of political tyranny. The global quality of the world is new; our knowledge of and sympathy with remote and diverse peoples, our involvement with them in practical terms, and our commitment to them in terms of brotherhood. What is new in the world is the massive character of the dissolution and corruption of authority, in belief, in ritual, and in temporal order. Yet this is the world that we have come to live in. The very difficulties which it presents derive from growth in understanding, in skill, in power. To assail the changes that have unmoored us from the past is futile, and in a deep sense, I think, it is wicked. We need to recognize the change and learn what resources we have.

Again I will turn to the schools and, as their end and as their center, the universities. For the problem of the scientist is in this respect not different from that of the artist or of the historian. He needs to be a part of the community, and the community can only with loss and peril be without him. Thus it is with a sense of interest and hope that we see a growing recognition that the creative artist is a proper charge on the university, and the university a proper home for him; that a composer or a poet or a playwright or painter needs the toleration, understanding, the rather local and parochial patronage that a university can give; and that this will protect him from the tyranny of man's communication and professional promotion. For here there is an honest chance that what the artist has of insight and of beauty will take root in the community, and that some intimacy and some human bonds can mark his relations with his patrons. For a university rightly and inherently is a place where the individual man can form new syntheses, where the accidents of friendship and association can open a man's eyes to a part of science or art which he had not known before, where parts of human life, remote and perhaps superficially incompatible, can find in men their harmony and their synthesis.

These then, in rough and far too general words, are some of the things we see as we walk through the villages of the arts and of the sciences and notice how thin are the paths that lead from one to another, and how little in terms of human understanding and pleasure the work of the villages comes to be shared outside.

The superhighways do not help. They are the mass media—from the loud speakers in the deserts of Asia Minor and the cities of Communist China to the organized professional theater of Broadway. They are the purveyors of art and science and culture for the millions upon millions—the promotors who represent the arts and sciences to humanity and who represent humanity to the arts and sciences; they are the means by which we are reminded of the famine in remote places or of war or trouble or change; they are the means by which this great earth and its peoples have become one to one another, the means by which the news of discovery or honor and the stories and songs of today travel and resound throughout the world. But they are also the means by which the true human community, the man knowing man, the neighbor understanding neighbor, the school boy learning a poem, the woman dancing, the individual curiosity, the individual sense of beauty are being blown dry and issueless, the means by which the passivity of the disengaged spectator presents to the man of art and science the bleak face of unhumanity.

For the truth is that this is indeed, inevitably and increasingly, an open and, inevitably and increasingly, an eclectic world. We know too much for one man to know much, we live too variously to live as one. Our histories and traditions—the very means of interpreting life—are both bonds and barriers among us. Our knowledge separates us as well as it unites; our orders disintegrate as well as bind; our art brings us together and sets us apart. The artist's loneliness, the scholar despairing, because no one will any longer trouble to learn what he can teach, the narrowness of the scientist— these are not unnatural insignia in this great time of change.

For what is asked of us is not easy. The openness of this world derives its character from the irreversibility of learning; what is once learned is part of human life. We cannot close our minds to discovery. We cannot stop our ears so that the voices of far-off and strange people can no longer reach them. The great cultures of the East cannot be walled off from ours by impassible seas and defects of understanding based on ignorance and unfamiliarity. Neither our integrity as men of learning nor our humanity allows that. In this open world, what is there any man may try to learn.

This is no new problem. There has always been more to know than one man could know; there have always been modes of feeling that could not move the same heart; there have always been deeply held beliefs that could not be composed into a synthetic union. Yet never before today has the diversity, the complexity, the richness so clearly defied hierarchical order and simplification, never before have we had to understand the complementary, mutually not compatible ways of life and recognize choice between them as the only course of freedom. Never before today has the integrity of the intimate, the de-

tailed, the true art, the integrity of craftsmanship and the pres-
ervation of the familiar, of the humorous and the beautiful
stood in more massive contrast to the vastness of life, the greatness of the globe, the otherness of people, the otherness of
ways, and the all-encompassing dark.

This is a world in which each of us, knowing his limitations,
knowing the evils of superficiality and the terrors of fatigue,
will have to cling to what is close to him, to what he knows,
to what he can do, to his friends and his tradition and his love,
lest he be dissolved in a universal confusion and know nothing
and love nothing. It is at the same time a world in which none
of us can find hieratic prescription or general sanction for any
ignorance, any insensitivity, any indifference. When a friend
tells us of a new discovery we may not understand, we may
not be able to listen without jeopardizing the work that is ours
and closer to us; but we cannot find in a book or canon—and
we should not seek—grounds for hallowing our ignorance. If
a man tells us that he sees differently than we or that he finds
beautiful what we find ugly, we may have to leave the room,
from fatigue or trouble; but that is our weakness and our de-
fault. If we must live with a perpetual sense that the world and
the men in it are greater than we and too much for us, let it be
the measure of our virtue that we know this and seek no comfort. Above all let us not proclaim that the limits of our powers
correspond to some special wisdom in our choice of life, of
learning, or of beauty.

This balance, this perpetual, precarious, impossible balance
between the infinitely open and the intimate, this time—our
twentieth century—has been long in coming; but it has come.
It is, I think, for us and our children, our only way.

This is for all men. For the artist and for the scientist there is
a special problem and a special hope, for in their extraordinarily
different ways, in their lives that have increasingly divergent
character, there is still a sensed bond, a sensed analogy. Both
the man of science and the man of art live always at the edge
of mystery, surrounded by it; both always, as the measure of
their creation, have had to do with the harmonization of what is

new with what is familiar, with the balance between novelty and synthesis, with the struggle to make partial order in total chaos. They can, in their work and in their lives, help themselves, help one another, and help all men. They can make the paths that connect the villages of arts and sciences with each other and with the world at large the multiple, varied, precious bonds of a true and world-wide community.

This cannot be an easy life. We shall have a rugged time of it to keep our minds open and to keep them deep, to keep our sense of beauty and our ability to make it, and our occasional ability to see it in places remote and strange and unfamiliar; we shall have a rugged time of it, all of us, in keeping these gardens in our villages, in keeping open the manifold, intricate, casual paths, to keep these flourishing in a great, open, windy world; but this, as I see it, is the condition of man; and in this condition we can help, because we can love, one another.

Rinehart Editions